Please re
fine is p
recalled
Unless o
renewed

DEVELOPING CAL: COMPUTERS IN THE CURRICULUM

Deryn Watson

Harper & Row, Publishers
London

Cambridge San Francisco
Mexico City   São Paulo
New York   Singapore
Philadelphia   Sydney

First published 1987

Harper & Row Ltd
28 Tavistock Street
London WC2E 7PN

British Library Cataloguing in Publication Data
Watson, Deryn
    Developing CAL : computers in the curriculum
    1. Computer-assisted instruction
    2. Programming (Electronic computers)
    I. Title
    371.3'9445   LB1028.5

ISBN 0-06-318382-X

Typeset by Inforum Ltd, Portsmouth
Printed and bound by Butler & Tanner Ltd, Frome and London

CONTENTS

ABOUT THE AUTHOR

Deryn Watson is lecturer in Educational Computing at the Centre for Educational Studies, Kings College (KQC), and Assistant Director (Humanities) of the Computers in the Curriculum Project. After reading Geography and Archaeology and Anthropolgy at Cambridge University, and taking a Postgraduate Certificate of Education at London, she taught geography in London schools, first at Haberdashers' Aske's school for Girls and then as Head of Department at Mayfield Comprehensive. Since the mid-1970s, she has been actively involved in the development of CAL materials for History, Geography, Economics, English and Foreign languages.

PREFACE

This book sets out to describe in detail a method of developing educational software for use in schools, and to place this method in a curriculum development context. The method discussed has evolved over twelve years through the work of the Computers in the Curriculum Project (CIC), based at Chelsea (King's College), University of London. I have been involved with this Project since 1973.

The first section explores briefly some issues relating to curriculum development. This leads into a discussion on the potential relationship between the curriculum and Computer Assisted Learning (CAL), and the style of CAL and model for development used by CIC at Chelsea. The second part describes in detail the operation of the model and is implications through:

- an examination of the stages of the development of a CAL unit;
- the setting up of writing groups and their *modus operandi*;
- identifying decision and design points during development;
- identifying general and specific guidelines and tools that have been developed to achieve these aims; and by
- discussing the variety of issues, including efficiency, management and relationship to the classroom, that are raised.

Throughout, examples are given of software to illustrate the points, and three chapters are devoted to tracing the course of development of certain units.

With the increasing interest in using computers in education, it has become apparent that an equal focus should be placed on the software as well as the hardware. There is very little written about methods of developing credible educational software, and yet many are now looking for evidence of good practice and an exploration of the relevant issues. The emphasis I have taken is on the totality of design and development issues; readers who are searching for a book on just hardware and programming must look elsewhere.

The model for CAL development explored highlights issues that are pertinent to a wide range of curriculum development concerns. This book therefore is not just a case study of one curriculum project; it draws on expertise gained by working in the project to explore practical as well as general issues in the area. At the same time it is hoped that the second section which covers detailed questions of CAL design including screen layout and the user interface, will provide a practical guide for other CAL developers of whatever model. Thus I hope that this book will be of interest to both those involved in developing software and those concerned about information technology in schools, as well as teacher educators and curriculum developers.

Throughout the book, the software examples I have used are those of the Computers in the Curriculum Project. Readers will detect a distinct bias towards the humanities. This reflects a natural slant caused by my own work. But I am also conscious that many books that address the field of educational computing, or the use of computers in the classroom refer only to scientific or mathematical examples. I hope this will help to redress the balance.

ACKNOWLEDGEMENTS

This book is the result of many years, of teamwork in the Computers in the Curriculum Project. For some time I have been a part of that team, all the members of which have formed our working environment, explored and produced solutions to problems, and contributed to my thinking. My thanks are due to all the members of the Project, both past and present, who have been my colleagues. Although this book represents my personal views on the development of CAL, these could not have been formed without the framework of the Project.

In particular I would wish to express my gratitude to the following CIC members:

● Bob Lewis, founder director of the Project, who laid down so many of the Ground Rules and who is responsible for my involvement;

● David Johnson, who encouraged me to develop a professional career in educational computing;

● Margaret Cox, for advice and personal encouragement;

● The current CIC team at Chelsea, under the direction of Margaret Cox, who have all supported and tolerated me during the writing of this book. They are Marianne Atherton, David Creasy, Alan Edis, Michael Figg, Richard Millwood, Ewa O'Donoghue, David Riddle, David Riley, Jean Seechurn, Royston Sellman, Colin Smith and Phil Wood;

● Richard Millwood and Royston Sellman in particular for their patience in educating me in technological matters;

● the many CIC co-ordinators and colleagues with whom I have worked over the years, and who have helped to formulate ideas and strategies where none previously existed, including Grant Alderson, Frances Blow, Jan Bright, Andrew Dean, Stephen Hurd, Ian Killbery, Michael Leveridge, Doug Masterton, Sophie McCormick, David Peacock, Keith Shaw, Peter Smith and David Want;

● the many teachers and programmers with whom I have worked, who are so numerous without whom there would be no Project, including Plaxy Arthur, Ross Bogart, Mark Bryson, Alan Greenwood, Simon Grummitt, Michael Headley, Alan Hills, Neil Howie, Charles Maltman, Rodney Mason, Diane Moody, Patrick Murphy, Tony

Payne, Ken Randall, Alison Rose, Andy Walters, Gill Waterworth, Angus Willson, Phil Wood, Jim Wynne, Ian Yates. There are many others I have not space to name;
● John Harris for his comments on the manuscript and helpful advice; and
● the administrative staff, Angie Donoghue and Sue Cooper, have always been so helpful. This book however could not have been produced without the invaluable assistance of Pat Dawkins, who as Project Secretary since 1973, has become adept at translating my scribbles and working to impossible deadlines. A special word of thanks to her.

I have enjoyed some extremely useful conversations and received advice over the years from many colleagues who work in the same field, including John Anderson, Mike Aston, David Benzie, John Coll, Jon Coupland, Fred Daly, Maurice Edmundson, Richard Fothergill, Diana Freeman, Michael Girling, Gabriel Goldstein, Alan Green-well, Terry Hinton, Ashley Kent, Rod Mulvey, Ken Parker, Richard Phillips, David Walker, and Norman Willis. My thanks to them and many others. In particular I would like to thank Hugh Burkhardt, Rosemary Fraser, Derek Esterson, Bill Tagg and other members of their teams in Plymouth and Nottingham, London and Hatfield for help and friendship over the years.

Finally, and most importantly, thanks to James.

THE FRAMEWORK

1
CURRICULUM DEVELOPMENT

The curriculum in most schools in the UK has changed in the last few decades. What I was taught as a pupil from 1950 to 1963 was different from the content, method and environment of my teaching between 1968 and 1975, which in turn makes an interesting comparison with the concerns of teachers with whom I work in the mid-1980s. Kelly (1980) considered that the rapidity of curriculum change in the last twenty years has exceeded that of any other period in the history of education. There has certainly been a growth in the literature on curriculum theory and curriculum practice, with an associated emergence of Curriculum Studies. This book however is about *curriculum development in action* through the work of the Computers in the Curriculum Project.

THE COMPUTERS IN THE CURRICULUM PROJECT (CIC)

This project was started in 1973, and has remained in operation almost continuously ever since, with the exception of a short break in 1977–8 whilst awaiting funding decisions. There have been two directors, Bob Lewis (1973–81) and Dr Margaret Cox (1982–) with Professor David Johnson as an interim director of for six months in the second half of 1981. The home base for the Project was always the Centre for Science and Mathematics Education at Chelsea College, which has recently merged to form a new Centre for Educational Studies at King's College (KQC) London University. I have been involved with the Project since its first meeting in 1973. I first served, while still teaching in London, on the Consultative Committee and chaired the Geography Panel. I subsequently worked as a development officer and project co-ordinator, and since 1981 as Assistant Director responsible for the Humanities. My perspective is therefore that of the teacher and curriculum developer, rather than theorist.

The Project was funded at its inception in 1973 by the Schools Council, who continued to support it in three separate phases of funding until the Schools Council was closed in 1982. Between 1980 and 1986 it was in receipt of three phases of funds from the government sponsored Microelectronics Education Programme (MEP). Since 1983 it

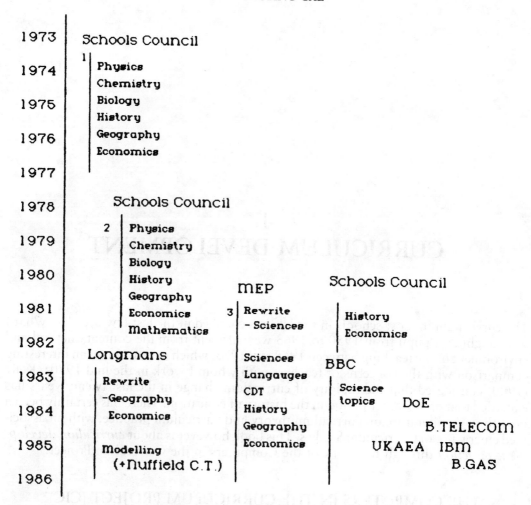

FIGURE 1.1 Historical pattern of the Computers in the Curriculum Project.

has also received funds for development purposes from a variety of sources including the BBC, the Department of Energy, the United Kingdom Atomic Energy Authority, the Nuffield Chelsea Curriculum Trust, the Longman Group, British Telecom and British Gas. Figure 1.1 reflects this pattern of funding. Between 1981–5 the project was in receipt of roughly £1.6m of funds from various sources. It also drew on hidden resources, in the form of LEA or other involvement that was not quantified. It is thus both a large-scale project and a survivor.

During this time the project has been actively involved in the research and development of Computer Assisted Learning (CAL) materials for schools, working always with a variety of disciplines and increasingly across discipline boundaries. These subjects include physics, chemistry, biology, history, geography, economics, foreign languages, English, craft design and technology (CDT) and mathematics. Whilst it has a strong central team, it also has the equally strong and active involvement of practising teachers in all stages of the development process. The materials that are produced in the form of

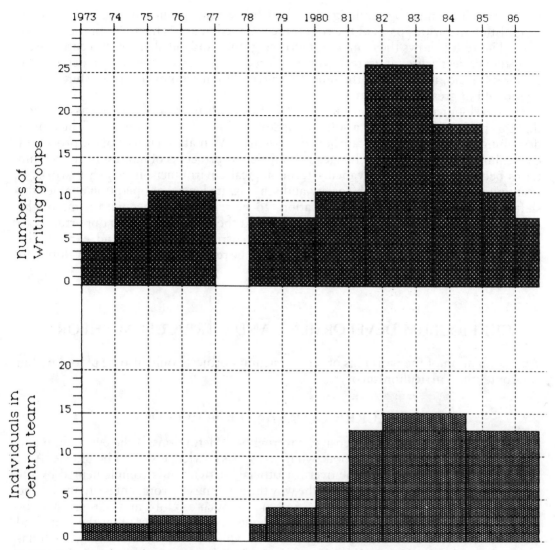

FIGURE 1.2 Numbers of writing groups and individuals in the central team since 1973.

computer assisted learning units, which include software and accompanying educational material, are published. Between 1981 and 1986, 141 units have been published. Most of these have been in versions for three machines. The project has had only a restricted remit from its funders for the dissemination of material. Members of the project however are frequently involved in in-service activities.

The project has changed in scale and scope over its life. A working model for development has emerged that is dynamic enough to accommodate shifts in both the technology and curriculum (Watson, 1983). During the first period of development there was a small centre, with the work dispersed in many regions. All the curriculum discussions and most of the programming took place through subject panels reporting to the director at the centre. The early 1980s, which coincided with a significant increase in both the funding and in the scope of the project, saw the development of a central team with curriculum and programming expertise while writing groups in Local Educational Authorities, in various parts of the country, continued to act as the focus of the creative work. Figure 1.2 shows the numbers of writing groups and members of the central team over the Project's life. It is this working structure that is explored in detail. The explorations do indicate that the model is currently undergoing a further shift; this is considered in greater detail later.

The development of materials in this field often leads to the unfortunate assumption that this project is really only a software factory. This is far from the case. The aim of describing the model is to indicate how developing CAL material is part of the process of curriculum development and change. This particular project is of interest in curriculum terms because the rapidly advancing technological environment in which it works is resulting in innovation in both society and schools. Its length of operation enables the shifts of opinion, emphasis and operations to be traced, together with some of the internal and external influences on those shifts. At the same time it is an opportunity to provide a case study of the workings of one curriculum project, and explore the guidelines that this project has produced that may be relevant to other CAL development groups.

CURRICULUM DEVELOPMENT AND CURRICULUM THEORY

An examination of the workings of one curriculum project could also be placed within the context of curriculum theory.

THE CURRICULUM AND KNOWLEDGE

The literature in this area is extensive, covering both definitions of the curriculum and the influences upon decisions about what areas of knowledge should be taught. A.V. Kelly (1977) reminds us that the overt or official curriculum is complemented by the hidden curriculum that emerges from the way the teaching environment is organized and the material taught. Informal activities in schools, such as clubs and outings, may be extra-curricular in definition, but some may have as much impact upon the pupil and how they perceive the learning environment as will the hidden curriculum. Nicholas (1980) has indentified interrelated factors to explain the increased interest in curricular concerns. The explosion of human knowledge in this century has acted as a focus. How can school knowledge be kept up to date? What should the children be taught? Upon what basis should decisions be taken to include or exclude areas of knowledge from the school curriculum? More resources are needed with associated implications for priorities and accountability. There are increasingly overt demands that education should be relevant to the needs of society and the economy. The curriculum must be tailored to provide pupils with both knowledge and skills, but also the experiences and attitudes needed in the adult world. A balance in what is taught to pupils must reflect the nature of knowledge, what society needs of pupils, and what pupils need individually. There is no consensus as to how the weightings between these three should be established. Nor is it clear whether such a balance should be determined by a prescriptive approach, that is identifying problems and remedying them, or by a preventative one that would anticipate the demands on education and plan accordingly.

CURRICULUM PLANNING, CHANGE AND DIFFUSION

What models do we have for incorporating a planned curriculum change in schools? What 'change agents' will facilitate or foster such development?

Models for curriculum planning have moved from a scientific task-analysis objectives approach (Tyler, 1949), through a framework of objectives for students' learning (Bloom, 1956), via a growing interest in the need for developmental, changeable objectives (Taba, 1962; P.J. Kelly, 1973) to an emphasis on the statements of principles rather than pre-specified goals (Pring, 1973; Stenhouse, 1975). A.V. Kelly (1977) considers that most would now agree that the educational curriculum, and models for its planning, should be viewed in terms of process rather than content or behavioural outcomes. Thus rather than 'analyse the task, prescribe the solution', there is greater emphasis on the exploring and identifying the central skills, concepts, ideas and methodologies of particular subjects, and on the involvement of classroom teachers in this task.

Macdonald and Walker (1976) argue that in order to understand curriculim change as and when it occurs, we need to look at models for the process of invention, diffusion and dissemination. Havelock (1969) proposed three models to classify the change process, that is Social Interaction, Research Development and Diffusion, and Problem-Solving. These concentrate on the styles of social systems and interaction between the innovator and the receiver of innovation. They emphasise the role of collaboration between the sender and the receiver and who exactly is in control of the change process. Holt (1981) has linked these with Schon's (1971) models for the diffusion of innovation, which are based upon variations of the centre-periphery pattern. These chart the relative import-ance of centres which are responsible for an innovation, and the diffusion and dissemina-tion of the ideas to the periphery, that is, the schools. Many might equate curriculum projects with a top-down centralized approach, producing a complete package that is delivered wholesale to schools. A proliferation of centres with different dissemination and support tasks is an alternative. The curriculum development that takes place in various local schools or teachers' centres is a reflection of a periphery based approach. This model ensures close links between the curriculum and the end-receiver – the pupil – but it may not travel very effectively to other peripheries or to any central point.

Where do teachers, pupils and curriculum development projects lie in these theoretical frameworks? Becher and Maclure (1978) and Nicholas (1980) see a growth of curricu-lum activity amongst teachers based in school departments and local authority centres. Shipman (1974) also reports on the successful adaptation of class teachers to the role of curriculum problem-solvers and change agents. Reid (1975) however reminds us that teachers may be regarded as the main source of curriculum stability rather than change, and also that curriculum planning needs to foster and facilitate change rather than perpetuate the status quo. Nisbet (1974) considers an infrastructure between centres of curriculum development and classrooms essential to provide the link between individual schools and prevent their sense of isolation.

A.V. Kelly (1980) believes that there is an essential requirement to allow freedom for the teacher to make professional decisions. Compared with most other countries, the teacher control of the curriculum in the UK at the moment is unique. Lawn and Barton (1981) however remind us how important is it to view curriculum development in the light of prevailing contemporary circumstances, both political and economic. Holt (1981) points out that the relationship between the various agencies – the local community, advisers and inspectors, teachers' centre wardens, local authority institutions, professional institutions and national curriculum projects, such as those funded by the Schools Council – and the curriculum of the school, is a function of the social and political factors which determines the style of curriculum development.

There is no consensus on how any development influences what actually happens in classrooms, or on the balance between whether change percolates through from outside or is stimulated from within.

CURRICULUM PROJECTS

The Schools Council was established in 1964 in the UK. It sponsored Curriculum Projects that focussed on subject specific areas, and operated a model for development that involved the establishment of project teams. The resultant outcomes, or material, were then disseminated. Blenkin (1980) considers that despite criticism of the Schools Council methodologies, it did act as a forum for the curriculum debate.

Accordingly, curriculum development in the UK in the last two decades has been very much associated with projects which were most often funded either by the Nuffield Foundation, or Schools Council (Stenhouse, 1980). The pattern since 1982 with the closure of the Council, has been more diffuse. Curriculum projects are undoubtedly funded to bring about change. Yet it is clear that a curriculum project by itself will not effect change without the mechanisms appropriate for dissemination, a receptive response in the classroom, and, in general, a climate that welcomes the notions or products that have emanated from the project. The notion of successful change demands not just flexibility and the ability to adjust to circumstances, but also that there must be some redundancy in the face of variability. It must be admitted that amongst the problems faced by curriculum development projects is the failure of the system to grapple with the noton of requisite redundancy. What part of the curriculum can be abandoned or altered to make room for the new?

Projects have to decide whether to approach this work by building either on the norm or the ideal. Despite the growing concern to look at the curriculum as a whole and not just from the viewpoint of separate disciplines, Stenhouse (1980) reminds us that Professional Subject Associations, such as the Geography Association, through their support and dissemination, are an important aspect of the landscape for curriculum projects. Projects that work across the subject boundaries, or in totally new areas of innovation, lack such support.

A PRACTICAL APPROACH

A project working in educational computing, which is inextricably linked to the introduction and use of new technology, has to attempt a practical solution for its *modus operandi*. The Computers in the Curriculum Project (CIC) has worked at a time of growing interest, both in society in general and education in particular, in the potential of microelectronics in the classroom. The Department of Education and Science has initiated two major national projects, in this field, the National Development Programme for Computer Assisted Learning (NDPCAL) 1973–7, and the Microelectronic Education Programme (MEP) 1980–6. A third initiative, the Microelectronics in Education Support Unit (MESU) 1986–91, is in the process of being established. At the same time, another govenment department in the UK, the Department of Trade and Industry, has sponsored a series of 'micros in schools' schemes that has resulted in the purchase of micros, peripherals and modem units by virtually all primary and secondary schools in the UK.

During the early years of the CIC project, it was estimated that 5 per cent of all secondary schools had access to some form of computing power, via a batch service or telephone link to a large mainframe. By 1986 the national average number of micros in secondary schools is thought to be around twelve. The reason for this rash of hardware is not totally related to education. The Department of Trade and Industry was concerned to promote British built micros and accompanying software. Nevertheless the Director of the MEP made clear that the aims of the programme (Fothergill, 1981, p. 1) were to 'help schools prepare children for life in a society in which devices and systems based on microelectronics are commonplace and pervasive'. Thus, all pupils should leave their schools aware of the roles and capabilities of the computers that they will meet in the adult world, and all pupils should be given the opportunity to expand their learning horizons through the use of educational software. The pressures on the system – political, technical and social – have produced a vibrant climate for a development project working in this field.

There are, on the other hand, drawbacks relating to the fact that the use of 'new technology' in the classroom can cut into previously established patterns of the curriculum, as well as classroom organisation, teacher's strategy and style. CAL material is bound therefore to be seen in some sense as a disruptive influence in the curriculum. Skilbeck (1975) distinguishes between curriculum change that may be planned by the participants who wish to change the situation for their own satisfaction, and change which is haphazard, which the participant may choose to accept or reject. He also draws a further distinction between change that builds upon the established system through the absorption and assimilation of new elements, and change which by being more disruptive and comprehensive provides genuine innovation.

Innovations that incorporate new technology tread a wary path between existing practice while attempting to explore the potential of the new. Computers in the Curriculum has over the years attempted to work through a practical approach that is focussed on the curriculum and its concerns. In this sense the following chapters report on the reality of curriculum development.

2
COMPUTER ASSISTED LEARNING

The development of computer assisted learning materials is prey to a variety of misconceptions, from the assumption that it's all about teaching about computers to the idea that such development is, in essence, a factory-line production of software. This is largely a result of a lack of clarity about what Computer Assisted Learning is, or can be.

DEFINITIONS

Any attempt to define Computer Assisted Learning (CAL) is fraught with interesting problems. A perusal of the literature in the seventies finds much confusion between *Computer Aided Instruction* (CAI) and *Computer Assisted Learning* (CAL). This is because this literature was leaning heavily upon the American experience where the term, CAI, was the norm. Such dependence on the term CAI caused confusion. Early work in educational computing often followed the 'programmed learning' path of the sixties – thus the instruction did not then, necessarily, relate to teaching and learning but rather to a tightly defined tutorial path. In its classic CAI form, the computer presents the student with a piece of text which is followed by one or more questions. These are usually of the multiple-choice type. Depending on the response, the student is routed to a second frame of text and questions, or to the same questions which are repeated, or to another series of related questions. This has been referred to as 'tutorial CAI', for the sequence of texts is selected according to the performance of the student. In 'drill and practice' CAI the student is not often offered the luxury of alternate questions. She/he is routed around the same loop until they respond correctly; they are then moved on to the next section.

For this style of operation the use of the term CAI is quite appropriate, however it is simply not synonymous with CAL. There are clear differences between instruction and learning (Maddison, 1983); CAL refers to using the computer as a learning resource to assist students in the totality of their tasks. Rushby (1979) and others (e.g., Fothergill, 1981) also refer to Computer Based Learning, and even Computer Based Education, but it is not apparent how either CBL or CBE can be distinguished from, or are subsets of CAL. It is more obvious how CAI, particularly as personified in drill and pratice programs, could be considered a subset of CAL.

Computer Managed Learning (CML) is clearly a distinct and separate area, that of using the computer to manage the learning sequence. The computer can define the students task, identify appropriate teaching materials (that may, or may not, be computer based), mark the work, record the results, issue reports, and assess, in the light of this performance, the next appropriate task. Nash and Ball (1982) state that whole courses can be derived in this matter and I know of one in use that covers a whole term of a Chemistry Undergraduate course in Sydney, Australia. Maddison (1983) refers to CML for administering the business of education in all aspects. This would appear to be somewhat sweeping but does emphasize the fact that CML delivers a system designed in the way that the teacher might ideally wish to manage the learning. Like CAI, it too is designed for use by an individual student.

However, in order to get the feel of the area that is referred to as 'Computer Assisted Learning', CAL needs to be viewed in two ways. Firstly, CAL must be distinguished from the broader fields in which computers are used in education; and secondly the term itself (CAL) must be covered in rather greater detail.

COMPUTERS IN EDUCATION

Hooper (1975) provided a classification of five uses of the computer in education, namely, in research, the teaching of computing, administration, management of learning, and as a learning resource.

ACROSS THE EDUCATIONAL RANGE

Computers for research

Computers are used in higher educational institutions, both in universities and in polytechnics for academic research. Using computers for solving problems that require excessive mathematical calculations, the exploration of large data-bases both in history and in the social sciences, the building and interrogation of concordances in literature, or design exploration through graphical capabilities, are but some of the many activities that are relatively common-place in institutions. The availability of such facilities is increasingly influencing the nature of research that is possible.

Teaching computing

Computer Science or Computer Studies Departments are now well established in higher education, and there has been an absolute rash of computing or computer studies departments in secondary schools in the 1980s. Examinations are reguarly set for students at the 16+ and the 18+ levels. These cover a variety of emphases, from computer architecture to programming lauguages and appropriate system applications. There appears to be significant argument between the various secondary and tertiary bodies as to what exactly constitutes an appropriate syllabus for pupils in this area. Some university lecturers would prefer pupils not to have done any computer studies at school, which is certainly somewhat reminiscent of those Economics lecturers who are appalled that pupils have been learning any Economics at school. Those who agree that computer studies is a subject appropriate to school, differ however about both the emphasis that should be placed on its various component parts; they differ as to whether programming should be covered in the maths lessons, or whether microelectronics should be covered in the physics lessons; they argue as to whether there is any need for a separate discipline of computer studies at all. This is all healthily reminiscent of the arguments about social science versus history, geography and economics. However, what is clear is that 'Computer Studies' as a course, is taught and is examined in large numbers in UK schools: for society and industry both place a premium on such studies.

Computers and administration

Computers are used extensively by educational institutions for a wide variety of administrative tasks, which include record-keeping, the indexing of resources, and timetabling. The authorities that run schools use them for pay-rolls and for the administration of school services; the application and regulation of entry to universities is computer-based; libraries are increasingly automated; and examination boards could not exist without them. It is commonplace for teachers and students to fill in 'computer-ate' forms and subsequently to receive information in reply that is clearly computer-generated. There is a widespread use of word-processing facilities. The increasing use of software tools, which were developed primarily for business uses, such as spreadsheets and large data interrogation packages, can only have an increasing impact not just on the handling, but also on the analysis of administrative information.

Computers for managing

The range of tasks that do constitute the management of learning, as defined earlier in CML, are not used widely in institutions. There are, however, some cases, particularly in the field of mathematics (the Hertfordshire Maths Project, Kent Maths Project) where it is used. Its appropriateness is particularly associated with both the pace of the individual learner, and clearly identifying the possible stages required. Its effectiveness, however, depends upon the totality of the system. More CML work has been reported to-date from the tertiary environment, the military, and from industrial training than from the schools.

Computer as a learning resource

This area embraces the way the computer assists learning in a variety of ways according to the design of the software. CAL therefore can be distinguished from use in research or administration of teaching about computers or from using the computers to manage learning, because the others are external uses of, or teaching about computers. CAL means learning with the assistance of the computer itself.

This is not to say that CAL does not sometimes embrace aspects of these other four. Hooper (1975) himself states that terms such as CAL and CML cannot have watertight definitions. History pupils in schools may embark on research using computers when seeking out data from local archives, encoding and interrogating it as part of a local history project; whereas pupils in English classes may use word-processors as part of their language work – though they will be using them for administrative reasons, they will also be using them as an aid to drafting, writing and exploring the structure of language. Computers may be used to control and manage experiments which are part of a science lesson.

INFORMATION TECHNOLOGY AND COMPUTER AWARENESS

There are two aspects of the use of computers across the range of educational activities that do not sit wholly comfortably within Hooper's classification; these may be considered distinct subsets.

Information handling

Handling information with data interrogation, viewdata, spreadsheets, or word-processing packages is one aspect with which the computer is particularly associated and for which it is particularly appropriate. Some would consider information handling to be an aspect of using the computer as a learning resource. Others would say the opposite, that it covers a much wider field of which CAL is only a small part. There is no doubt however that whatever framework is used, information handling by means of the technology is a distinct part.

Computer awareness

Another distinct aspect that also cuts across other discussions is computer awareness; that is for pupils in schools to become aware of the potential and pitfalls of computers and of the variety of ways in which they may be used in society. Some consider that this is an integral part of teaching about computers and place this within the domain of computer studies. Others advise the setting-up of separate computer awareness courses, or courses on 'Information Technology'. It may be difficult to justify totally separate courses, but there is no doubt that schools will be considering a computer awareness policy, just as they are recommended to develop a total policy in other areas, for instance in language as a consequence of the Bullock Report (1975). In essence, the use of computers in society should be mirrored wherever possible in schools, so that the all pervasive influence of the technology is seen to be understood and controlled by the teachers, pupils and administrators within their school environment. For, just as pupils can take a critical exploration of media – through studies of television, the press or advertising, often spearheaded by the English Department – so too will pupils need to study the role of computers generally – in business, the storage and flow of information, the control and monitoring of equipment as well as issues of confidentiality and data protection.

Computer awareness for the pupils will be achieved most naturally if they are educated in establishments that do not necessarily run computer awareness courses, but which openly and clearly use computers wherever appropriate. The one which may have greatest impact, because it should reach the pupils in a variety of forms through different disciplines, is CAL.

CAL

There are a variety of ways in which the constitute parts of CAL may be viewed.

PARADIGMS OF LEARNING

Richard Hooper (1977) in the National Development Programme in Computer Assisted Learning (NDPCAL) final report stated that 'the easiest way into a definition of CAL and CML is to say what they are not' (p. 81), and also that 'CAL, and its twin, CML, as defined and developed in the programme [i.e. NDPCAL] are characterized by a versatility of application, some of which have nothing to do with programmed learning at all. Even those applications which do derive from the programmed learning tradition, for example the computer acting in a tutorial role [often called CAI – Computer Aided Instruction], are not very reminiscent of programmed tasks' (p. 10). Macdonald *et al.* (1977a) in the same report, focused their evaluation on CAL student interactions; 'it is in the process of interaction [learning in a CAL environment] that the promises for an effective computer–related pedagogy are delivered or denied' (p. 43). An understanding of CAL comes, therefore, also of an understanding of the constituent parts, or variety of activities, that can be usefully included within the term. During their work, Macdonald *et al.* (1977b) developed a typology of student interaction which they held in a matrix against four paradigms of CAL – instructional, revelatory, conjectural and emancipatory – which they defined to accommodate the major ways the developers in the NDPCAL programme conceived of the curriculum task.

The *instructional* paradigm is drawn from the ideas of programmed learning and depends upon the subject content being broken into small parts. Each part can be treated independently, consquently there is an opportunity for reinforcement at each stage for the learner. It may be the most obvious mode for a machine that is associated with accuracy within a testing environment. This application is manifested in programmed learning units, drill and practice exercises (or even to use the latest term 'structured reinforcement'). Such exercises on a computer often defined, therefore, as CAI, offer the particular advantage of limited but immediate feedback compared with the more traditional worksheet.

The *revelatory* paradigm guides the student through the process of learning by discovery, in which the content and related theory are revealed by progress through the unit. Hence the name which reflects the assumption of the gradual unveiling of the key concepts during the learning operation. The use of simulations on computers is considered a classic example of this paradigm and is undoubtedly a method of capitalizing on the particular assets of computers.

The *conjectural* paradigm covers that area where the student learns through his experience at experimentation of exploration of any topic. Thus the computer may assist in the student's articulation and testing of his own ideas and hypotheses. This suggests an environment for modelling whereby the student himself has the opportunity not only to examine, but also to change the internal working of a model.

The *emancipatory* paradigm hinges upon the concept of the computer reducing the amount of inauthentic labour of the learner, thus releasing him for more significant work which is an integral part of his learning. This mode covers the facility of the computer to handle large quantities of data or large tedious calculations. Thus in one way the computer is being used as a tool to relieve mental drudgery. In this sense if often may appear in parallel with other paradigms.

This methodology of distinguishing CAL occurs in other writings from individuals who were involved in NDPCAL – (Rushby, 1981, 1984; Hartley, 1981). Although not necessarily totally adequate, it does provide one of the few attempts at a more rigorous look at the variety of learning activities within the definition of CAL, and thus is a useful reference base. With the emergence over the last decade of a great variety and complexity of CAL, much of the software does not fit into only one category, but often embraces two.

Maddison (1983) is critical of this approach, in that it places undue emphasis on CAI and that the formulation of the third paradigm, *conjectural*, is weak. Conversely, I have found these paradigms useful in that the *instructional* enables CAI firmly to be located as a small subset with CAL, while the third covers the interesting question, 'What shall I do?' and this I explore further in Chapter 3.

ARTIFICIAL INTELLIGENCE

One of the most active areas of research with respect to the use of computers in education has been in the field of Artificial Intelligence (AI), that is the computational modelling of cognitive activities. In the UK there are now strong centres for this work among which are the universities of Edinburgh, Sussex, London, Exeter, Lancaster and the Open University. Their great challenge is to represent knowledge in the detailed and precise fashion that is necessary for it to be reproduced using an effective computer language. Some areas of work are exploring the problems of interpreting natural language, others in developing a means to teach learning strategy. A good impression of the work can be gained from Howe, (1978; 1983) and O'Shea and Self (1983).

Two aspects of their work impinge upon the development of CAL and an understanding of the term. Firstly, much of their writing suggests that the only worthwhile CAL is that which is developed for AI purposes. Self (1985) indeed expresses considerable surprise that the Computers in the Curriculum Project should be principally interested in the curriculum. O'Shea and Self (1983) have made it clear that their work lies in using AI as a source of ideas, and combining these with what they consider to be the computers' distinctive properties. They list processes, such as remembering and accessing relevant knowledge, revising and extending knowledge, and using knowledge appropriately. They place them in juxtaposition with some of the computer's properties, that is it can make decisions, it is reactive, it understands. In many ways I am in agreement with their ideas and look forward to seeing them in execution. What does slightly disturb me is that some of the AI programs that have been produced, while no doubt exciting in their design from an AI viewpoint, are poor educationally. Developing a sophisticated list for the capital cities of the world is neither geography nor is it the sort of learning wanted in geography. Hopefully some more exciting educational examples of CAL will emerge from what is clearly a powerful field of research. What is important to realise is that the AI approach, while valid within its field, is not the only approach to either developing CAL or the purposes to which CAL can be put.

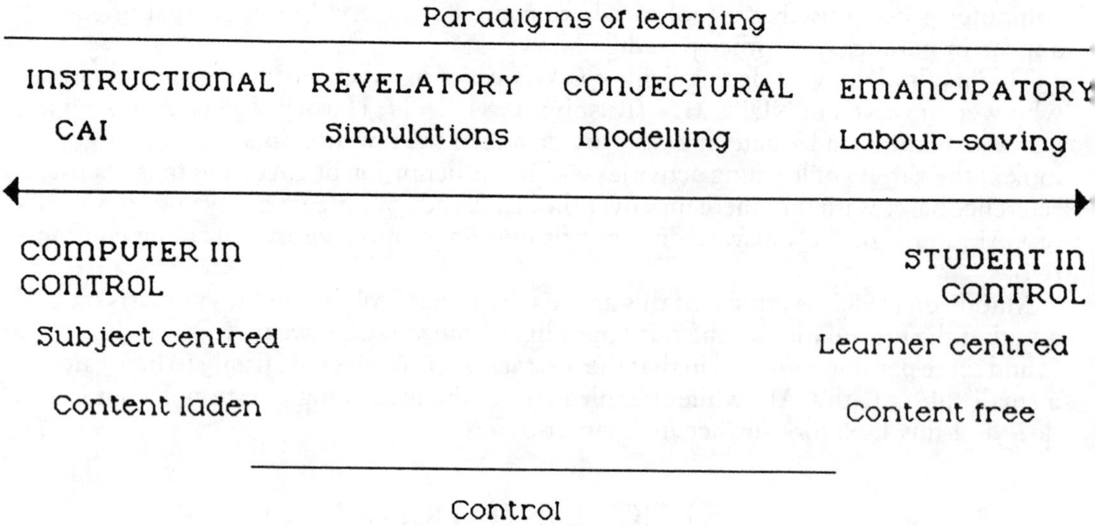

Paradigms of learning

INSTRUCTIONAL	REVELATORY	CONJECTURAL	EMANCIPATORY
CAI	Simulations	Modelling	Labour-saving

COMPUTER IN
CONTROL

Subject centred

Content laden

STUDENT IN
CONTROL

Learner centred

Content free

Control

FIGURE 2.1   A spectrum of control between the computer and the learner (after Wellington)

WHO IS IN CONTROL?

Across the four paradigms of Macdonald *et al.* are traceable levels of control. In instruction, the computer could be considered to control or be in control of the student. Emancipatory however suggests the student is in control. A spectrum of control between the computer and the user has been drawn by Wellington (1985) in association with the paradigms (Figure 2.1). This is another way of exploring the value of these categories; however, it also throws an unfortunate emphasis on the computer rather than the software. This, like the phraseology of O'Shea and Self in saying 'the computer decides' or 'it understands', suggests an emphasis on the assets or properties of the hardware rather than the style of the software. As Terry (1984) states, we must be careful not to endow some innate intelligence to a computer. It seems to me that a focus on the properties of CAL centres more readily on the interrelationship of educational software and the learning operation.

STYLES OF CAL

Other methods of classifying CAL depend more heavily on the 'style' of software, which puts software into type. Thus, drill and practice, tutorial games, simulations, and databases can each be related to the activity the CAL unit generates. Wellington (1985) has drawn up a scheme into which these types fall, based on four categories – teaching programs, learning programs, tools, and open-ended use. Thus 'drill and practice' are teaching programs while Logo is placed under open-ended use (Figure 2.2). Ranged across these four categories is a parallel strand starting with how much the computer 'programs' the children under 'drill and practice', compared with the children programming the computer under open-ended use. Wellington himself points out the similarity between this method of categorisations and the paradigms of Macdonald *et al.*

   Matrices which use these styles of CAL are often used to indicate where the style may fit into a particular aspect of learning in a discipline.

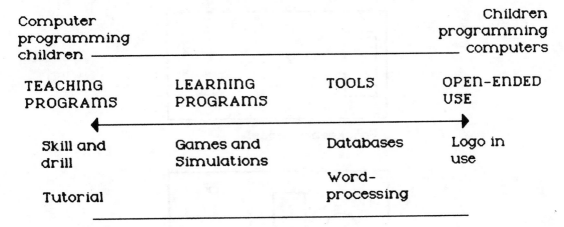

FIGURE 2.2 Types of educational program (after Wellington)

CLASSROOM ORGANISATION

A further strand of classification looks not at the level of control or the subject appropriateness of the style, but at the way the software can be used in the classroom.

Shepherd *et al.* (1980) when addressing themselves to the issue of how large groups of students can use one computer, refer to four models of student–teacher relationship with one classroom (Figure 2.3). The models range from

- the position of a tutor acting as a *gatekeeper* between the students and the computer, allowing students access only when and as they feel it is appropriate;
- the computer acting as a *barrier* between the students themselves, and the tutor thus insulating himself from the students;
- the *diversionary* in which the students in turn may exclude the tutor; and
- the *partnership* in which tutor and students work together with the computer.

These models are possibly more related to the tertiary than secondary world, although they have been used as a basis for consideration by Hassell (1983). They were also drawn up when the term 'a computer' referred to a terminal of a mainframe. Another way of looking at classroom organisation is to focus on the physical location of the hardware, and consequently how each arrangement will determine different styles of use. Weigand (1984) identifies three methods – whole class teaching, group work and cafeteria. (Figure 2.4). Note he is referring to a microcomputer.

Whole class teaching with one micro and more monitors, which is often associated with the phrase 'the electronic blackboard'. It must not be assumed however that the CAL used in this mode follows an expository style. Maddison (1982) devotes a whole chapter to the electronic blackboard as a classroom aid and the way in which the moving screen becomes an extension of a tool all educators have used at some stage.

Group work, in which small groups of pupils cluster around 5 or 50 micros, each using the same piece of CAL.

The cafeteria in which the class is organised into groups, but because there is only one micro, each group comes up in turn to work at the micro either when it is free or when they have reached an appropriate part in the work.

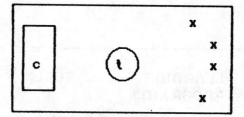

Gatekeeper model

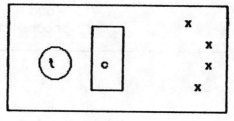

Barrier model

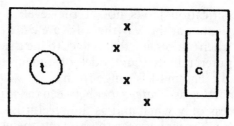

Diversionary model

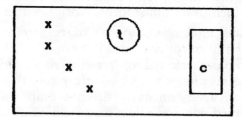

Partnership model

c computer   t tutor

x students

FIGURE 2.3   4 models of classroom organizations (after Shepherd *et al*)

Whole class teaching

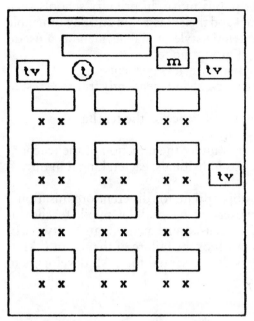

t teacher   x pupil
m micro   tv monitor

Group Work

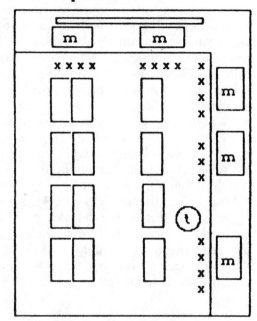

t teacher   x pupil
m micro   tv monitor

Cafeteria

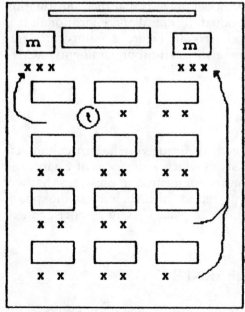

t teacher   x pupil
m micro   tv monitor

FIGURE 2.4   3 models of classroom organization (after Weigand)

In many classes, particularly in science laboratories in secondary schools, a circus of activities is organised around which groups of pupils move. In primary schools such handling of a diversity of activities is more normal and their classroom and day timetable are organised accordingly. Weigand sees the cafeteria style of management as a useful compromise between the whole class mode and group mode.

Payne, Hutchings and Ayre (1980) consider five user arrangements:
● Where one or two pupils only per lesson, are working independently from the rest of the class.
● Where small groups run the program without reference to the teacher.
● Small groups in which the teacher is a participant.
● Where a whole class is working as a single unit under the direction of the teacher.
● Where the whole class of pupils are working as individuals, each taking it in turn to run the program.

Obviously different styles of CAL are more appropriate for different organisational systems, and different styles also provide a variety of methods of pupil, teacher or computer control. Not all circumstances, styles, organisational methods and software fit into neat categories. Leiblum, (1981) suggests much of the failure of the use of CAL is due to the lack of attention given to these issues. It is essential for CAL developers to consider *all* these factors.

THE TEACHER'S ROLE

Classroom organisation frameworks presuppose that teachers who are going to use CAL would have these same perceptions of CAL and how it can be used. This is obviously not always the case. Freeman (1983) provides a model for teachers decisions to use CAL that is based on a survey taken in Hertfordshire. This model suggests that their information field is divided into four groups – social, institutional, technical and educational. It is only the last two which directly involve the classroom. Figure 2.5 illustrates this descriptive model. Notice that the educational field also uses the four paradigms of CAL, relating them each to a style. Thus:
● Instructional – skills,
● Conjectural – games and simulations,
● Emancipatory – statistical analysis,
● Revelatory – information retrieval.

In the educational field a fifth factor emerges, namely, fitting into the curriculum. It is this fifth factor, with the related paradigms and styles which is the focus of Chapter 3.

This model also highlights the combination of environments and pressures that will influence not only the teacher's and institution's perception of CAL, but also the style of use and range of take-up. It adds to the opportunity to place CAL in a wider context.

CAL AND THE LEARNER

Most of the literature defines CAL in relation to the learning operation, although the internal classification beyond this may be more hazy. Baker (1984) when writing about curricular implications, states that since instruction does not necessarily lead to learning,

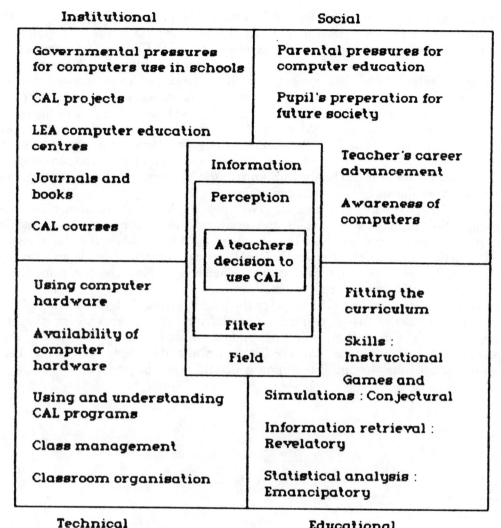

Institutional

Governmental pressures for computers use in schools

CAL projects

LEA computer education centres

Journals and books

CAL courses

Social

Parental pressures for computer education

Pupil's preperation for future society

Teacher's career advancement

Awareness of computers

Information

Perception

A teachers decision to use CAL

Filter

Field

Using computer hardware

Availability of computer hardware

Using and understanding CAL programs

Class management

Classroom organisation

Fitting the curriculum

Skills : Instructional

Games and Simulations : Conjectural

Information retrieval : Revelatory

Statistical analysis : Emancipatory

Technical

Educational

FIGURE 2.5   A descriptive model of behaviour; a teachers decision to use CAL (after Freeman)

more enthusiasm may be generated by the practitioner for software which creates discovery learning (CAL).

Jenson (1980) is concerned about the falseness of using CBL as a term, since we do not refer to BBL (Book Based Learning) or FBL (Film Based Learning) (sic). Shepherd (1983) also questions the appropriateness of the term at all by suggesting it is placing a false emphasis on the computer over other resources. Perhaps this also explains why Nash and Ball (1982) attempt no definitive statement of CAL in their book, although they define other terms, and do place a commendable emphasis on the issues of learning and teaching.

Jenson (1980) is concerned at the undue emphasis on technology when he states that the identification of the computer as a conveyor of teaching material and its association with educational technology, when taken together, has caused the present rejection by teachers of the computer as a medium, because they reject educational technology.

Fraser (1984) in writing about the work of the ITMA project makes it clear that this work has concentrated on developing CAL as a teaching aid in the classroom. It is important that this is not construed to be synonymous with CAI for as she states later, the aim is to design material that will make a qualitative difference in teaching and learning. Laurillard (1983) also comes in heavily on the side of learning, by writing that the real point of using computers in education is to help students learn more effectively. This welcome emphasis on 'quality' and 'effective' gets closer to the core of the role of CAL than does the definition in Megarry (1983), which rather covers all educational computing, by saying that CAL is where teaching and learning in any part of the curriculum are aided by some application of the computer; the role of the computer can be as a teaching aid or it can be student centred; the latter approach is becoming more significant with the spread of microcomputers.

Hartley (1981) provides us with a range of types of CAL – from tutorial, illustration and simulation, problem-solving skills, and the assimilation of computer-based teaching materials. These are similar to both the paradigms of Macdonald *et al.* and to the styles of Wellington. Zinn (1981) is simpler; CAL is learning about, with and through computers. Papert (1980) is quite categorical, when he states that computers may affect the way people think and learn.

Defining and categorising CAL exposes the issues surrounding the development of CAL and its use in the classroom much more effectively than a neat classification. The Computers in the Curriculum Project has and continues to explore a variety of these aspects of CAL, usually where the words interaction and learning both occur. These form the basis of the Ground Rules upon which the work depends.

3
COMPUTERS IN THE CURRICULUM – THE GROUND RULES

Any curriculum development takes place within a framework which provides the parameters, the consensus of ideas around which the participants will explore and work. These ideas may be rigidly drawn up from the first in a classic objectives approach, or may emerge as the nature of the work dictates its own framework. Whether the process becomes embedded in a formalized model, or remains a lose conglomerate of ideas, there has to be a commonality that draws the project team together sufficiently for them to feel that they are all participating in the same work. The commonality is not the framework, but rather the principles that help to shape it. Thus an understanding of any model for development depends upon an understanding of the commonality or philosophy. As such, this philosophy then acts as the Ground Rules – the basis upon which the participants do their work. For the Computers in the Curriculum Project, the Ground Rules lie not in the computer and its assets so much as in its understanding of the term Computer Assisted Learning.

The Computers in the Curriculum Project has from the first not been particularly interested in the instructional/tutorial (CAI) or management/assessment (CML) role. Not only has it always referred to its work as within the broad field of CAL, indeed the very title of the Project makes clear that it sees the role of CAL as being one integrated within the curriculum. Lewis (1981; 1983) makes this clear, by placing the emphasis on the role of the computer as an additional learning resource which may assist in achieving existing pedagogic aims and thereby provide new learning possibilities through its power.

Thus, the CIC 'philosophy' of CAL is that we should explore and develop ways of *using the computer to assist both the learner and the teacher in their tasks within the whole curriculum area.* This is not to deny the significance of other approaches, but simply to say that they are not the area the CIC is either interested in or has tackled. In practice, this philosophy suggests that the computer should be used from an educational perspective. This inevitably colours the way the facilities and attractions of the computer need to be handled. This may seem a relatively esoteric point, but it becomes important in the execution of development.

In the early days of microcomputer hardware, the machine would arrive with a manual that seemed to be designed to confuse. I have quite fond memories of my first exploration of a microcomputer – one had to reach a page in the manual that was already numbered in the hundreds before there were any clear indications as to how to turn the system on. This was a classic example of a manual written by individuals who rightly wanted to explain what they saw as the most salient features (often the machine architecture), but who had failed to address themselves to the issue of how a new user might want to use it. Even worse, the naive, i.e. non-computerate user, was not considered at all. The initial pages of most micro manuals almost inevitably teach you to write a simple program in BASIC. The number of new users who want to turn on a computer, load in some software and run it, are legion. Yet using software comes lower on the list of priorities than writing your own.

A CAL philosophy that places pedagogy first will always begin from the viewpoint of how to use the hardware for learning purposes and not of using the necessarily most attractive features of the hardware. A significant amount of educational software tends to address itself primarily to the most obvious assets of the computer – i.e., it is a fast number calculator. This is the only explanation of the large number of statistics packages that have been developed; indeed CIC developed two such packages, one for geo-graphers and the other for biologists, in the mid-seventies. From fast number crunching to accuracy testing is but a short step. This is why CAI has flowered so much in those educational environments where a premium is placed on checking and reinforcing skills. Hence the plethora of drill and practice programs.

I was first introduced to this style of program in the early seventies. As a geographer looking to find out what this machine could do for me, I was shown a program that tested the user's knowledge of the captial cities of the world. Whilst this was impressive in so far as it went, and provided an accurate method of checking such information, it was not the sort of geography that I or others were teaching in our classrooms. Despite the fact that this was a method of utilizing the power of the computer in the classroom, this was not information that I considered desperately relevant; for the rote testing method was not a style of teaching I would use either. The inappropriateness of much 'drill and practice' still appalls me – many of these programs, from testing the order of the kings and queens of England to testing your mathematical multiplication tables, represent a backwards step educationally. The computer certainly is an asset in accuracy testing; however, harnessing it indiscriminately may not be educational. I believe that CAL is about utilizing the computer in a much more imaginative way.

INTERACTIVE DISCOVERY LEARNING

Interactive discovery learning is a phrase that attempts to summarize a combination of attributes of the type of CAL in which the CIC is interested. The majority of types belong to the second and third paradigms, that of revelatory and conjectural, while many also combine the emancipatory aspects. In order to provide more details of what this acutally means, I will explore a variety of styles of CAL and styles of associated learning in an intermingled fashion. They do not fall easily into categories, because when taken as a whole they are intended rather to provide a flavour than classification.

SIMULATIONS

An exciting and illuminating use of the computer is to develop a model and embed it in a system that enables the model to be explored – thus the wide range of simulations that have been developed.

An educational simulation is a useful method of simulating an environment that it is otherwise not possible to explore within the confines of the classroom. Initially taken up in the Sciences, it has been used with vigour in the Humanities and Languages too.

The justification for the use of simulations firstly resides in their ability to explore areas that are otherwise inaccessible through time, speed of process, expense or even danger. Pupils can explore the environment within a pond (POND) over a period of many years, and see the relative balance of the population of herbivores, plankton and fish through annual cycles; they can also see how this balance is altered by fishing or pollution. The chemists can simulate the planning and production targets of an aluminium smelting plant (DALCO) and drive the processing machinery as if they were actually in charge of the factory. The physicists can 'send a rocket into space' to explore issues of gravity and propulsion (NEWTON); they can simulate nuclear decay (RADACT). None of these would be feasible within the classroom. This justification of simulations has been referred to by a variety of writers (Shaw, 1981; Rushby, 1979; Harris, 1980; Hartley, 1981).

Using simulations however is not just a matter of bringing environments into the classroom. The pupils must be able to explore the environments – not just to watch an operation passively, but rather to explore actively and relatively quickly the associated variables and their behaviour under a variety of circumstances. Thus in POND, by varying the number and rate of fishermen in any season pupils can see the impact immediately that occurs on the delicate balance of plankton, herbivores and fish in the pond over a period of time. They can do this even more drastically by polluting the pond. Pupils can change the angle of projection and speed of the rocket and see what effect this had upon the rocket's orbit. Pupils can change temperature and oxygen levels to produce the best aluminium processing combination. Thus in all cases the pupils can conjecture about the nature of the environment through changing one or more variables – they can ask the question 'What would happen if. . .?' (Lewis and Want, 1980a).

Such an environment is open-ended. Exploration can be tightly directed by the teacher – problems can be set to force the exploration along certain paths towards a best-fit solutions. A best-fit pattern however can often be achieved by a variety of equally satisfactory paths. This is one of the more fundamental assets of CAL, in that it can provide an environment where a combination of paths can achieve similar results. The teacher can also set loose goals that demand that the pupils explore in a variety of directions in order to appreciate the intricacies of each combination of the variables and their behaviour. The purpose of setting a problem is not just to achieve one combination of solutions, but rather to explore the various factors that have to be considered. Use of such simulations suits the teacher who wishes to facilitate their pupils' own discovery. While in no way wishing to suggest that the simulation of an environment to be preferable to actually experiencing it, there can be little doubt that appropriate CAL simulations provide one of the most easily grasped of the assets that computers can offer the field of education.

Simulations can be used for both known (or real environments) and for theoretical (or conjectural ones). Their use and impact in the classroom will depend not only upon their pedagogic appropriateness, but also on the support that the software has through its accompanying notes. Many teachers would consider it important to compare results obtained from simulation software, with 'real world' data, where possible. The notes will need to define the limits of the simulation and explore its educational context. These may also illustrate how such simulations are often aimed more at the concepts rather than content of a subject.

EXPLORING A MODEL

Sometimes simulations will be developed and used in order not just to find a best-fit pattern, explore the interaction of the variables, or discover the implications of the environment, but rather so as to expose the model itself and its workings. The 'transparency' of models becomes important in some educational tasks. There is a program, MALTHUS, based upon the Malthusian model of population projection, which considers the interplay of food, population and mineral resources in a finite world. The aim of the program is not just to explore the interaction between its three main parameters but rather to explore the Malthusian model and consider just how adequate it is as a method of analysing future population trends. MALTHUS in operation suggests that within fifty years there will be major famines and war as the world's population competes for diminishing food and mineral resources. Has the Malthusian model taken enough relevant factors into account? Is the assumption that the available food supplies are fixed valid? What else needs to be considered? Is the supposed behaviour of population when faced with famine accurately modelled? These questions could not really be considered without the computer emancipating the student by doing all the model calculations both speedily and in a variety of appropriate combinations.

Using simulations to analyse the behaviour of the variables in any one environment is a useful pedagogic goal. To this can now be added the exploration of the adequacy of a model itself as a reflection or indeed qualification of an environment, either known or theoretical. Such a secondary goal of analysing the model as well as its behaviour goes a small step towards the 'peeling back' environments discussed by the AI community (notably by Howe, O'Shea and Self). I think it is important to remember however that in the educational environment there may not necessarily always be the need to 'peel back' the simulation and explore the model itself. These demands vary according to the aims of the exercise and the ability and age levels of the pupils involved. It should be understood that a simulation depends on a model that is often a subjective intepretation of the behaviour of variables in one context. The models which are used in CAL simulations are simple; they often may not include all the possibly relevant variables as these would confuse and decrease the chances of the educational aim of the simulation being achieved. But these models may oversimplify or skew the overall pattern. The teachers and CAL developers designing a model have to decide on the relative balance and weightings of the variables in consultation with as many others as possible. What matters is that the exact nature of the model, and its limitations, are made clear to the teacher in the accompanying notes , who may then in turn expose it to the pupils. It is also important to remember that teachers often teach a simplified version of events to twelve year olds, a more complex version to fifteen year olds, and a yet more complex version to 18 year olds. CAL simulations will often reflect this ; indeed they can be geared so that a different style of 'peeling back' emerges. The pupils can explore let us say 4 parameters at first; later they can move into a second stage where more parts of the model are exposed.

Which ever model the simulation is based on, it is important to remember that modelling an environment is not a method of reproducing reality exactly in all its detail and complexity. Rather it is a methodology for exploring certain of its constitutent parts, and indeed for providing a classification of the way those parts are seen or thought to interact in reality. Use of models and their exposure and discussion by pupils becomes a valuable, but familiar activity (Riley, 1984).

BUILDING MODELS

There is another aspect to using models that relates to this, namely, providing an environment for the pupils to build their own models on the computer. It is in this area that the development of CAL and some of the AI work is converging. The AI community is concerned to provide pupils with languages to explore rules which the computer will execute; hence Logo and turtle geometry. Although coming from a different perspective, CIC has already developed one modelling system, with applications for physics, chemistry, biology, geography, economics and mathematics (Dynamic Modelling System DMS). Note that the application of modelling is still seen as within a curriculum focus. Further work is planned for the development of a modelling system for use in a variety of scenarios. The core of the conception lies not in the actual modelling, but in the tools to facilitate such modelling.

The humanities have used CAL simulations as well as the sciences, and have arrived at the position of being most concerned with modelling, but via a somewhat more varied path. Some aspects of modelling in the humanities may at first seem relatively straight-forward – e.g. modelling population growth using the UN Demographic model for future predictions. Other areas, notably in Economics, have been much harder. Hence the model is used as a method not of emulating known events or behaviour, but of interpreting them in the light of political, economic and social opinions. When modelling the economy of the country, do you use Keynesian theory, or a monetarist approach? How do you decide on the weightings within the variables, particularly with a simplified model? Not only are such models subjective, but they can rarely be tested for accuracy against reality in the same way that a model of Newtonian behaviour can in physics. This does not mean that you do not develop CAL simulations in these areas, it simply means that much more time is often spent on the model definition, and that such a model cannot be satisfactorily incorporated until the behaviour of its variables have been properly tested by its performance in the developed simulation. Model development in the humanities therefore tends to be a particularly creative activity.

This is not all; some 'models' of behaviour have been described in the classroom but never adequately tested in the accurate fashion that developing a CAL program demands. The 'correctness' of such descriptions has often been called into question by quantifying the model, when its subsequent behaviour may not match that which has been expected. Some CAL authors have had to go to considerable lengths to develop a credible CAL model (PUDDLE and COSBEN) where only descriptions of an environment or behaviour had previously been possible.

QUALITATIVE MODELS

A yet more complicated factor in this perception of CAL simulations is that the disciplines of the humanities have not wanted to tackle only those aspects of their subjects and models that are quantifiable. Exploring cost-benefits for example (COS-BEN) is not just a matter of placing the cost of building or improving roads against the deficits of keeping open a branch railway line. How do you quantify inconvenience to passengers; how do you quantify the loss of amenities if you build an airport, the threat to wildlife, or the interference with a rural environment by development? Both economics and geography cover a whole myraid of issues such as these. However, because they are not immediately quantifiable, or more dangerously, they are often given false monetary values, it does not mean that they should not form a basis for planning CAL simulations. Indeed simulating an environment in which a problem has to be explored and a solution found, where there are a variety of inter-related factors, some monetary and some not, is an important part of social sciences syllabuses and also of what actually happens in the adult world. A notation for human values and attitudes is needed because they are real and important variables which need to be balanced with the more readily quantifiable ones, be they monetary, or passengers per mile, or whatever.

Historians have faced rather similar problems. In developing simulations of events and behaviour in certain circumstances, they have come up against the inadequacies of using numerical algorithms as a method of representing the complex inter-relationship of related causal factors. This is a problem that is also faced by the geographers and economists. Describing a situation has, in the past, enabled a more accurate analysis to be avoided. Being forced to produce a clear sequence of cause and effect, plus related ranking according to the combination of events and strategies both across and through time, has forced historians to be more careful about what they have previously been able to describe. Such descriptions are composed of a combination of facts and opinions about events in the past. Models therefore reflect the historians' opinions about events and sequences.

An example of this style of work is contained in ARABIS, a program that explores the issues of the conflict in Palestine in 1947. It is a counterfactual game based on the United Nations plan for the partition of Palestine in 1947. The aim of the unit is to help students understand certain aspects of historical causation in the context of the Arab–Israeli conflict. The program enables the student to select from a number of variables, which are the various policy discisions of the relevant powers, to make a series of combinations and find out immediately what the supposed consequences would be. Obviously these consequences reflect the historians' opinions of the interrelationship of the factors at work and are therefore an interesting source of discussion about the conflict itself. Science models may be about content that can be tested, whereas history models are used more to generate an understanding of what history is.

Developing such multi-layered models that are dependent more on a combination of relational factors than numerical ones poses a problem in programming terms. The required programming languages are simply not available to address a representational method of linked factors. It is not insuperable however – ARABIS and another similar program, AMWEST have both been developed by CIC in BASIC. Ennals (1984) has referred to this problem, and values PROLOG as the language that provides the solution to this style of problem, as do Nicol, Briggs and Dean (1986). Certainly the CIC team, once they had developed and refined the ARABIS model, was able to replicate it within half a day in PROLOG – a task that had taken over three weeks in BASIC. But could they have done this if they had not already conceptualized the model sufficiently for it to be developed already? We need a tool to help us formulate such multifactorial models, not just replicate them. PROLOG only seems to be an interim solution. Complex models of this relational type end up with such a sequence of brackets in PROLOG, or square brackets in Logo, that the developer is often left counting brakets in an attempt to unravel the declared relationship. The humanities are in fact still awaiting development of an appropriate language or software system that specifically tackles the modelling of this style of thinking. Translating it into a numerical form in the interim is adequate but insufficient. This issue of modelling is central to CAL in both its current use and future directions.

GAMES AND ROLE-PLAYING

A somewhat different aspect of using CAL simulations has also emerged that relates closely not only to the emphasis on the learning aspect of CAL, but also the relationship of such material to the curriculum. Quite a few CAL simulations use a role-playing environment. Such simulations can be referred to as games but it is important that they are not left in such a loose a category (Watson, 1984b). Firstly, these sorts of games are nothing like the 'arcade games' that are written for home computers. Secondly, they do not necessarily combine a strong competitive element, of two individuals or teams set against each other. Thirdly, they do not necessarily have a top score or best answer. Some CAL role-playing games may incorporate these features, but the majority do not. What is important about role-playing games, whether board ones or CAL ones, is the educational environment that is generated during the progress of the game, rather than the achievement of a solution.

A couple of CAL examples may illustrate this point. In WINDS, the pupils are invited to adopt the role of a sailing ship's captain, and to sail between any two of the six available ports in the world, using only the wind as the source of power to their large square-rigger. They decide which date to set sail and respond to the information about the wind speed and direction by choosing which of the 8 compass points and directions in which to sail. Thus they slowly navigate towards their destination, facing the hazards of the sea as produced by the model of the wind zones in the simulation. They are learning about the wind zones and their seasonal shifts by acting out the role of a sailor on the oceans. They learn to choose the date of departure carefully according to the seasons and destination, to avoid being trapped with little sea room in areas of frequent gales or hurricanes, to plan to use the winds to their advantage rather than struggle against them. They can emulate the voyages of discovery. Not only are there no fixed routes or best voyages in this game, but the pupil is conjecturing and exercising decision-making in the light of evidence and knowledge discovered during the exercise. Place a group of pupils around the keyboard to work through this simulation and the group discussion over choices and rationales behind choices becomes, I believe, particularly rich.

In economics a game called WORKER invites pupils to adopt the role of a manufacturer of supermarket trolleys who has to allocate each shift of the thirty workers in the factory to the three tasks – cutting, shaping and welding wire. Initially 600 units of wire are bought at the beginning of each shift, and an examination of the rapid results in terms of both completed trolleys and using all the workers (i.e. not leaving them idle for want of work reaching their department), results in the pupils reaching a best-fit ratio between the three. Pupils may increase the amount of wire bought in order to try to maximize production. Once they feel confident that they have established an appropriate distribution, they can use the part of the program that introduces economic shocks. How should they respond to the message 'maintenance work in the cutting department reduces productivity in this shift'? Then they may use the 'new technology option' to explore the implications of using new equipment. The analysis of the results achieved in the previous shifts, and the discussion amongst the students on how to reduce the number of idle workers, or to increase productivity, is an important part of the whole process. Adopting the role of the manufacturer in charge of the operation places the pupils in a useful context to learn economic concepts or ideas, such as the Law of Diminishing Returns.

Role-playing provides interesting and, therefore, a motivating environment for pupils, and it was often used in classes before the arrival of CAL. Role-playing games on a computer expand the variety and style of simulations that are possible.

PROCESS SKILLS

The exercising of process skills by the pupils using CAL does not appear in any major paradigms or category, yet it has recently emerged as an aspect of CAL that I find of particular interest (Watson, 1984a; 1985). During the use of a role-playing simulation, the pupils are not just examining the question '*What would happen if . . .?*', that is 'what would happen if I sailed East now?' or 'what would happen if I moved more men into the Shaping Department?' They are also being forced to take decisions, and so to ask the question '*What shall I do . . .?*' If a simulation offers structured paths to the problem, the pupil has to concentrate on which variable to change next. In a more open-ended enquiry however, the choice of where to explore and which part is thrown upon the students. Thus they are involved not just at random or in an opportunistic fashion, but encouraged to develop a hypothesis and follow through a strategy to test such a hypothesis. Thus for example, 'I think, it must be easier to sail round Scotland than to be battling into the Channel against prevailing South Westerly winds'. 'OK, let's try it out in four different seasons and see if it works'.

Although this is not obviously always appropriate, either through the content or the conceptual basis of the CAL unit, I feel that CAL can act as a catalyst for the development and exercise of such process skills and that this should be considered during development. It does reflect the increasing emphasis with which process skills are to be seen in the main syllabus of secondary school subjects. Within the pattern of paradigms that places an emphasis on the student learning activity rather than the assets of the computer, there is clear scope for some interesting work on the way the learner is encouraged to conjecture, hypothesize and make decisions. In this sense, a simulation is not only encouraging the question 'What would happen if. . .?', it is now placing emphasis on the pupils asking questions of themselves. Thus the intention has shifted from an analysis of the model by way of changing the parameters, to an analysis of the user's response in a variety of scenarios (Watson, 1984e).

Such active decision-making or posing and testing a hypothesis is clearly fostered by simulations which are designed to offer such opportunities. In WORKER, the pupils may say 'If we reduce the shapers by two, there won't be enough welding work' or 'Let's work on the basis of always needing at least more cutters than anywhere else'. An open-ended environment designed to encourage discovery learning naturally provides an opportunity for the pupils to explore and exercise such skills.

COMMUNICATION BETWEEN PUPILS

An interest in decision-making and the posing and testing of hypotheses leads naturally on to looking at the role of the computer in fostering communication skills. This aspect became increasingly apparent through the CIC work in languages, both with English and Foreign Languages. Here the demands of the subjects means that the teachers are concerned to develop units that do not concentrate on reading or writing skills, to the exclusion of listening or talking. It is important to these disciplines to look at all aspects of communication together rather than in isolation. Rather than be despondent about the current limitations of the technology, language teachers have set about designing units that would force a level of discussion among the pupils, both at and away from the keyboard.

This is very much in accord with the general 'ground rules philosophy' of CAL that CIC has followed hitherto. I hope it has already become apparent that the emphasis of style of use amongst pupils has been on *group work*. This partly is a reflection of reality, for during much of the design life of the Project, there have not been single micros available to all class members; consequently units had to be developed with whole classes or groups of pupils in mind. Such expediency has been valuable in exposing the positive benefits of fostering group work among pupils around the keyboard. In particular I sometimes view the development of computer rooms with 20–30 work stations with some concern, as there is a danger that the provision of computers in this configuration constrains the way CAL units are both perceived and used, and may lead to a returned emphasis on drilling or testing the performance of an individual student.

A small group of pupils working together at the keyboard can generate some significant discussion. Chatterton (1985) has already reported on the increased on-task discussion amongst chemistry students when using a CAL simulation. Cummings (1985) has also reported a valuable level of discussion in upper primary pupils on a geographical exploration. This discussion can be fostered by the role-playing units where decision-making and hypothesis-testing often becomes a natural group activity. Certainly feedback from our trials on a variety of subjects has reported on the increased levels of discussion and the 'interest' generated amongst the pupils. So the question to design for is not just '*What shall I do?*', but also '*What shall we do?*', '*What would you do? Why? No – lets try this? What shall we do next?*' This encourages interaction amongst the pupils at and around the keyboard, as well as between the teacher, pupils and the machine via the software (Figure 3.1).

The English working group chose to develop programs which had the specific aim of encouraging a discussion and analysis of words and their meanings by pupils. One of these, Call My Bluff (CBLUFF) is based on a game in which up to four teams compete in choosing the meaning of an obscure word from the three that they were offered. The words can be chosen from files which contain examples of words for instance from Elizabethan English, or from Johnson's Dictionary. It may not be clear what part of speech the word is, and the three offered meanings could be for a noun, verb, adverb, etc. The purpose is not that the pupils should know or learn any of the words and their correct meaning, but rather that they explore the likely possibilities. What does the word sound like? Does it look like another word you know that has a similar meaning? All this forces the pupils to talk about words, which was the main pedagogic purpose for the development. This is a neat extension of the rule that there is not necessarily a best route or single best-fit solution to an exercise; it is a natural concomitant of a philosophy that

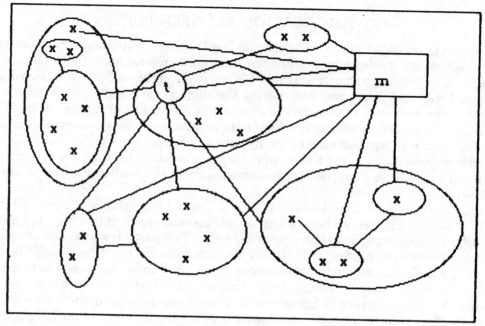

ꬼ teacher   m micro   x pupil

FIGURE 3.1   The interactive CAL classroom.

places the emphasis squarely on the learning operation, rather than the completion of a correct sequence.

This example also exposed another problem – the English teachers were determined to provide a facility for the users to be able to build up their own files of words rather than only use those available in the pack. CIC had already produced some programs (DEMOG, PUDDLE) where the teachers had been encouraged to build up their own data files, but this had usually been more on the periphery of the unit. There was a demand for a simpler method to be made available for the teachers to be able to build up and store their own files of words to use with CBLUFF, without having to be expert at programming, or break into a BASIC list. The form of open-ended, or generic software, is now becoming increasingly useful and will be considered further in the next section.

DATA HANDLING

Data Handling falls into one of the 'categories' of use of a computer, and is related to both the emancipatory and revelatory paradigms. It also acts as the basis for much of the work on 'Information Technology'. In reality, the facility that the computer has for handling data is only significant if there is an educational need to handle data. Which data? Why? What questions do you want to ask of it?

It was the historians in CIC who first began to make significant pleas for data interrogation packages to make specific use of specific data sets (CENSUS). The demand came from their own discipline concerns: the need to explore further the resource material that makes up part of the crucial evidence of history (Labbett, 1980; Killbery, Labbett and Randall, 1979). Exploration by hand or eye of reams of data returns means that one tends to pick out the obscure or odd, rather than overall trends or matched patterns. Putting such data on the computer enabled searches and analysis to be made. Yet there were very real concerns that putting the data on computer meant encoding it – actually reducing the richness of the historical veracity (the variety of spellings of the name Annabel, the myraid of minor job descriptions) into letter or numerical codes. This was not satisfactory, so variable field sizes were required; codes had to be devised to use with, rather than replace, this richness. It was also important that the interrogation software could accommodate matches between fields – thus 'equal' and 'not equal' to be placed with 'less than', 'greater than' and 'between'. Secondary searches of initial subjects must be possible so that one can search deeper into as well as across the data.

All this was because the historians wanted to be able to pose questions such as: 'How many children under the age of sixteen worked in England in the 1870s?' 'What sort of households did they live in?' 'How many siblings did they have?' 'Was it more, the boys or girls?' 'How many children under the age of sixteen already lived in households other than those of their parents?' Thus the imperative for putting the data on the computer and encoding it was due to pressure from historians, rather than from computer scientists (Watson 1984c). Freeman and Tagg (1985) have reported on the use of data-bases in a variety of classrooms. Now that some teachers in the humanities regularly use computer interrogation of data, they are in a better position to demand the appropriate style of interrogation software, and certainly, a better user interface. This will in turn influence the design of generic software.

Files of data are often incorporated as an integral part into other CAL units. Apart from the one experience of developing this large historical data handling package, CENSUS, the CIC Project has more usually turned its attention to the role of data within a wider exercise, such as the word files for the language game (CBLUFF) and village records for a biological role-playing exercise (RELATE). Currently, there is great interest in general but in the CIC in particular in the development of *generic packages*, that is, programs into which the user enters his own content within the framework provided. CIC has been working on a narrative generator (SCRIPTWRITER) for some time. Heppell (1986) has reported on the value of using generic packages, developed for the business world, in the classroom.

There is a tension between totally open-ended systems, such as a word processing unit or spreadsheet, and a totally closed CAL simulation that the user cannot customize for his own purposes. Our experience in developing a great variety of simulations makes CIC cautious about the idea of a 'simulation generator'. On the other hand, within a clear framework with working examples, we have seen through CBLUFF and DMS the value of enabling users to use frameworks for the incorporation of their own data or models. There are two clear issues to be resolved. Firstly the file handling of the material to be incorporated into the unit, whether for a series of team records or a file of words, must be given as much attention in design as the CAL unit itself. Ready-made example, or files, must be incoporated into the whole unit to provide a template of the total idea, and also for those who may not wish to customize by the incorporation of their own material. Secondly, the desire to develop an open-ended system must not dictate the shape of the unit to such an extent that its essence is lost or squeezed to an unacceptable degree. The pedagogic need for a generic unit must be clear. Such units do not necessarily spell the end for specific one-off simulations.

In the future, the new generations of software should enable us to interlink professionally-developed data packages, such as word processing or a spreadsheet, to the specific CAL unit that wishes to draw upon them. The interfacing between such general packages and the main unit will possibly become one of the main features of CAL development in the late 1980s.

RELATIONSHIP WITH THE CURRICULUM

Following such ground rules, it becomes apparent that educational software should be devised and developed to be incorporated into the educational curriculum if it is to be of any benefit to pupils.

The richness of the variety of CAL is partly a reflection of the richness of the pedagogic concerns to be found in schools. CAL can support and enhance some of these concerns. Familiarity with CAL and its attributes by educational practitioners will ensure that they take into full account its potential in extending the curriculum. But it is most unlikely that a radical shift will come by imposing the 'benefits of IT' on schools without any regard for the concerns of schools and their curriculum. The same problem occurs in the home education movement. It has been suggested that using computers will enable pupils to learn at home rather than in the classroom. Quite what style of learning is being referred to? CAI and CML? Expecting children to learn in isolation in their own homes, away from contact with other learners, must be of concern. An emphasis on the machine as a medium for delivering a message should not make the assumption that the style or content of the message is desirable.

ENHANCING THE CURRICULUM

CAL, by nature of these ground rules inevitably works in partnership with the curriculum that it has been designed to explore and serve. Thus the key question in developing CAL is not 'What are the assets of the computer that I can capitalize on?' This places the emphasis too much on the computer and may lead to drill and practice, or the development of large data bases to no educational purpose. Rather, 'What areas of the curriculum do I have problems with or are difficult to teach?' Can the computer help?' Exploration along these lines will then lead to the later but more significant questions that are currently being addressed, 'What areas of exploration and learning are now possible with the computer that I could not have conceived of before?' 'How can using the computer not just enhance but even extend my perception of the curriculum?'

This means that the bulk of CAL should have a clearly defined location within the curriculum. In the UK this currently means a location within a discipline, whenever the subject content and concepts are used and provide the basis for CAL. There is good reason for this, secondary teachers see themselves as teachers of a particular subject and will look to History CAL, or Music CAL or Biology CAL, as they will also look at Music films, or Geography tape and slide sequences. The point of entry into the medium comes on the whole, in secondary schooling from the discipline base. In primary schools this operates more around their areas of work, such as communication skills, number work and project work.

This is not to suggest however that CAL can only serve the requirements of subject-based skills and knowledge. There are many concerns, and in particular concepts, which CAL can address that occur in more than one syllabus – often across groups of subjects, such as the sciences or the humanities. Moreover, there are pedagogic aims such as the development of process skills, that cut across a broad sweep of subjects. Many of these aims indeed could be considered to be central to any curriculum which took as its base the disciplines of thought pupils should be able to exercise upon leaving school. Interdisciplinary or cross-disciplinary movements come and go; CAL is certainly an extremely useful medium for addressing concerns outside the domain of the single subject by drawing them together around the commonality of a topic, for instance the geographical, historical and economic aspects of canal building in eighteenth century Britain (CANAL). Indeed Killbery (1984) has extended this argument further by examining the role of the computer as 'guest expert' in the classroom, by providing the detailed information, concepts and variables to be explored from the view point of more than one specialism. In CIC, I have been struck ever increasingly by the commonality of aims, and indeed content and concern, that emerge from a variety of writing groups in different subjects. Each individual discipline approaches these commonalities from a variety of perspectives which lend specific colour to each specific discipline. CAL can capitalize on both the colour as well as the commonality

It is the place *within the curriculum* of CAL that makes the role of 'generic' or 'content-free', or general-purpose software so interesting and yet often misconceived. Data collection and interrogation packages, or general framework software tend to be white elephants unless they can be tailored, or have been designed to accommodate from the first, the nature of the data to be analysed, and the style of interrogation. Such data handling packages then become more specifically useful to educationalists. The newer generation of specific packages that are now becoming available will make this task easier.

Ensuring that CAL is developed in tandem with the curriculum can still lead to some fairly esoteric developments that pick and touch upon odd, often unconnected, areas of the curriculum. This *random-pecking approach* (Watson, 1982), while possbily valid as far as CAL and the curriculum is concerned, ignores the third part of the partnership, namely the teacher, who plans and delivers the curriculum. If software is produced which matches a teacher's curriculum concerns on perhaps six occasions throughout the school of eleven to eighteen year olds in any one year, there is little incentive for that teacher to ensure that the hardware is available, familiarize herself with both the hardware and the software, and plan the management of the machine in the classroom and the lessons. A more regular availability of CAL, just as a more regular availability of film (Watson, 1984b) would ensure that such concerns were as commonplace to the teacher as setting up a laboratory experiment, organising a field trip or using the videotape recorder. Until using CAL is seen as a regular and integral part of the curriculum as those other activities now are, it is better for CAL to address specific areas of the curriculum. Thus, if history teachers teaching a known syllabus to 13–16 years olds have at least six or eight CAL units that address that particular area and integrate specifically with their concerns, then there is a greater chance that those teachers will explore the potential of CAL to them and their teaching. This policy may be appropriate until incorporating software into the curriculum becomes more commonplace.

CIC has tackled this problem by working closely with *other curriculum development projects*, in history, geography, economics, languages and science in an attempt to produce software that addresses specific topics. This also has the benefit of ensuring that the software is developed by those who are exploring and extending their own subject-based curriculum. Thus the resulting software will be in touch with the latest thinking on the curriculum rather than reflecting the concerns of yesterday's classrooms.

Of course there are certain aspects of, or topics in, the curriculum that are bedrocks and those CAL units which tackle them have a long shelf life. On the other hand, it would be false to suggest that the curriculum is a static animal. Any comparison of the average class in the 1950s with that of the 1980s, in terms of syllabus content and context, and examination style would expose this fallacy. The curriculum sometimes shifts in significant bursts, as with earthquakes – with the associated chaos before the landscape (of curriculum) settles into its new form. Other aspects slowly but inexorably change – as with the shifting apart of the tectonic plates, one inch every ten years, down the central spine of Iceland. Either way, in combination the curriculum must be seen as a moving beast rather than as a static animal (Galton and Moon, 1983). The development of educational software must take place, therefore, within the context of the ever-changing concerns and manifestations of the curriculum.

ACCOMPANYING NOTES

Few pieces of CAL stand alone; they need accompanying notes for a variety of reasons:
- to explain the overall purpose of the unit;
- to identify any specific models and define the working limits to the variables;
- to suggest ways the unit may be used;
- to provide support documentation such as images; and
- to set appropriate introductory and follow up exercises.

The notes firmly embed a piece of software in its educational context. I have not used the term courseware, which some use just for the notes, whereas others use it for the whole pack. Also I dislike the implication that a CAL unit with the accompanying notes can provide in itself a self-contained educational course.

There was a period in the early 1980s when such notes accompanying software were derided – why not put all relevant information on the screen? There are a whole variety of answers to this: you can get much less information on any one 24 × 40 (or 80) character screen, and layout is less sophisticated, than on a printed sheet of A4 or A5 paper. Information should be presented in the most appropriate medium – and the computer is not very good as a page-turning tool. More importantly the notes provide a discussion point around the various ways the software can be used. Recent in-service initiatives suggest that rather than less documentation, we need more to help bridge the gap between the novice user and the potential of the software.

If these notes are to be taken seriously then they should be produced with as much care and professionalism as the software which they accompany. Hastily written dot-matrix script, Roneo'd onto A4 sheets stuck to the sleeve of the five and a quarter inch disk do the contents of that disk a disservice by downgrading its validity through the immediate impression it gives. Of course, the converse is also true – glossy well-presented material can give a spurious credibility to the content of the software. Nevertheless a mismatch between the care taken over the notes and the actual software is unfortunate.

EVALUATION

CAL should be evaluated in the educational environment for which it is designed. There are two types of evaluation: a formative evaluation during and as part of the development process, and evaluation of the product once complete. Whilst I shall write more of the former as part of the CIC development process in the second part of this book, of the latter there is woefully little. Indeed, there must be a growth of such evaluation for the health of CAL. As ideas in the development and execution of CAL change, the developers need to be able to draw not just on their experiences and pragmatism, but also on some external assessment of the educational role, and successes, failures, weaknesses and strengths of CAL as it is used in the classroom. Other curriculum work is able to draw upon a variety of opinion culled from research enterprises. CAL must be included in this pattern.

As Walker (1983) emphasizes, there is a need for the systematic and rigorous evaluation of the available materials. Unfortunately evaluation is seen too often in a more simplistic format – similar to a review of the software and what it does as a method of informing the potential users about it. Other forms of evaluation are drawn up to suit criteria which makes the software acceptable for purchase or use by one school board or authority. Miller and Burnett (1986) have indicated how potentially restricting such evaluation criteria can be.

If we are making claims for the role of CAL, then these have to be substantiated. At the moment, the only evidence I can use is taken from our 'formative evaluation form' which is reported in more detail later. Case study reports exist of classroom practice using computers in the Exploring Microcomputers series (Chandler, 1983; Watson, 1984a; Smith 1985; Wilkes, 1985). Some extremely useful reports have emanated from ITMA, where they used detailed classroom observation as a part of their CAI development and research process (Ridgeway et al., 1984; Fraser, 1983). But we need many more, and soon.

EXTENDING THE CURRICULUM

There is however another aspect to ensuring that CAL is developed in association with other curriculum developers and their associated concerns. Becoming familiar with the (currently) relatively limited role of computers within the curriculum and classroom will ensure that its potential has a greater chance of being extended in the future. Computer specialists, however wonderful they may believe their machines or the latest systems software to be, will never influence what will happen and is going to happen within education from outside. If educationlists become involved with the current technology and are able to use software that matches their current concerns, they are all the more likely to see how it can be used still further, not just so as to enhance the curriculum but also to extend it. Developing simulations that extended the range of laboratory experiments was a start; moving into model exploration, or the break up and analysis of texts, is an indication of how the computer may become an essential ingredient in the same way that both field and laboratory work is in schools today.

There is no doubt that information networks and the power of new hardware and software environments could have a significant influence upon the curriculum. I am not simply referring here to the potential for ensuring that the pupils know about the technology that they will meet in the adult world. The very nature of the syllabus and perceptions of the relative importance of content, concepts and process may undergo a fundamental shift with an environment that facilitates the fast downloading of facts from a variety of sources while also providing an oportunity to set up and explore declarative models. This shift within the educational spectrum will only be possible if education is a partner in the exploration of the potential of the systems. This makes it incumbent upon the educationalist to know and understand quite what is happening in the technology, but also for technologists to treat educationalists and their environment with respect. Developing CAL for the 8 bit and 16 bit micros that will be in school at least until the late 1980s may seem unexciting and outdated from a technological point of view. If it means that by the 1990s the educational world has a clearer understanding of the potential and limitation of newer environments, then the use of these systems will have an influence upon the curriculum in ways that I and others cannot possibly predict.

In developing CAL, there are clear interests from the curriculum, the hardware and software. Which of these is actually the dominant factor? For CIC we work with a combination of interests breathing over our shoulders – the technology, the curriculum, the teacher, the pupils, and the classroom environment. It is within this context that the method for developing CAL which has slowly emerged can be viewed; and this is described in Chapter 4.

4
A MODEL FOR CAL DEVELOPMENT

During the life of the Computers in the Curriculum Project a clear philosophy has emerged which has been outlined in the Ground Rules of Chapter 3. Conjointly with this, a model for the work has evolved that provides both a stable framework for operation, and yet one that is sufficiently dynamic to reflect the shifts of emphasis in both the curriculum and software domains.

Developing software for use in a range of subjects in schools is a highly volatile activity, prey to a rapidly changing hardware environment. It would be too easy for the dictates of that environment to grossly influence the shape of the product. While there is a necessity for a deep understanding of that environment (Millwood, 1983; Riddle, 1986), nevertheless the central purpose of the framework is to produce a natural marriage between the curriculum and the hardware, and so develop materials that reflect a philsophy which says that the CAL must serve education more than the system upon which it depends. Figure 4.1 illustrates this. The style of CAL units that provide a learning environment for the pupils to explore and gain a better understanding of the topic as a whole clearly influences the nature of the development model (Squires, 1981; Watson, 1981, 1984e; McCormick, 1984)

THE MODEL

The basis of the model lies in a large team that reflects a combination of expertise in hardware, software, the curriculum, and schools. This requires a team which not only contains the professional expertise in each area, but also will build and maintain the bridges between them. This team consists therefore of the following:
● Classroom teachers in a variety of sujects,
● Curriculum developers,
● Professional programmers,
● Systems analysts,
● CAL developers.

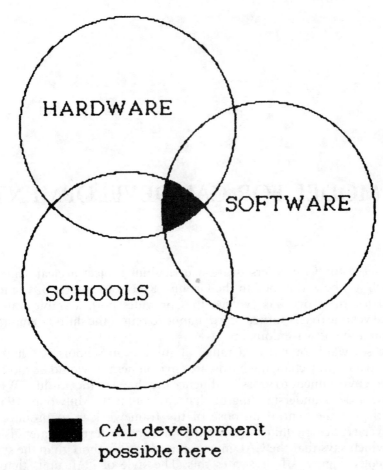

FIGURE 4.1   Three interlocking spheres of influences on CAL development

It is important to appreciate that these component parts are brought together at the beginning of any new CAL development. They may subsequently be involved more heavily at different stages of the development. But it is fundamentally a team approach.

TEACHERS

Creative and energetic teachers are essential for the development of good software. There are a variety of reasons for this.

● The teacher of a given discipline provides a practical understanding of his or her subject's syllabus. It must therefore be the geography teacher and not the physics or 'computer studies teacher who also programs' who designs the material, in order to avoid programs for Geography lessons that reflect the way a physicist happens to have been taught that subject some thirty years earlier. The latter would be nonsensical, and yet reflects the way any software produced in this way can creep readily into the classroom through the lack of useful software in a particular discipline.

● A teacher knows instinctively a variety of ways a topic may be taught in the classroom and areas of learning difficulty. This experience and pedagogic skill needs to be trapped and transformed into good software principles.

● Teachers who are actively involved in the classroom also provide a level of practicality and understanding of classroom organisation and management. Software that takes a long time to use, that covers a particularly esoteric part of the curriculum, and has to be used by all pupils simultaneously may simply be neither practical nor desirable.

● These teachers probably do not have to have any great initial understanding of either computers or CAL. It is their professional expertise as teachers that the team needs to provide credibility and relevance to its curriculum work. Teachers who are in the classroom would prevent the development of such software. This means that they may need a CAL awareness introduction before they can begin work.

● For the average teacher today being introduced to software designed by someone who is either without expertise in teaching the subject concerned or in the realities of the classroom could be positively harmful. It could well give a false and narrow perspective of the potential future role that resource may hold for the discipline. The value of CAL is that it should reflect and enhance current teaching practice in schools; it should not look over its shoulder to past practices that were related to particular structures or beliefs, and perpetuate them just because they lend themselves to a programmable framework. Equally, unless educationalists become involved in the development of software, the future value of CAL in extending the curriculum cannot be explored.

These points are covered quite succinctly by Bork (1980, p.42) when he states that 'Teaching is still teaching whether done by computer or any other device . . . really effective educational materials are coming in almost entirely from those who are very much involved in the teaching process.'

Who are these teachers and how can they be identified? Two agencies are used in identifying appropriate teachers. Firstly, it is important to work closely with Local Education Authority (i.e. school boards) subject advisers. They know the teachers in their own Authority, know those who are keen and those able to take on new commitments, know the Headteachers who will be sympathetic and supportive of teachers who will become involved. The second is other curriculum developers and their projects.

CURRICULUM DEVELOPERS

The inclusion of curriculum developers from other educational projects ensures that appropriate and current areas of the curriculum are tackled. With the development time for software running at a minimum of two years, a perspective is demanded that is innovative rather than reflective (Watson, 1982). Where there are no specific projects in hand there will always be key figures within the field who can be contacted through the relevant subject association or college, institution, or faculty of education.

A close relationship between CAL and curriculum development is built up through the teachers who have either been actively involved in the development of curriculum materials, or who have been involved in their trials and dissemination. The teachers associated with such projects are already used to analysing in some detail what they require of a particular area of the syllabus, or how to flush out conceptual understanding through topic specific content, and the related teaching points. These are often highly critical innovative teachers who bring a sharp cutting edge to the debates during development. CIC has worked with such teachers from a variety of curriculum development projects, including the Schools Council 16–19 Geography Project, the Schools Council History 13–16 Project, the Economics Education 14–16 Project, and the Secondary Science Curriculum Review.

The catalyst for the relationship between CAL and curriculum projects lies not just in the active involvement of the associated teachers, but by the association of one of the key 'actors' or development officers from a project with which CIC works. With each of the co-operative joint working parties with the aforementioned curriculum projects there has been a particular individual from that project who has played an important part in the team. Often that individual has taken on the role of group co-ordinator. They provide, in essence, the link not just with the practical implications of their approach, but with that project's own philosophy and 'ground rules' of, say, history or science.

PROGRAMMERS

Software needs to be written by professional programmers. There are reasons for this, and for the issues that result.

●Writing software that will survive and can be supported on a variety of machines is not a job for an amateur. Teachers who have taught themselves BASIC and code in their spare time will produce programs that are satisfactory for their own particular requirements, but rarely appropriate beyond their own schools.

●In education, no single microcomputer dominates and so, CIC has developed a strategy that enables the software to survive the changing hardware environment (see Chapter 7). Most commercial programmers are expected to work in one language and implement on one system. Educational programmers are working increasingly in a variety of languages and need to be familiar with sometimes as many as three microcomputer systems

● A programmer from an educational background, or with distinct educational sympathies, may be better than a commercial programmer because there needs to be some tolerance of the misconception that teachers may have about the machines capabilities, and also a willingness to provide a variety of CAL awareness components for the team to inform and help them write appropriate unit specifications.

● A good educational programmer will be less influenced by the visions of the future of a specific machine, while at the same time attempting to take the maximum advantage of existing hardware to ensure that good software will survive the vicissitudes of change. This requires a clearly structured logical approach to programming.

● The programmer on the whole has to work within much tighter constraints than the teachers. Not only do they have to adhere to some strong rules for development, but considerations of screen design and user interface dominate rather than the most elegant ways of coding.

Some teachers in the group do themselves program, or go down with a bout of 'computeritis' when they first acquire a machine. With very rare exceptions, these are not the people who should code the programs; the teachers are members of the writing group on account of their educational professionalism and not because of their amateur coding. Some teachers, however, once they have started programming, find it easier to explore their ideas by using code, particularly when developing a model. Though they are in the minority the team needs to accommodate those teacher/authors and persuade them to allow the programmer to take over at a certain point so as to provide professional polish. Nevertheless, over the last decade some key teacher/author/ programmers have emerged, providing extremely valuable inputs to the team as they act on the bridges between the component parts of the team. Newer software systems and authoring languages should in the future allow us to involve such teacher/authors more constructively.

SYSTEMS ANALYSTS

Systems and program analysts have become increasingly important in the light of the educational programming environment described above. In 1979, CIC published some thirty-five units written in BASIC to run on Nova mainframes. In 1980, these were converted to run on three micros – the RML 380Z, the Apple II and the Commodore Pet. By 1983, the Pet was no longer of any significance in UK schools, instead the new Acorn BBC Model B had to be accommodated, and a further forty-five more titles were published. By 1986, CIC had published another sixty plus units written in BASIC on three micros. CIC had also by now ensured that they were network compatible (for stand alone use) for the RML Link and Econet 2. New development work is currently underway using both Pascal and Logo as well as BASIC and a new procedural library. Two new host machines (the IBM PC and the RML Nimbus) are involved, while the Apple Macintosh is increasingly used as a graphics development tool. *Programmers therefore need recourse to a combination of hardware and software specialists.*

● It is essential to have a clear understanding of the machines for which software is being developed, including their various versions of BASIC, the machine architecture, the way they address graphics, and all those special features which make up each particular machine, down to the idiosyncracies of each version.

● These same hardware specialists need to keep a weather eye open for each new development that comes along that may have either a direct or a marginal impact upon the hardware to be used in schools in the future. Assessing the possibilities of transfer of software to a new host machine is done in collaboration with those educationalists on the team who try to assess the impact of what equipment is eventually likely to be found within schools. It has to be admitted that this form of crystal ball gazing is very hard. In the early 1980s computer memory was becoming very cheap. It seemed safe to develop software that needed 56K of memory. However, firstly, the new DTI scheme supported only a 32K machine, and then the Acorn BBC machine only came out with 32K. A significant amount of time then had to be spent devising means of condensing programs that had been developed on the assumption that memory would be automatic rather than a luxury.

● Peripherals are quite as important as the host machine; printer configuration for each micro has to be able to cope with the variety of printers that may be used. Similarly, networking existing machines causes headaches. It can be really quite difficult to transfer file storage software that has been designed for use on one machine for stand alone use on a network station without a considerable re-jigging of the internal file structure.

● Advice is always needed on the way any programming language is used to ensure that the most logical structure is adopted in both general and specific routines. This is particularly important, on the current micros where real development space is at a premium. Though 32K only may be available, it must be remembered that the style of user interface, graphics, and help routines can eat into that space very rapidly. Even in the newer 16 bit machines, with 256K or even 512K of space available, the space available is often drastically reduced by the language and graphics facilities.

● Analysis of the most appropriate structure for designing a program is also needed from someone who has particular skills at those problem-solving aspects of the task.

● In order to facilitate the issues of software portability and programming efficiency, these specialists of CIC have over the years developed a series of software tools and guidelines, which will be examined in further detail in Chapter 10. These provide a coherence to the work and a framework within which each programmer writes their code.

● The role of commercial software tools has become more integral to the overall work of the project. Thus there is a need to explore new tools as they emerge and to assess their value in relation to the home grown ones.

It is this everchanging programming environment that makes such professional support for the programming team essential. The links these individuals have with hardware manufacturers and software suppliers are just as important as the links between the teachers and their curriculum development projects.

CAL DEVELOPERS

These are a new professional group that has emerged during the operation of the model. Some teacher/author/developers and programmer/developers have become co-ordinators of subject writing groups, and by spending much time on development issues, have become specialists in CAL screen design and the user interface, as well as providing a link across different writing groups. Increasingly they can recognise the germ of an idea and help to tease out during discussions the most appropriate route forward for development.

An aspect of the perception of such individuals is their awareness of the variety of ways different subject groups have tackled CAL development. They bring to working groups, and the planning of new initiatives, a perspective that encourages lateral thinking. Their experience is essential in any CAL development that is to take place across a variety of curriculum areas.

An essential component in this structure in the development is the development of *mutual respect* between these educators and computer specialists (Watson, 1986). This respect is fostered by the CAL development co-ordinator, and by the fact that most members of the team fulfil two roles, the analysts also encode CAL units, the teachers are also often curriculum specialists, and the CAL co-ordinators both develop and design units and manage this development.

These co-ordinators act as both a catalyst for ideas and as the bridge between the two areas of work – the programming and the educational. They tend to be the focal point at which the combination of ground rules resides.

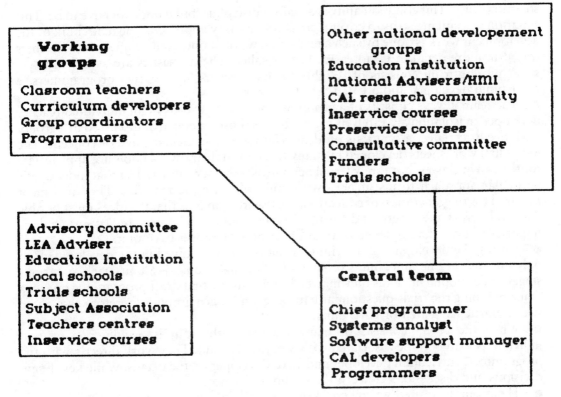

FIGURE 4.2   Relationship between a group and the centre

HOW THE TEAM WORKS

The CIC team is composed of a series of small subject-based working groups reflecting this combination of skills in various locations across the country. Each working group is often linked to an innovative curriculum project in one subject. These groups both draw upon and influence the skills of the central team where the core of the programming and CAL expertise resides. This relationship between one writing group and the central team is illustrated in Figure 4.2. This system has emerged to accommodate the finding and developing of 'good ideas', and then to see those ideas turned into sound imaginative CAL units.

A devolved team which nevertheless has a home in a local host institution helps to provide contact and credibility with a variety of local bases of curriculum innovation – from Foreign Languages in Lancashire and Cumbria, to History in Leeds and Bradford, Craft, Design, Technology (CDT) in Devon, and Geography in Kent.

A WRITING TEAM

The core of the model lies in the successful drawing together of a writing group that has a common unity. This common unity is usually a discipline, but it does not have to be. This situation is changing so as to cover a cross-disciplinary approach. The main bulk of the development work is done by such a team. The work of one team, from start to finish, is traced in more detail in Chapter 12. But its salient characteristics are as follows.

● A writing team consists of roughly twelve teachers, one or two programmers, a curriculum developer and a CIC CAL developer.

● The team always consists of a group of teachers. The ideas of an individual teacher developed in isolation are rarely as productive as those amended or discussed in a group. CAL needs to reflect a synthesis of ideas relating to a particular topic or concept. The individual worksheets developed by many teachers in their own schools are appropriate for their own classes, but rarely travel beyond as they inevitably reflect that individual's particular approach to his or her own pupils who use the material. The investment required for the generation of educational software demands that the ideas must be able to travel across the length and breadth of the country. The *peer review* principle is important in the development and modification stages of a CAL unit.

● During the development, a writing group is rarely involved in the development of only one unit at one time, but is often 'seeing through' some 4–6 units each at various stages of development. Thus they may be looking at the first draft program for one idea while planning the trials questionnaire for a second. Each group is therefore associated with a particular batch of CAL units.

● While the group consists of many teachers/authors, it is usually one or two individuals who become associated with a particular unit. They work directly with the programmer, curriculum developer and CAL developer on the details, while key design decisions and discussions concern the group as a whole.

● The group is located wherever a keen LEA adviser, or another curriculum project base, or key individual have been identified. Thus teachers in the north west of England were drawn together at a centre for foreign languages. The curriculum developer, who was a key figure in the foreign language world, had been involved in developing a scheme of foreign language graded tests that were used in those LEAs, and was based in the local College of Education. He provided the links to the LEA advisers in the two authorities who identified the teachers.

● Whenever possible, at least one of the programmers should be located with the group. Sometimes it proves impossible to locate a programmer in the place where the writing group is based, in which case one of the central team programmers should travel regularly to the area.

● The curriculum developer's home institution provides the home base for the writing group, and the home also for the programmer.

● The group will meet for regular sessions as the local conditions and the secondment pattern determine. Where teachers may be travelling long distances, a two day residential workshop, held roughly three times a year, may prove to be the most appropriate arrangement. In others, a half day and evening twice a term may suffice. The frequency of the meetings depends both on the flow of work and the various stages that have been reached in the development process a CAL unit (see Chapter 5).

● Sometimes the LEAs have managed to provide secondment on a regular weekly basis for some members of the writing group. Other LEAs have provided whole term's secondment. The ebb and flow of the work very much depends upon this rather individual pattern which is quite peculiar to each working group.

● The curriculum developers need secondment from their host institution for between

10 and 40 per cent of their time to co-ordinate the work of the local writing group. Their tasks are two-fold, to make the detailed arrangements such as the calling of meetings, paying expenses, etc., and more importantly to work regularly with the local programmer on the flow of work in hand in between the group meetings.

● A member of the central team, the CAL developer, has usually been the one to take the initiative to set up the group. He is closely involved with the writing group, especially at the early brainstorming stages. He needs however to avoid cramping the style of the local group co-ordinator. He provides the link between the writing group and the central team. The CAL developer usually has responsibility for more than one writing group – thereby bringing a lateral perspective from being actively involved in geography as well as history, or science as well as economics.

● The programmers who are centrally based are often working with two different writing teams, so they also can bring to each a different cross-referencing perspective.

● It usually takes up to a year of negotiation with an LEA, a host institution, and/or a curriculum development project to establish a writing group. Funds have to be sought, personnel identified, and machines located before the real work begins. Much of this work takes place by building upon individual contacts. As CIC gets older these contacts have become more numerous, as teachers who were members of earlier writing groups move to other posts and then instigate discussions on the setting-up of new writing groups. These individuals may then become group co-ordinators/CAL developers.

● The involvement of local teachers and close contact with the LEA subject adviser over a period of two or three years with one writing group can be a useful focus of professional development in the field (Watson, 1984d).

THE CENTRAL TEAM

For 12 years CIC was based in the Centre of Science and Maths Education (CSME) at Chelsea College, London University. In 1985 this merged with two other London colleges, Queen Elizabeth and King's; a new college King's College London (KQC), and a new faculty of education known as the Centre for Educational Studies, were formed. While a significant proportion of the work has taken place at the location of the writing group, the central team had taken an active developmental role, and not just a managerial one, from its Chelsea base (which itself had four different locations). CIC has often been called 'the Chelsea Project' in the world of educational computing.

The director, and since 1980 two assistant directors, have been based here. They not only provide a managerial base, but are individuals who have built up the CAL development expertise and the main curriculum and educational issues. Other individuals who have CAL development experience have also been based centrally – at one time there were three individual managers with particular responsibilties for science, humanities and languages. This was when the project was made up of 17 writing groups.

The Chief Programmer, Systems Analyst and Software Support Manager are based at Chelsea and provide the support for hardware and software issues. It is important that they are in an environment where they work together rather than in isolation. This includes provision of all the hardware likely to be found in schools, as well as other machines that are either used in development or are being investigated. This is a large recurring expenditure and requires space.

Quite a few of the project programmers are based centrally. This is because the funds which enable a programmer to work with a writing group may only cover a percentage

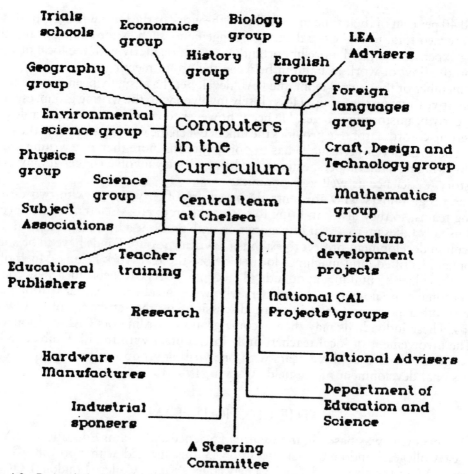

FIGURE 4.3   Project links in 1985 – the whole team

of a person, but for a three year period. The doubling of function makes it more likely that those who are working to two writing groups will be based in London rather than at one regional location. CIC did for one two year period, have two different writing groups based in one city, each of which was served by the same programmer, but such a coincidence is rare.

The final tidying up process, which described in more detail in subsequent chapters, generally takes place at Chelsea rather than at the location of the writing group. Here all the machines are located, the office support staff is available for the production of final manuscripts, and one of the directors or managers usually plays a major editing role and sees through the flow of a whole series of units in their final stages.

Figure 4.3 illustrates the total team.

SUPPORT STAFF

The central team, as well as the writing groups, must have an appropriate supporting staff without whom the scheme could not operate. Two secretaries are the minimum for the flow of work that is generated, and some technical assistance. The secretaries at the CIC are often in receipt of notes for units from various writing groups, and so have become familiar with an enormous variety of handwriting, or indeed scribble, styles. With size, the project has also found the role of an administrative assistant useful, to combine the tasks of conference organiser, information officer and trials overseer.

RELATIONSHIPS BETWEEN CONSTITUENT PARTS

CROSS-LINKS BETWEEN THE CENTRAL TEAM AND THE WRITING GROUP

As can be seen from Figures 4.3 and 4.4 the central team and writing groups may be viewed from different perspectives by the individuals who make them up, or by those who are looking for a centre/periphery type of analysis. This diversity of viewpoint could cause tension and confusion in the team, but in fact can be a strength as long as the two parts are seen as equal partners and not as two groups competing for the ascendancy. Each needs the other.

The various functions within the project as a whole are not necessarily fulfilled by separately identified individuals, however expertise in hardware, software tools, programming languages, the curriculum in various disciplines, and editing, must all be available for the writing groups to draw upon. Sometimes the expertise resides within the central team at Chelsea (King's College); at other times it resides with an individual who is located with one of the writing groups. For instance, almost invariably the subject

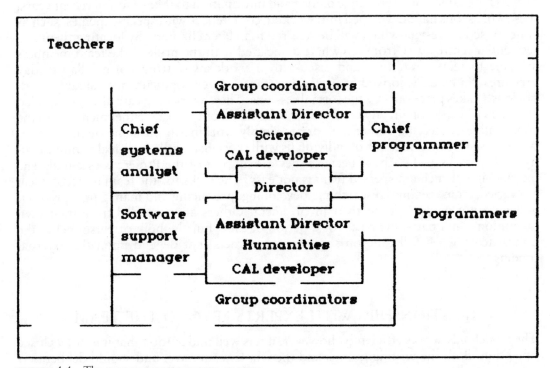

FIGURE 4.4   The management structure or maze

curriculum specialists are more likely to be found in various locations each acting as a curriculum developer and group co-ordinator to one writing group. One particular writing group may be particularly interested in developing CAL units that are team games, so their allocated programmer has the task of identifying, or building up, specific routines and screens to tackle this aspect. When another group looks at a team game, the programmer in the region will be drawn upon for advice. In this sense, it is important to note the value which is placed on individual expertise within the team, rather than a more hierarchical approach of responsibility. Obviously there are several managerial issues which the directors/managers/co-ordinators have to face with respect to ensuring a through flow of work, and responsibility to the funders. But the creative development side is very much a team activity.

How does a project team which is dispersed across the four corners of the UK keep in touch?

● Two *newsletters* appear regularly – the first a general one to keep all the writing teams informed of the various activities in the subject areas as well as general current concerns. The second, PATCH, specifically addresses programming issues and keeps the whole team updated as to the current position, solutions to old problems and points the way forward to new potential problems.

● Project *workshops* are held annually. It is rare for any writing group, as a whole, to meet or exchange views with another writing group. In the 1970s when there were fewer writing groups involved, the whole project would meet annually for workshop. With the increase in the size of the project in the early 1980s this was no longer possible. Instead each writing group sends its co-ordinator, and possibly one of the teacher members of the group to the workshop. All programmers come, as do all the members of the central team. This enables an interchange of idea and information to take place. In recent years, these workshops have developed into working conferences with specific themes, such as issues of screen design, which will be referred to in later chapters. By locating them in a residential centre away from anywhere associated with the project, the team members are able to relax, fraternize and discuss their work away from normal day to day pressures. Software is looked at in various stages of development, but valuable work obviously takes place outside the formal sessions. These workshops are always attended by others who are not directly involved with the work, but who are either members of the consultative or steering committee, or are simply working in the same field.

● A loose *personal network* of individuals with specialists skills, who feel a commonality in their tasks and purpose because they are all part of the Project is essential. The interlocking of such a dispersed team is not easy. The tasks for the team to accomplish are varied, from creating, researching, developing, producing and managing a product. Some are not paid at all for their involvement. Others are seconded from their own institutions on a part-time basis for a period of time, but the bulk of personnel in the central team work full time on short-term contracts that depend upon the external funding.

RELATIONSHIPS WITH EXPERTS BEYOND THE TEAM

The model only works efficiently, however, if it is well understood that it is not a closed operation. Both the writing groups and the whole team have, and should deliberately foster, links with the immediately available networks to which they are naturally attached.

- The first natural network is the curriculum development project or subject specialists with which many individual working groups are associated. A member of the other curriculum project team attends meetings and takes part in discussions in the writing group. The CAL co-ordinator regularly attends meetings of the other project. Other project schools act as trials teachers for the material. This ensures that curriculum thinking behind the materials is always to the fore in minds of the group.

- The Local Education Authority advisers are an important network for advice and concerns about all schools and teachers, not just those associated with innovative curriculum work. It is important to remember how 'selective' the teachers can be, who become involved in a writing group. The advisers provide a clear link to the perceptions and concerns of the 'average' teacher. They thus remind the group, and indeed the whole team, of the spectrum of 'clients' for whom the CAL is being developed. Most importantly, they also remind us that the clients are in fact the learners who will be using CAL. The pupil's concerns are kept well to the fore, not just by the regular discussions about the user-interaction in the actual development, but also by the country-wide perspective the advisers provide.

- Many members of the team, either the co-ordinators, CAL developers or teachers are also members of their subject association. The CAL developers do foster links both with these associations and with the growing number of sub-committees these associations now have covering the domain of educational computing in their particular discipline. This gives another layer of perspective to all the overall concerns of subject teachers, through their annual conferences. This awareness is fed back both for the detailed deliberation of the writing groups, and for the overall management and strategy planning of the whole team.

- CIC builds up a list of those schools where no teacher has been involved in the development of that particular subject writing group, but who will do a detailed trial of the whole CAL unit, both the software and courseware. This contact back to schools is always most salutary and results in interesting tensions in the trials feedback. Sometimes the writing group has become so involved in the development of a unit that it takes trials in the schools to point out some of its basic inadequacies – for instance, a complete run needs at least ninety minutes, but no class of the age level at which it is aimed ever has that block of time available. On the other hand the trials schools can display such a naïvety and ignorance of software that the writing group are reminded of, not only how far they have travelled in experience during their work within the team, but how many basic and fundamental problems there are that many teachers have yet to overcome. There are many reasons of a practical and organisational nature which explain why there is still relatively little CAL used in the classroom.

- Each writing group is based in a host institution; this may be the same as the one in which the central team is based (Chelsea (King's College) in the case of CIC), or another, for instance, a polytechnic, college of education, or teacher's centre, in various other parts of the country. The programmers and co-ordinators will have access to members of other departments, including education, subject faculties and the local computing centre. All this provides a wide base of interest and pool of expertise with the common theme of education running throughout.

- There is also a formal method of advisory groups associated with specific subject writing groups where the various interested parties, such as host institution, LEA, curriculum development project and the wider team are represented, and who meet to discuss and monitor progress of each writing group. This is complimented by a Steering Committee which advises the directors of the whole team, with representation from the wide range of interested parties and observers in this field, including HMI's representatives from national bodies such as CET, and the DES. Some members of these groups have been friends of the Project for a long while and provide a breadth of perception that those of us working within the Project may lack. At the same time representation of new educational initiatives, such as TVEI, enable us to keep firmly abreast of current issues.

● Links are also deliberately fostered with the hardware manufacturers. CIC has maintained close links with manufacturers for some time and has been involved in planning discussions; it has also been consulted by them on educational issues. Nevertheless, the relationship with manufacturers is a difficult one as it has to be recognised that the home or business market, rather than the educational one, is likely to have the most influence on hardware producers – and yet education needs just as good a programming environment as commerce.

The Project as a whole deliberately fosters relationships, both national and international, with other similar projects or groups. It is essential in fact that such contacts are made and maintained in order to prevent the work atrophying. CIC has maintained these through the basis of the following:

● Regular meetings with other national development groups, including ITMA, ILECC, AUCBE, Homerton College and Netherhall School Software.

● Attending conferences in educational computing, presenting papers and discussing the work in general, as well as with subject specific presentations at subject association annual conferences.

● Taking part in in-service educational initiatives, by lecturing and running workshops at the various regional and national INSET conferences.

IMPLICATIONS

There are implications that devolve from the model and its constituent parts, and how they interlock. These in general can be reviewed under the headings of time, space, resource and management.

TIME

The most important implication is time. It takes time to set up and operate the model. Once the model is operating, it builds upon the continued growth of experience of the team members – the spin-off in terms of value and richness of experience naturally increases, the longer the model is able to operate. Although most writing groups naturally last for only about three years, as the teacher members' interest and commitment either moves on or wanes, there have, however, always been some individuals who have maintained, and even increased, their involvement. Some members of the central team have now been working with the project, on short-term contracts, for seven or more years. Some co-ordinators were members of orginal writing groups in 1973–4.

Long term involvement can result in staleness, or in an isolation of ideas. In this field however, where the technology itself is changing so rapidly, it is very hard to become insular. It is difficult for this author to be neutral on this, as I have actually been involved with the project since its inception in 1973, and worked directly within it for eight years. Nevertheless, there are always dangers when a curriculum project becomes too institutionalized, or when it continues to develop the same type of materials in the same way. CIC has gone through shifts of emphasis, and is currently undergoing a new shift. But the danger of staleness must be recognised.

● Programmers must be employed full-time to work in this field. It is a professional commitment and requires time.

● The curriculum developers who become group co-ordinators also need time; the pattern that has worked more successfully than any other is a percentage time secondment – anything from 10–50 percent from their institutions for the period of time that a writing group is operating.

● The CAL developers, who also tend to have directorial and management roles, need to be employed full-time to both organise and develop the 'outside' links and yet be an integral part of the work of the team. They must keep their hands 'dirty' through active CAL development all the time.

● The teachers who form the basis of the working groups do need secondment release from their schools to be arranged so as to be involved with the work. CIC has operated a variety of patterns, according to what has been found to be possible for a particular Local Education Authority either to arrange and or to afford. It is essential for all members of the writing group to be able to meet for at least one whole day in a term. Ideally, on top of this they will also have a half-day or a one day a week secondment to pursue the development of the unit in between group meetings. Sometimes this is possible for some, but not for all the teachers, for some of the development period; that is, two and three teachers in the group may get a half day a week's secondment in one year, then another pair may get it in the second year. This will naturally influence which of the units is to be developed most speedily, and also in which order. Conversely, the pattern of secondment may be able to fluctuate according to the pace at which some units are being developed. Occasionally local authorities have been able to arrange a full-term secondment for one of the teachers.

The variation in the pattern of secondment certainly influences the identification of some units for development, as the key authors are able to spend more time on it. On the other hand, some LEAs are prepared to arrange secondment for an individual once they know which members show signs of being most actively involved. Despite this, it is important that the secondment pattern does not impinge upon the sense of unity of the group as a whole, otherwise the peer group 'feel' comes to be lost. There are times when teachers who want secondment cannot get it, because of the particular circumstances of their school, and yet they have been the major author of the unit.

The absolute ideal is for the group to be able to meet in an environment well away from their teaching posts; either at the host institution where the CAL co-ordinator and programmer are based, or in a residential centre. One CIC group, based in the North West met once a term for three years in various residential centres in the area where there were no distractions for any of the group and consequently they were able to concentrate on the work. This certainly has implications for the funding, but when it has been possible to arrange, these two day residential workshops, the pace and progress of work achieved at them has been significant.

● The meetings one per term are also attended by the various members of the whole team who have been associated with the particular group, for instance, one of the manager/CAL developers, one of the systems experts. In between these meetings, the programmers and authors working on a particular unit will meet either at the host institution or the author's school to iron out particular points. However it is also necessary to appreciate that coding takes time – and there will be periods when there may be little meeting going on, but there will still be plenty of work.

● A CAL unit needs time to generate and develop fully. Coding up the initial idea usually is little reflection of how the finished unit may look. It goes through key shifts – firstly at the brainstorming stage, then at the specification, followed by one or two development drafts, and also following trials. This pattern of development is traced out in more detail in later chapters. But there are times when there is no active work taking place on a unit, while the authors mull over the ideas and possible directions in which the development can go. Such pauses often inflicted by the pressure of other work in the project, are a most valuable way of stepping back and analysing the real scope of the unit. Such time is difficult to identify formally, yet I feel it is important.

●The time configuration for the operation of the model therefore works on a mixture between writing group members who combine these tasks with their teaching or lecturing tasks, and CIC team members who combine their tasks across a variety of writing groups.

Each writing group needs at least three years available to it. In that time, one group can produce roughly between six and ten CAL ideas and can see most of them through to publication. The important aspect of allocations is the length of time that is needed. One single unit cannot really be developed in less than one year; ideally eighteen months to two years should be allocated, and in reality it more usually takes between two and a half to three years. This will be explored in further detail in subsequent chapters. It must be remembered that this time allocation includes both the development of CAL design awareness and the failure of some ideas. The second set of ideas from a group usually takes a shorter time to define and get to a clear specification stage. Cutting back on time for the operation of this model cannot be recommended.

SPACE

All writing groups need a sense of identity. Most have been associated with a particular institution and with a curriculum area. In the 1970s most writing teams were not related to an area, but were really one individual in one location who was kept in touch with another, working in the same subject, in another part of the country. The isolation of this work was inhibiting and led to the clear need to identify and locate working areas. This aids the sense of belonging to a specific sub-group of a larger team. When there are groups culled from more than one location to work in the same topic, space has to be found in one institution so that a sense of identity can be fostered when amongst a diverse group. This is often done centrally at Chelsea (King's College), but it can and has occurred elsewhere.

● Space and resource allocation in a host institution is not necessarily as easy to arrange as it might seem, and such allocation needs to be negotiated early on in the establishment of a group so as to avoid headaches of a petty sort interfering with the flow of work and the co-ordinators time.

● Having a 'home base' for the project has been of increasing importance, particularly in relation to an education faculty. It has aided a significant sense of identity, both internally to the team, as well as externally, to both the funders and the users of software.

RESOURCES

Personnel, space and time allocations have natural implications on resources. That is, the level of funding needed to operate this model is obviously significant.

● This model assumes a professional approach to curriculum development and this expects the model to work through the employment or secondment of the appropriate individuals.

● The level of expertise of all those involved does not come cheaply. Good programmers who are going to build up a particular expertise in CAL design and development are on the whole not found in a school leaver who wants employment for six months. Key co-ordinators and CAL developers are rarely young inexperienced teachers, but rather those who have already begun to move up the educational career structure. After all, it is their very experience in education that is so valuable. The salary level of these key personnel is not minimal, nor should it be.

● One key problem is the inability of this model to reward financially the teacher members of the writing group. They are employed full-time by their LEA, and the model works on finding the resource to fund the LEA for secondment or supply covers for the teachers. They work extremely hard, often in their own time. A system of honoraria is sometimes able to be used. The nature of the funding from various sources which expect to see a return for their investment makes a royalty share difficult. Yet there is no reason why the model could not allow for this. It is the constraints of the funding agencies that exerts the greatest influence.

● The real implication of this model is that *educational software is expensive to produce*. But so is an educational television programme. Costs should be compared with other significant resources – the development of a CAL unit should not be compared, as it so frequently is, with a textbook. Further chapters give an indication of the total costs and refer to man years of resource. It must also be remembered that there are gains beyond the obvious one of having CAL material available.

● There is no doubt that the involvement of so many practising teachers from the classroom in the actual development acts as a basis of long term in-service teacher education in its own right. At this critical period of time, many teachers have attended only 'CAL awareness' courses, lasting a few days, which have been in effect, a 'Cook's tour of Information Technology' and left them more confused than ever, a pool of teachers in an LEA who have been immersed in the detailed issues of CAL development through CIC is invaluable. Indeed, it is noticeable how many of the teachers who have been involved with the Project in this way have moved into posts of responsibility in the light of their expertise thus gained.

Members of the team also gain professional development through the involvement in curriculum development as well as management skills.

Some impression of actual costs is given in Chapter 13; for the last five years the Project has been working on a combined annual budget of around £350,000.

MANAGEMENT

The task of managing and directing a team based on this model is not simple. It is complicated by the fact that most individuals involved with this, as with many other curriculum development projects, have gone through no formal management training. Experience from other aspects of educational work will help, but a project is peculiar in that it cannot necessarily draw upon known structures which are either accepted generally as being appropriate for the work, or rules which the individuals who make up the project team will understand as being in operation. Various factors emerge.

● There are definite areas of responsibility where a pyramid of hierarchical responsibilities may be seen as appropriate, particularly within the project as a whole.

● This is reinforced in CIC by the position of managers who are responsible for specific specialisms or areas of work, for instance the Science Manager, the Chief Programmer.

● An emphasis in team-work and creativity cuts across a managerial hierarchy in the development work itself. This may be difficult to operate in practice if an assistant director responsible for humanities attends a meeting only as one of a team discussing a new idea for a unit. The director may perceive himself as only one of the team but others may be inhibited, or give undue weight to the directors contributions, because of his role in the whole project, rather than in that specific writing team.

● Writing teams can only work on the peer review principle. In practice, the operation of the central team can also only work on the peer group principle. Thus in the work and position in the central team it should be the respect and role of the professionalism that dominates, rather than the managerial role individuals undertake.

● The hardest area to manage is not a single writing team, or the Chelsea based group, but the links between the combinations.

● Responsibility has to be taken by known individuals for:
— the work of any one writing group, through a co-ordinator,
— the work of each identified specialist area, through the managers,
— the overall linking and managing of these two to make a coherent whole, through a directorial team.

The latter has to take responsibility both within and beyond the project, that is to the funders and home base institution. In this way a hierarchy of responsibility and associated management is inevitable.

Figure 4.4 illustrates the management structure or maze of the total team. Notice how the strands between specialisms help to make the formation confusing enough for no single pyramid to effectively operate.

The *main management task* is to dovetail the various aspects of the work into a coherent and logical flow. The main focus is on the through-put of CAL units from initiation to publication. CIC maintains a data-base that gives, at a quick glance, an idea of how many units there are at certain key stages. It also shows the loading of current work, or work in the pipeline, for individuals. Into this must be dovetailed time for other aspects, such as the development of new software tools. The co-ordinators and editors also keep separate charts of their authoring and editing commitments. The directors are juggling with space to explore new initiatives and write new proposals, as well as chasing up progress in the areas for which they are responsible.

Most of these tasks are dynamic, and the status or stage of work changes more frequently than maintaining large flow charts would warrant. Accordingly managing the flow is organised in CIC principally through two sets of meeting – that of the directors (fortnightly) and the management team (executive) that consists of all the subject or technology managers which meets monthly. Progress of groups and units, problems either general or specific, issues that need to be raised are brought to these executive and directors meetings, often with the pre-circulation of discussion papers and progress reports. The regularity and frequency of meetings are aimed to help to maintain the unity of the team.

EVOLUTION

This model may appear to be a fixed static beast. In reality it has evolved over a long period and continues so to do. Members of the Project in 1975, would find it difficult to recognise either its size or complexity in 1985. At the time in which I am writing (1986) there is a shift in scale and emphasis which has already resulted in the closure of a number of writing groups. New writing teams may operate for specific purposes such as cross-disciplinary work, or an exploration of modelling, but may be drawn from those individuals already skilled in CAL particularly for the more complicated design explorations and for the leading-edge work that CIC is planning. Such CAL may be designed more to extend rather than just enhance the curriculum. Integrated research projects may influence the nature of the development. All these will dictate a shift in the type of team to serve the work. The model as outlined reflects the work we have undertaken hitherto.

Unless there are credible curriculum projects whose personnel are involved in 'getting their hands dirty' in educational software, then education will always have to accept the tools, both hardware and software, that are presented to it and just make do. The voice of experience persistently discussing the issues such as software tools, peripherals, and languages in the light of education's needs is more likely to be listened to. Although the educational market is not as large as that of the business or the home computer market, it is a steady one and specialists who can draw upon computing and educational expertise are thin on the ground. This model provides one environment for the development of such expertise.

More detailed implications of the operation of this model will emerge in practical examples of various stages of development, through an exploration of guidelines for development and subsequent chapters. In no way, however, am I suggesting that it would be appropriate to transport this model totally and impose it on other environments. However, by exposing it in detail, I hope to raise the issues that any CAL developer must face. In order to place such a strategy for development in a wider context, Chapter 16 briefly reviews other CAL development models currently in operation.

SECTION II

GUIDELINES AND EXAMPLES

5
STAGES IN THE DEVELOPMENT OF A CAL UNIT

The total process, whereby a piece of CAL starts with the germ of an idea and ends up as a fully published unit, could be viewed in the light of a flow of events. Some activities take place concurrently; others follow a stepped sequence. A linear progression through the process must not be assumed. Sometimes parts of a unit follow totally separate strands only to merge together later. Nevertheless a distinct set of stages of development can be identified; within each stage there are a combination of operations which have to be fulfilled before that stage is complete and the unit moves to the next. These stages naturally reflect the roles within a team.

In CIC, five distinct stages of development occur. They relate to the nature of the team approach that has been identified earlier, but the main structure is a reflection of the distinctly separate feel that is given to each stage of the work. Figure 5.1 illustrates the flow of work through the five stages of Idea, Development, Trial, Modification and Publication. The figure gives a rather idealized identification of two strands, programming and writing activities. In reality the two are highly intertwined – as is indicated in the subsequent text.

FIVE STAGES

THE IDEA

This is the key 'brainstorming' part, this is how good ideas are to be found. Although the nature and character of a unit may change during development, the soundness of the initial groundwork in this stage is important.

● Identification of teachers, curriculum developers and host institution for the formation of a new writing group; introductory sessions on CAL awareness to include looking at CAL in other subjects.

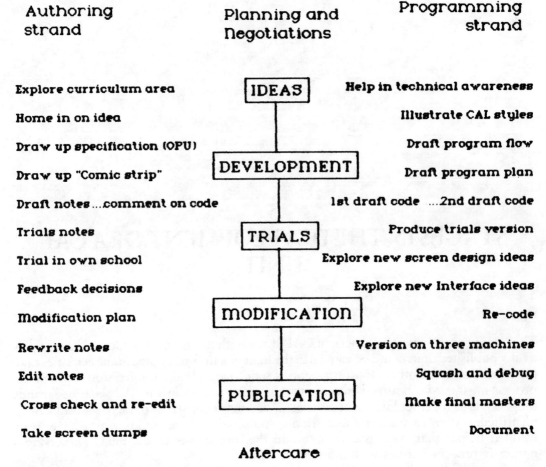

Authoring strand	Planning and Negotiations	Programming strand
Explore curriculum area	**IDEAS**	Help in technical awareness
Home in on idea		Illustrate CAL styles
Draw up specification (OPU)		Draft program flow
Draw up "Comic strip"	**DEVELOPMENT**	Draft program plan
Draft notes...comment on code		1st draft code ...2nd draft code
Trials notes	**TRIALS**	Produce trials version
Trial in own school		Explore new screen design ideas
Feedback decisions		Explore new Interface ideas
Modification plan	**MODIFICATION**	Re-code
Rewrite notes		Version on three machines
Edit notes		Squash and debug
Cross check and re-edit	**PUBLICATION**	Make final masters
Take screen dumps		Document
	Aftercare	

FIGURE 5.1   Stages in unit development

● Discussion on both the curriculum and areas of teaching difficulty which leads members to home in on appropriate topics; programmers indicate particular facilities of micros that may interest them.

● Identification of specific ideas; and the extent of the content; this task often results in four or five ideas which may all get followed through to completion.

● Each idea evolves, after discussion, to some paper based points which cover the following:

– selecting priorities of educational aims and objectives – why this topic? How is it taught at the moment? Are there problems that turning it into a CAL unit might solve?

– Identifying the extent of the content, which may involve some subsequent research into the subject matter.

● A consideration of a mathematical, or qualitative (possibly a multifactorial) model on which the calculations or structure of the program may be based.

● Following a pathway through the program; what do we want the learner to do and in what sort of sequence? A further look at variety of styles of user interface.

● Initial attempts at designing the screen layout; drawing up a comic strip.

- Some initial coding and feasibility of certain aspects of execution. Consultation by the programmer with the central team on the overall plans and an exploration of various methods of execution.
- Producing a clear specification for the programmer upon the basis of which it is agreed by the group, the CAL developer, and by the programmer that it is sufficiently sound to proceed.

DEVELOPMENT

This is the really exciting, creative and most fruitful part of the whole operation. During the ideas stage, the teacher in the group will often feel insecure about their role, their lack of expertise in the face of these computer specialists, and about the technology in general and how to get going. The role of the experienced CAL developer is crucial here at building the initial bridges across the two levels of experience which will receive heavy use in this next stage. These bridges are based primarily on respect for each others' skills and professionalism. In the ideas stage, the programmers' professionalism is already clear. In the development stage, the partnership becomes more equal. Apart from anything else, it is a creative yet practical time; progress is clear and tangible.

- Main coding of key modules in the specification takes place; draft screen designs are produced and the initial user interface mapped out.
- The groups respond to the initial execution of the idea. This often results in quite major revisions of their specification as intentions become clearer. Occasionally the execution spins off further ideas that move away from the original intention.
- The model being used is tested for robustness and appropriateness; the programmer requests appropriate limits to variables to be able to see if realistic results are produced. At this stage fundamental problems, or a lack of balance, within the model can be exposed through the testing of the outward variable limits.
- There is a debate between the 'fudgy' descriptive models of the teacher and the programmer who needs an exact algorithm; or a debate on how to simplify a horrendously complex model, but known to be academically respectable, into a size that is compatible with the machine. The teachers often ask the programmer to continue with the rest of the program while they 'sort out' the model.
- The group debates in greater detail the educational objectives in order to clarify the aims which the model must achieve; this may help solve some of the modelling problems.
- The teachers begin to explore the logical links between key sections of the program, and debate the relative merits of a totally open-ended piece of software versus the more directed learning path. This influences the design of the user interface.
- Tensions in peer groups need to be calmed as each individual author's methods and style of teaching become exposed to debate during the above discussion. These peer group discussions are powerful but can be traumatic, and a keen eye and the active involvement by the group co-ordinator and CAL developer are needed at this time.
- One or two teachers emerge as the authors for the unit when they are cajoled into the need to begin to write notes for teachers and students to accompany the software.
- Various sections of code are beginning to be merged to form a coherent program.
- The programmer frequently consults with systems analysts and other programmers in the central team when tricky issues emerge.
- Draft notes begin to emerge from writing group; often teachers have not written this sort of material before except for themselves. A lack of confidence at this new role also

has to be overcome and their confidence nurtured. Editing help is provided both by the group co-ordinator, and the CAL developer.
● The contents of the notes are scrutinized by the group and curriculum project advisers to clarify curriculum aims.
● Trials evaluation sheets are written, with a particular emphasis on a section covering the particular subject and learning aims intended by the developers. Sometimes an author will do a dummy run of the software in their own classroom to explore some of the questions that need to be asked in the trials.
● Program and notes need to be welded together by cross-referencing; screen dumps are taken for incorporation into notes.
● The authors determine style and wording of error messages and check their occurrence.
● The programmer has to decide early on about any particular machine constraints to avoid during development, and accordingly consults with others in the central team.
● The programmer has to decide which machine will be used for development of trials version; this is tricky, as often teachers have two different machines available in their schools. The ideal is to conduct a trial on more than one machine, but this may be very unrealistic due to having to produce a version on two different machines which will both then have to be modified. Sometimes the software is developed on hardware that is not, but will be shortly, available in schools. This can cause problems!
● The authors and coders debate hotly the relative merits of driving through the program, despite reminders of CIC standards.
● Notes are edited and prepared for trials distribution.
● Trials' teachers are sought (up to twelve) who have access to the equipment on which their trials program will run, and who are prepared to try out software in the classroom and fill in questionnaire for response. They are also asked if they are prepared to receive a visit from a teacher and programmer to watch the trials in action.

TRIALS

This is a stage for both satisfaction and apprehension. In all creative work, it is very positive to have a physical product that is both robust and formal with properly produced notes and artwork ready for trials. The teachers are able to use something in their own schools, so as to test out their own ideas in reality. The LEA adviser can begin to see that this group may have really positive results and something tangible can be shown to the Chief Education Officer to justify the expenses, meetings, and general involvement in the scheme. For the teacher, something tangible can be shown to their Head to justify any secondment they have had. They can hold their heads up in front of colleagues as being involved in something outside the normal confines of school. For the teachers, this makes it worth all the insecurity and fears they went through at the early stages. The CAL designer can often see the teachers positively blossom at this stage. The fruits of their professional development have begun to emerge and this affects the development of other units that are still at an early stage.
● The trials' programs and notes, forming the complete unit, are sent out to the trials' school; this is accompanied by the detailed questionnaire.
● Copies are also sent to all members of the working group.
● Copies may be sent to funders for comment, and also shown to the advisory group that has been set up to monitor the work.

- The authors, in their own schools, begin noting problems and bugs in the unit and contacting the programmer directly about them.
- The trials have to run for quite a few months so that as far as possible, a unit can be trialled at the point in the curriculum that the teacher would normally cover the topic. This can influence the pace of work and projected trials date.
- Letters are sent out to remind trials' teachers for responses by the cut off date.
- The co-ordinator, advisers and some authors may demonstrate the trials software at in-service courses.
- The co-ordinator and CAL developer may demonstrate the unit at about this time at a CIC Project workshop.
- The meeting is fixed for team to consider trials' feedback.
- While one unit is on trial the group is continuing to develop other units in their batch.

MODIFICATIONS

Surprisingly few units are dropped immediately after the trials stage. There tend to be two periods when units are dropped – either half way through development or half-way through the modification stage. Units are dropped for the following reasons:
1. the idea and/or its execution are not gelling enough and it has to go back to the drawing-board, to emerge as a virtually new unit or be scrapped entirely;
2. the programmer cannot solve an intractable coding problem;
3. the author cannot complete the notes in any satisfactory way;
4. by general consensus in the central team, the unit just is not good enough, even though it received a favourable trials response.

The modifications stage is a difficult one. The programmer may be asked to re-do, or re-arrange, scrap or start new code – all of which is time consuming and frustrating when the trials' version may have seemed to work perfectly well. New ideas with regard to screen design and user interface may need to be incorporated. The authors may not see the need to 'polish' up the notes so as to make them more acceptable for publication. It is easy and tempting to ignore trials comments; but reality will often suggest that they themselves know there are rough edges that need polishing. Also the different ways the unit has been used in trials needs to be incorporated into the notes. So this is a period of hard slog. It tends to go in two phases – getting the unit right, and polishing up all the last details. The latter is very difficult, for without that extra polish a unit may be finished to all intents and purposes, but is not good enough for publication. It is very difficult also to get the group to stop the development. 'Lets just add this. . . . Wouldn't it be nice to include . . . ' are comments all too frequently heard during this stage. And of course, some of these extras are excellent, and time and space may need to be found for their incorporation.
- Trials questionnaire forms analysed with respect to program performance, useful-ness of the notes, subject considerations, and the general acceptance or rejection of the unit in terms of its value to the trials teacher.
- Working group gives feedback from their own use.
- Working group consider what aspects to incorporate into the program and notes.
- Group decides whether to scrap unit if its improvement seems intractable.
- Programmer given modification specification.
- Discussion on any screen design and user interface changes.
- Author given writing tasks by CAL developer who now assumes role of editor.

● Difficult discussions as members of group differ in way it is thought unit should be modified – should they be minor, or very major modifications. The very major ones often reflect the fact that the author now wants to turn the unit into something grander or larger – by adding a bit here, and a bit there. They are often really specifying a new unit, or certainly a 'son of' unit.

● Other units are also being discussed in the group. The author of Unit 1 finds himself rather isolated, involved in the slog work, while the rest of the team is concentrating on the new ideas, or developing the notes for Units 2 and 3. Their principle involvement with Unit 1 is almost finished while the single author carries on, with the help of the group co-ordinator.

● Programmer produces version of the program, on one machine, in the light of trials modifications. Colour combinations of screen display chosen.

● Front page designed, using some artwork from within the program.

● Modified notes typed (word processed), revised and edited.

● Editor and CAL developer discuss print style, size, layout and related features with publisher, to agree a format for the series as a whole.

● Program transferred to other machines. Decisions taken about screen layout modifications in the light of other machines capabilities; modifications made.

● Notes checked against program for consistency between the two.

● Artwork is checked with publisher for feasibility; relative merits of screen photos or printed screen dumps are discussed. Front cover design and titles discussed and agreed by the participating bodies.

● Artwork is checked, redrawn as necessary, and provenance noted for copyright clearance.

● Final typing and top copy produced of notes, artwork, screen dump and working version of program for each machine.

● The CAL developer, who acts as the series editor and overall manager of the group, has to decide when to call a halt; authors and subject co-ordinators will receive 'final copy' but they then ask for further modifications. Programmers will want to condense, and crunch, just re-write a bit more code. None of these extras can be accepted without careful thought – any new feature introduced at this stage will often have knock-on effects across the unit, which causes yet more checking.

● The CAL developer insists on receiving a final, bug-free copy of program, with front page, that will run with no problems from programmer.

● The CAL developer gently refuses the latest set of modifications requested by author and insists on receiving final copy of text by certain date.

● Editor resists attempts of other CAL members of central team at suggesting improvements and alterations in the light of latest decisions about screen design, for instance, 'do we bounce or roll the cursor through a menu of choices?'

PUBLICATION

During the previous stage, the work of the unit becomes centred increasingly upon the central team, as it leaves the provenance of the writing group. It may have taken over two years for a unit to pass through the first four stages. By now, the teacher/authors are well into the development of other units, or the group is now disbanding. All the program finalizing and checking and text organisation at this stage takes a surprising amount of time. It is sometimes nine months before the unit is actually published after the receipt of

manuscript – and this is short compared with some books. This stage, therefore, requires patience – it is the last, but also an important ten percent.
● A complete manuscript with the screen dumps and artwork is sent to either the publisher or printer. A working version of software on one machine accompanies the text for purposes of cross-checking.
● The program is given again a standard checking procedure known in CIC as 'finalization'. It is debugged, error traps checked, condensed further if necessary, and checked for performance against final text and screen dumps. It is even at this stage that simple spelling mistakes are noticed; or suddenly the program accepts an inappropriate negative value where none has previously been input. All this has to be corrected. A final master version on each machine is prepared by incorporating any menu selection, and is sent for multiple copying.
● Program documentation has to be prepared; including REM statements, variable lists, and a clear discourse on any model, the way it is coded, and the way is should work. The programmer has been encouraged to keep relevant documentation up to date during development, but drawing it together can be very tedious, especially when they are now planning the coding for a new idea.
● The editor approves artwork sent back by the publisher.
● Galley proofs are checked against text and software. The programs are mastered.
● Page proofs are checked with both artwork and screen dumps in position.
● The Publisher collates the printed material and copied software.
  Publication is then complete. This is of course not the end of the life of the unit; its usefulness is now tested in the market-place.

IMPLICATIONS

These stages presuppose that the initial groundwork in the identification of general curriculum area, location of working group, identification of individuals and successful application for funding has already taken place. The approach to setting up these initiatives is considered in Chapters 4 and 12. There are inevitable implications in a staged framework for the development of a unit. Firstly, how to ensure that there is a progression through the unit, that is the management of the flow of work, and secondly the issues of post-publication aftercare and support.

MANAGING THE FLOW OF WORK

Each group co-ordinator has a responsibility for the work of one writing group and has to nurse each unit through the stages. He or she will draw up with the CAL developer a timetable for each unit, identifying the constituent jobs to be done. Working to an ideal of two years for the development of one unit, he or she will usually prepare the chart on the basis of key dates in the school year where meetings or workshops of the group can take place. Figure 5.2 illustrates one progress chart.
  The chart for one unit cannot be seen in isolation. The group is often developing two or three, and sometimes as many as six ideas at any one stage. The programmer will begin work on the first good specification received. The third one in the line may then have to wait 3–6 months before it is given any coding attention. The flow of work then becomes a practical rather than theoretical pattern – which code is ready determines the

2

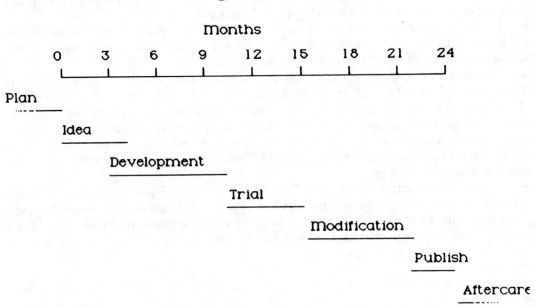

FIGURE 5.2   Progress plan for one unit

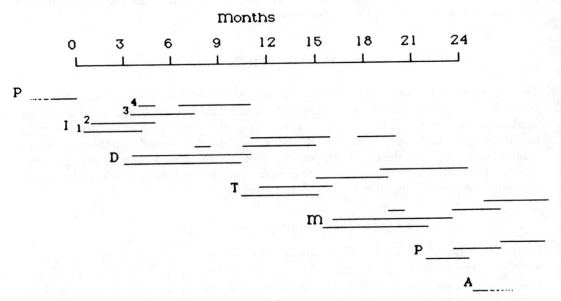

FIGURE 5.3   Progress plan for 4 units

units that are discussed at the next meeting. There will be a burst of effort up to trials, as the trials dates are fixed some while in advance. Figure 5.3 illustrates the progress chart for a group of four units.

The flow of one group's units, however, also have to dovetail into the flow of work from other groups, especially when any shared programming facilities are involved. The

CAL developer responsible for this and other writing groups will be keeping a combined flowchart to interface with the general Project data base. There can be hold-ups in the flow of development of one unit due to circumstances that the group co-ordinator is unable to influence – such as the development of a new routine, or a backlog of editing. Consequently, progress charts are a means of keeping track of the flow of work, and ironing out problems that emerge. This is part of a juggling act between the variety of individuals involved at the different stages.

Figure 5.4 illustrates the areas whereby people who are part of the whole team are involved at various stages, from planning the concept of there being development, through to the aftercare. It will be seen from this that not all 'actors' are involved at all stages – some may appear at two periods but separated by a variety of activity in between.

The main core of each writing group tends to be more involved at the idea, development, trials and early modification stage. The central team members, however, are involved in a more dispersed way at the beginning, with a concentrated burst of activity at the modifications and publication stage. Altogether, however, the units are always '*ours*', rather than '*mine*'. Members of the CIC team will read this last sentence with amusement and disbelief as I have always maintained a high profile for 'my work in the humanities' and 'my humanities units' in the internal team discussions!

SOFTWARE SUPPORT

Despite the most professional and rigorous of checks, errors can be spotted in a unit, either in the software or in notes, after it has been published. Developers who fail to recognise this, ignore the problem at their peril. Textual errors can be handled either with errata slips or by amending the master file before the next printing.

Small bugs, or even major model problems, can and do occasionally occur. This is usually found out when a user inputs a value that has hitherto not been checked and it causes problems. The simple classic is for a negative number to be input when only positive variables are expected. This sort of thing should have been checked at the publication stage, but can still creep through. With complex and uniqe models however there is always the possibility that its behaviour, under extreme conditions, is not correct. These can be sorted out as long as there is both adequate program document-ation and a team still available to undertake such support.

Another aspect of aftercare is the keeping alive of a good educational idea by transferring it to a new machine that has appeared on the educational market. It is so sad to see software virtually die within a year of publication because it does not run on the machine that has suddenly appeared and swept the scene. CIC has developed a library of software routines (see Chapter 10) which facilitates such transfer. It was used with conspicuous success when the BBC Model B was launched.

It is most unfortunate that many of the authorities responsible for the purchase and distribution of machines in schools fail to realise the significance of the perpetually changing hardware scene. Software development has rarely enough time to catch up with the changing hardware, with the result that the hardware tends to be used more for computer studies, or with general purpose packages often produced for the business rather than educational user, than for CAL. The introduction of machines into schools could now afford to have a period of consolidation, with the maintenance of existing technology so that the software that is now available can be used regularly in schools and

	Negotiating	Planning	Ideas	Development	Trials	Modification	Publication	Aftercare
Curriculum Project	x	x			x		x	
LEA Advisers	x	x			x			
Host Institution	x	x	x	x	x	x		
CIC Directors	x	x			x		x	x
Funders	x				x		x	
Group coordinator	x	x	x	x	x	x	x	
CAL developer	x	x		x		x	x	x
Programmer			x	x		x	x	x
Writing group			x	x		x		
Individual author			x	x		x	x	
Advisory Committee		x			x		x	
Trials teachers					x			
Groups schools					x			
Chief programmer				x		x		
Systems Analyst				x		x		
Software support manager				x				x
Series editor						x	x	
Other writing groups					x			
Publisher							x	x
Teachers trainers		x			x			

FIGURE 5.4   Involvement in the stages of a unit

incorporated into the curriculum. The introduction of the 16 bit, or even 32 bit environment will then be related to a clear understanding of the role and potential because educators have not just seen, but also regularly used, educational software.

Good educational software can outlive the machine, and even generations of machines, for which it was originally designed. Conversely a good idea can be seen to be poorly executed because with direct transfer the design still reflects the earlier generation of machines. Thus the unit written to run on a teletext type of mainframe transferred poorly to an 8 bit micro. Software from the 8 bit micro may not look too good in the 16 bit environment without the addition of certain educational user interface features, e.g. a mouse, with which users will become familiar. This means that a unit will need sometimes not only to be transferred but also re-written to take additional features into account. This is a very time-consuming operation – but for those units that have the core of a good idea, it is worth it. In CIC, the unit, MILL, was originally developed in 1974 on a mainframe and published in 1979; it has been transferred directly to run in teletype form on micros; since when it has been rewritten and published (in 1986) to take into account graphics and the latest user interface, and this version has already been transferred, as part of a pilot scheme, to run directly on the RML Nimbus and the IBM PC.

DISSEMINATION

The core of the work, that is the research, development and production of CAL units, does not have a distinct and separate dissemination stage. By implication, the dissemination of these products, the CAL units, is in the hands of the publisher who markets the material. It would be unfortunate if the impression was given that CIC had neither considered nor involved itself with issues of dissemination. This has been done in a variety of ways.

Lectures, seminars and workshops

Members of the Project are regularly called upon to give presentations at a variety of in-service and pre-service courses, at local, regional and national levels. Topics covered include CAL in a variety of subjects, CAL in the curriculum in general, CAL in the learning operation, the evaluation of educational computing materials, as well as program design and implementation issues. In 1980 the pressure on the team was so great that the Department of Education and Science awarded funds for the Project to run two lecture-training courses in order to spread the load (Watson and McCormick, 1981). The Project Steering Committee advised against allowing these tasks to snowball to such an extent that they impinged upon development time. The Microelectronics Education Programme (MEP) then adopted a high profile in the in-service area through regionally based centres and the development of associated materials (Rushby et al., 1981). Preparing and giving lectures and workshops on various aspects of the work does act as a useful catalyst for thought; the perceptions of the attendees and feedback from such presentations is invaluable. There has been an increasing interest in the last few years in the CIC model for the production of CAL.

CIC is based in an education faculty, within the faculty's own Educational Computing Section. This Section and the Project is increasingly in receipt of visitors on both a short and long term basis who come to explore and discuss educational computing matters. The Section mounts in-service courses in the field, and has a growing commitment to both the masters and research programmers in the college.

Conferences, exhibitions and committees

Project members have regularly presented papers or workshops at the main academic conferences in the field of educational computing both in the UK and overseas. CIC has been represented at every biennial CAL Symposium since their inception during the days of NDPCAL, and is also represented at various IFIP (the International Federation for

Information Processing) TC3 (Technical Committee 3 – Education) working parties' conferences, as well as the IFIP World Conference. Exhibits with the CAL units on working display are mounted, often in conjunction with our publishers, at these and other events.

Members of CIC can be found on various national committees in this field. Two members served on the MEP In-service Advisory Group for Computer Based Learning. Members of the Project also sit on various Subject Association working committees on educational computing, and have contributed to some of the recently commissioned 'Curriculum and Information Technology' documents produced by the subject associations for the Department of Education and Science, including those of the National Association of Teachers of English, Association of Science Education, Geography Association and History Association.

Direct contact

By far the most significant form of dissemination about the Project and its philosophy of educational computing takes place through the direct involvement of teachers in the development work and trials. At one stage in 1983, the Project was able to name over 300 individuals and their schools who were either members of a working party, or were on the trials lists. Such involvement of teachers in the work, as an integral part of the Project, keeps the Project in close contact with the classroom, acts as a form of in-service in CAL for the teachers (Watson, 1984d), and as a dissemination base for CIC.

It is not clear, however, how efficient this is in influencing the take-up of the use of CAL in the classroom. The use of CAL will be determined by a number of factors, including the availability and control of hardware, the availability of software, costs, management issues, organisational issues and the overall acceptance of the general disturbance this innovation can have on teaching styles and strategies. A curriculum development project can only contribute a part to the totality of these issues.

6
UNIT SPECIFICATION

Few good ideas emerge in a vacuum. Even once the environment for development has been generated, the authors still need a mechanism for translating the idea into a specification to be used by the programmers.

With the plethora of rules and standards that the programmers themselves have to follow, they rightly expect to at least be given a clear specification upon which to work. This, unfortunately, is rarely the case. The Project has been through a variety of attempts to provide guidelines for authors for the production of such a specification. These guidelines have inevitably acted as a framework for the idea to emerge, rather than a complete and exact specification. The examples given in other chapters will illustrate in detail quite why. Basically, a good idea needs the chance to breath, change and emerge during the development. I know of very few CAL units that, when complete, are exact replicas of their specification.

Nevertheless, the formal drawing up of a specification is an important stage in development, not least because the team has to clarify its ideas enough to be able to communicate them to others.

FORMULATING THE BRIEF

The brief for teacher groups reflects the clear Project philosophy identified earlier as CIC Ground Rules. These ground rules cannot be assimilated from scratch by new developers; indeed their significance only really emerges through experience. A synopsis of the philosophy, can be presented fairly easily in the form of the statements itemized below.

- It is not envisaged that any program will be designed according to a strict path of learning, but rather along a sequence of guidelines.
- No form of computer assessment of the student is to be considered as part of the overall design; but the material is to be designed for direct student participation.
- The material is to be an integral part of a wider teaching unit.

● The material is to be flexible in design so as to offer the teacher a resource pack to be used in his own individual way.

● The subject area must be part of the accepted curriculum in that discipline.

● The material should avoid covering topics already sitting easily in the teaching framework, unless it provides a useful compliment; thus beware of designing software only for its own sake.

(Watson, 1981, p.11)

More recently I have found it helpful to compliment this brief by demonstrating other CAL materials to new teachers and developers. In particular it is useful to use software from other disciplines to show them the range of ideas and styles that are emerging and which they can consider.

KEY QUESTIONS

In formulating a particular idea, and preparing it in a style leading up to a specification, the teachers are encouraged to be specific in answering the following questions:

1. For what age and ability level of student is the topic aimed?
2. How is the topic currently taught?
3. In what area do particular difficulties arise?
4. What pre-requisite knowledge is required?
5. Along what detailed path would you like the students to travel to gain a real understanding?

THE OUTLINE OF A PROPOSED UNIT (OPU)

An understanding of the ground rules and the answers to the above questions form the basis of a pro-forma, which is known as the OPU (Outline of a Proposed Unit), which has to be completed before the development of a unit can really begin. This pro-forma has two purposes, to both strike at the heart of the objectives, and to make more concrete this difficult period of development (Lewis and Want, 1980a). The basic OPU is outlined below.

Outline of a proposed unit

Part A   The Topic
Curriculum Area and Year
Specific Topic
How is the topic currently taught?
List 2 or 3 questions which students should be able to answer after studying the topic.
What aspects of the topic will the computer cover?

Part B   Comparisons with Traditional Teacher
What are the difficulties faced by students in their study of the topic?
How is it envisaged that the new unit will help with these difficulties or improve the
  students understanding?

Part C   Program Description
Outline sample dialogue showing parameters which the student will control.
What model is to be used?
What parameters are unseen by the students?
What limits to student input should be
(a) mandatory and
(b) educationally recommended?

This OPU has acted as a basic specification for many years for the programmers; it also reflects the curriculum concerns that lie at the heart of CAL development. It suffered from a number of faults however that have emerged during development. In particular there were programming and screen design aspects that became prominent.

MODELS

Many programmers suffer severe problems with the model specification given to them by the authors. Essentially, within many circumstances the appropriate design of a model depends upon the programmer knowing all the equations of the model, all the symbols to be used, and the limits of each variable, before work begins. More usually, however this information is simply *not* available at the beginning. This can occur for a combination of reasons:

● The model may be a new simplified version of a more complicated model already in existence, for instance the one CIC had to devleop from the UKAEA for REACT. How to simplify the model to make it both manageable, valid and digestible for the educational environment may not be known until after various drafts have been produced.

● The model as required may not have existed previously, for instance in the development of PUDDLE (Riley, 1984). A rough outline of the model can be used for initial stages of development, but the behaviour of the model is only exposed by its performance in the simulation. This then results in further work and the addition or deletion of various equations or variables, until the model itself can be said to have been expressed completely.

● A mathematical model may be the only, but not the most satisfactory way of expressing the combination of issues to be explored. Under these circumstances the author can only explore and change a draft program until the results match those required for the purposes of the unit.

● In some cases, a model as such does not lie at the heart of the unit. Instead, it is the logical framework that needs to be known, for instance, a crossword. This logical framework may be obvious to the authors, but not to the programmer.

All these points simply indicate one of the great values in using simulations, because they force us to explore and formalize models hitherto unused or only roughly verbally expressed. This is a great strength of computers in education. Nevertheless it does not make the task of the programmer any easier. It can be particularly hard in certain humanities developments where authors have not been used to expressing their understanding of their subject in the form of quantitative models, and where the programmers simply haven't grasped that the fundamental logic the authors are expressing, does not sit comfortably with an arithmetic algorithmic expression. Indeed it is the coming together of these two aspects that is making the search for new approaches to a modelling environment that satisfies the logical requirements of historians and geographers so interesting in the mid 1980s.

THE DYNAMIC SCREEN

The basic OPU takes no cognisance of the dramatic impact the microcomputer can have with its graphical capabilities. The OPU rightly reflects the educational concerns and the need for an outline of the model to be used. But the assumption in the original OPU was that the pupil would be working through a dialogue structure, and that the execution of the model would determine the visual face of the unit. The possibilities of the hardware have overtaken both these assumptions, so much so that guidelines for both the Screen Design and User Interface are given separately.

It is clear that authors now need to spend a considerable amount of time thinking about, and even visualizing, a sequence of screens through which the unit progresses. Indeed, it is not just a sequence of screens, but how different parts of one screen, and in which order, will change.

It is much harder to express these ideas to the programmer. The best way at the moment seems to be via a comic strip.

THE COMIC STRIP

Many authors in the early 1980s, while struggling with the impact of graphics, were at the same time struggling with an appropriate user interface. The programmers in the meantime were using a programming framework that turned a dialogue interaction into an option keyword structure. The resultant mismatch of aims between the two parts of the team required a solution. This was the drawing-up of a detailed comic strip of idealized frames.

At first new sections were added to the existing OPU.
● Proposed Screen Layout 'Comic Strip'. Please draw a series of consecutive screen displays in each rectangle to show the different displays at each stage of the program.
● If a model is not appropriate, give some indication of the logical framework within which the program fits, e.g. the game sequence.
● Specify any special or unusual features required, e.g. animation, colour, printout. . . .
● Give references to provide information on the topic for the programmer.

The role of the comic strip part of the OPU is therefore similar to that of the 'Storyboard' outlined in Alexander and Blanchard (1985). The problem with drawing up a comic strip and the associated dialogue is identical to that of the model – the authors will only have relatively hazy ideas at first; these ideas grow and become more concrete when they are presented in draft solutions in code. These additional parts to the OPU indicate that a method was required to formalize the thinking on screen design and use, as well as educational aims and model definition.

At one stage a writing group rather desperately attempted to draw-up exactly on a series of grid sheets representing the screen, and including all the dialogue each frame they thought they would want. This was a monumental task that took up a huge amount of time. Naturally as development progressed and ideas changed, that time was wasted; new ideas were formulated in discussion and directly noted by the programmer with no formal OPU stage in between. Attempting to formalize all the details at too early a stage in the development is counter productive.

PARTNERSHIP

While the need for the development of a specification is necessary, to act as a formulation of authors ideas and as a brief for the programmers, it has been clear over many years that developing CAL is a creative activity in which both the teacher authors and programmers work in collaboration together *throughout* the development. For this reason the word 'Outline' in OPU has as clear meaning, and should not be confused with a 'specification' as it is normally used in programming circles. An investigation into how others develop CAL has indicated the importance of the 'Specification Stage'. The way that CIC specifies units differs fundamentally from these.

This can be criticised quite rightly from a management point of view. Indeed the funders have from time to time expressed grave concern that the style of specification identification allows for a woolly development cycle that does not hold up to management scrutiny. This may be the case, but as a practical methodology I believe more creative CAL has been developed using the outline rather than specification approach.

SOFTWARE DESIGN TOOLS

An interesting further development has recently taken place. A program, INDFARM had been developed and run through trials; the author was working on some inconsistencies in the model, and this was combined with further work on the screen design and user interface. These latter two are inextricably linked. The coder tried out a variety of methods of representing the information on the dynamic screen. One attempt caused weeks of work of character definition on the RML 480Z and was almost immediately rejected by the development team. It was clear that we had to be more efficient in our method of defining the screen and interface for the programmer. After a couple of intensive hours around a blackboard while we thrashed out the main issues again, the coder went to the Apple Macintosh. He drew up the frame for the screen, and carefully put in the current picture changes and associated user dialogue. We then sat down with this complete visual record of the current unit, and worked out the new design both at the screen, and on paper. The coder drew the frames on the Mac, we then checked each combination of user prompt and response again, and the timing and change associated on the screen as well as the sequencing through the model. After checking and double checking, the artwork was then drawn on the Mac and transferred across to the RML host machine. Not only that, but the programmer then drew up a complete comic strip of the flow of the program on the Mac, to be checked out and verified by the authors, before total implementation.

This raises a whole new series of possibilities, namely that of using the newly emerging systems to explore designs by sketching out on screen rather than on paper. I realise that many people will breathe a sigh of exasperation, and ask themselves why I have not referred to the use of authoring languages as a means of teachers specifying and developing their own code earlier. For many this appears to be the most appropriate method of translating the authors' educational aims by placing the tools directly at their command, rather than having to work through the intermediary of a programmer.

This is not, however, what I am proposing, even at this stage. Authoring languages may be of some use in developing the structure of the program and the inherent model. The current manifestation of many authoring languages are still fairly crude, especially in their front end. The emergence of tools such as Macpaint and Macdraw on the Apple Macintosh has helped the programmer to explore appropriate designs in both the case of INDFARM and also with SCRIPTWRITER. Using software tools in the design process, by either teacher/authors or programmers is very different from suggesting that authoring languages can do the task. Tools now available on machines however do indicate the directions in which the design process may move in the future. This will be particularly relevant for methods such as those of CIC, whereby the unit's development is seen to be a creative process, and the tools are needed for such creativity, rather than simply as methods of implementing a fixed idea. The development of SCRIPTWRITER has been aided by the Apple Macintosh because the software indicated ways in which the user could handle the idea of moving texts and words through windowing techniques. Even with other tools to implement the ideas, there still remains a large amount of hard work and thought needed between the author and programmer in terms of definition and understanding of the logical sequences that will then come to be implemented by the design tools. Neither the tools themselves nor the languages will do the job of outlining and then developing the unit.

STAGES OF SPECIFICATION

Most units therefore go through at least two stages of specification:
1. the *outline stage* which concentrates on the educational issues and inherent program logic or model; and
2. the *comic strip* stage which concentrates on the dynamic screen in which the flow of the unit in the execution of the idea needs to be thrashed out, together with the associated user interface.

   This method of outlining the basis of the unit and then its execution all depend upon all the participants in the development having a clear understanding of who the CAL unit is being designed for. As the experience of the members of writing groups, and the project as a whole, deepens, so the method of defining a detailed specification on paper becomes more refined. The role of specification devices such as an OPU and COMIC STRIP is to formalize the communication that is required between the team members at the appropriate stages in the development. How this works in practice will be explored in later chapters of the book.

7
PROGRAMMING AND SOFTWARE TOOLS

The programmers in any CAL development team will need guidelines as to the hardware they are designing for and the languages they can, or are expected to use. The guidelines for the programmers in the CIC team are embedded in a variety of software standards and tools, that have either been developed in-house or adopted from other sources. These 'rules' have expanded over time as the programming tasks have become more complex. Behind them all, however, lies two overriding concerns – the *portability of software*, and the need to provide *development tools*.

Following the dictates of its philosophy, CIC has considered software development as an activity that is integral to educational concerns. Thus software should serve, respond to, enhance, and possibly extend the curriculum. It cannot do this if it is too closely tied to one transient piece of hardware. The variety of machines in the school environment come and go with alarming speed. There is no reason why the life of educational software should be dictated by the life of any one machine. Indeed, it seems positively criminal for an interesting educational idea that has been developed into a complex CAL package, to be discarded because the technology on which it runs has now become old fashioned. Accordingly the software in which the educational idea is embedded must be developed, in so far as is practical by a method that will make it as machine independent as possible. This philosophy enables the Project to reach a wide educational audience which has an ever-changing variety of hardware facilities.

The policy of guidelines for programmers does not end with the production and maintenance of the tools for transportability. Help is required with regards to the structure and logic of programs, if the developers are to achieve a code that is not just idiosyncratic to themselves, but instead one that is accessible to the other members of the team, that can be transferred to other machines, and that can be maintained after publication.

A LANGUAGE STANDARD

The principle tool, and indeed the first that emerged in the mid-1970s, is a standard for the use of BASIC. Throughout development in the 1970s and in the first half of the 1980s the language of coding has been BASIC.

The first BASIC standard, is a modification of the proposed ANSI Standard. This standard was originally developed in the mid-seventies when the Project together with another project based at Chelsea, the Chelsea Science Simulation Project (CSSP), was working within a reasonably consistent hardware environment – namely a printing terminal attached to a remote mainframe computer. Due to slight variations in BASIC as implemented on these machines, a standard of BASIC was defined. This meant that programs could be, and were, distributed in the late 1970's in punched paper tape form from Chelsea across the UK, indeed across the world, so that the CAL units were used in a great variety of schools and colleges.

With the advent of microcomputers, and the subsequent development of the Sub-routine Library, a further tightening of the language standard was required; thus, the BASIC standard became an integral part of that development. Various versions of BASIC were common to all the 8 bit microcomputers that were then appearing in the educational environment. The project standard had to be the equivalent of a BASIC Common Denominator that would run on all the machines.

This standard is published in the *Subroutine Library Manual* (Millwood, 1983). Examples of the tone and rigour of the BASIC standard is given below:
- Strings must not exceed 255 characters.
- Integer type numeric variables cannot be used.
- AND, OR and NOT should not be used as arithmetic operators.
- IF relational condition THEN statements. ELSE is not allowed.
- GOSUB, GOTO line number. The line number could be a variant.
- RETURN must be used to exit from a subroutine.
- DEF is the keyword for function definition. Function definition must be on one line only and have only one argument. DEF statements should be on separate lines.

VARIATIONS TO BASIC

Increasingly, variations to BASIC are being used with the changing demands of development.
- Sometimes for specific features, a machine version of BASIC is used. If this is the case, the equivalent machine version has to be fitted in for each different environment on which the software will run.
- For the sake of speed, some parts of a program are written in machine code.
- When there is a deliberate policy to implement a unit on only one machine, so obviously that machine's version of BASIC and machine code can be used with impunity. This has only occurred once in CIC, with the BBC Science Topics Series.

OTHER LANGUAGES

It is apparent at the time of writing (1986) that the value of BASIC has now virtually been outlived. This is for a variety of reasons:

1. BASIC is no longer appropriate as the use of interactive screen graphics and a sophisticated user interface become the standard for CAL units.
2. The increasing reliance on file handling demands a more sophisticated logic than that offered by BASIC.
3. The new 16 bit generation of microcomputers coming into schools do have available a greater variety of languages on them.

Investigations in CIC are under way on the appropriateness of various languages, such as Logo, PROLOG, LISP, Pascal and C for various tasks. This has certain implications:

1. As the design of software becomes more sophisticated, the team will probably need to work in more than one language. The language will be chosen according to the task.
2. Some units may be developed in a combination of languages, e.g. C and PASCAL for different coherent parts in any one program.
3. The team can no longer rely on everyone having the same basis of expertise, but rather to share the expertise in different languages. Each language that is used, will have to be worked following a standard to enable the sharing of skills and again the transfer of code.

Thus a relaxing of the rule to use a standard in one language simply means that work is required to identify a version or standard to be used in two or more languages.

THE LIBRARY OF SUBROUTINES

The introduction of microcomputers with graphics facilities in the late 1970s caused a series of problems. Each microcomputer not only had its own version of BASIC, but also a host of other facilities, including addressing its graphics, that were unique. This problem had already been faced by another project, the Computers in the Undergraduate Science Curriculum (CUSC) in which, in the 1970s, Chelsea were partners with Queen Elizabeth College, London, and Surrey University. This project developed material that had to be used with a wide ranging variety of graphics terminals. In order to achieve this, the main part of the program was isolated from the graphics part (written in BASIC or FORTRAN) which was developed in various forms for each different type of graphics terminal. The terminal in use, in any one establishment, determined the graphics subroutines used with that program. This was published as the CUSC Graphics Package (Chapman 1977). When faced with the similar but more extensive problem, that is with the other features of microcomputers unique to each piece of hardware as well as the graphics, CIC had to develop a similar policy.

THE PRINCIPLE OF SUBROUTINES

A Library of Subroutines was developed for use on microcomputers initially by Lewis and Smith (1980) and subsequently refined, after reference to Newman and Sproull (1979), by Millwood (1983). In essence this provides a framework for code to be written for a theoretical machine. In reality, the theoretical machine has to reflect the commonality of characteristics to be found in the actual machines upon which the software will run. This commonality determines the rules for the theoretical framework. Thus, if one of the real host machines has a graphics area that covers only the first 20 of the 24 lines on a screen, then that becomes part of the theoretical standard.

At the time of initial development, the host machines that determined the standard

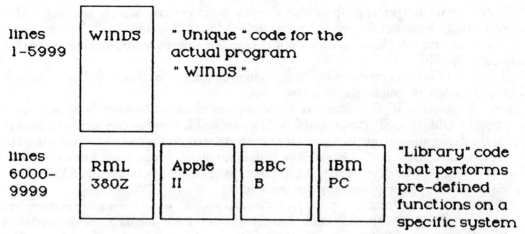

FIGURE 7.1   The library structure

were the RML 380Z, the Apple II series and the Commodore Pet 3000 and 4000 series. Subsequent modifications to the Library have taken cognisance of the experience of incorporating the BBC model B microcomputer.

THE PRACTICE

In essence, the library is based upon a split in the program. Figure 7.1 illustrates this for the program WINDS, with the four libraries that could be attached to it. The unique part of the program is written in the first section – between lines 15 and 5990. Lines 1–14 are reserved for machine specific utilisation, while lines 5990 to 5999 are reserved for REMarks on the use of the library. The Library of Routines (MINLIB) itself uses lines 6000–9999. These lines are divided up roughly into sections on input and output, numbers and strings, graphics and file handling. There is a library of subroutines for these sections written for each of the host machines. At each location in the library is found the code for a specific task as it operates in that machine.

When the programmer writes a program, it contains large numbers of GOSUB statements which refer to a location within the subroutine library. Its simplest example is in the message 'Press RETURN to continue'. This is located in the library at line 7320: REM Press to Continue. Every time this is required, the coder routes the program to 7320. This will then set the sequence for the message, 'Press RETURN to continue' to be displayed, and a wait until the RETURN key is pressed before returning to the flow of the program. All the major routines a coder needs are handled in this way.

Thus every program essentially contains two parts – the unique attributes of a particular program, and the subroutine library that executes those attributes on a particular machine. With the RML version of the library, it will run on an RML 380Z or 480Z. In order to run on a BBC machine, the RML library is replaced by the BBC library. Thus as long as the BASIC standard and Library have been adhered to, the program is automatically transferable to as many machines as have a subroutine library developed for them.

Very few programs will fit into this pattern perfectly. There may be some features of a particular program that need recoding for each machine. In this case, the code is carefully documented and located for ready recognition and recording for a new machine version. This task can be done by any programmer who is familiar with the characteristics of the second machine, without having to necessarily familiarize themselves with the whole unit under development.

LIBRARY EXTENSIBILITY

Once the library has been full developed, it can and has been extended as new machines have appeared in the environment. The Acorn BBC Model B, appeared in 1982. It fell within the standards set by the library, so a new BBC Library of Subroutines was developed. Within a six month period over forty library based programs were transferred directly across to run on this new machine. It was ironic that the BBC BASIC contained in the new machine was extremely attractive to developers, but many of its features were outside the BASIC standard and so could not be used without compromising portability.

Other machines, notably the Commodore 64, did not come up to the minimal standard required by the Library. The flaw often lay in the graphics configuration or in the lack of graphics statements in the version of BASIC supplied. Equally a machine may fulfil the standard but it may not be expected to be taken up in schools.

Currently the Library has been extended by the addition of versions for the IBM PC and the RML Nimbus. This means that software currently running on three 8 bit machines can now also run on two 16 bit ones. Of course, these units will not be using the unique environment of the 16 bit hardware. On the other hand, a piece of sound educational software is not going to die just because it will not run on these new machines. We are, therefore, able to make a large library of CAL available straight away to institutions with these new machines.

A NEW LIBRARY

The same pressures that are causing the demise of BASIC, also affect the usefulness of the BASIC Library of Subroutines. But it will not die without a replacement.

The chief programmer and systems analyst have both been interested for some time in the value of PASCAL, particularly from a procedural point of view. In order to emulate the features of BBC BASIC, the first development which actually used the language was a procedural Library (PROLIB). This has now been turned into a procedural library in Pascal for use in PROBASIC and PASCAL. Development work on this new library of routines is still underway. It is hoped to make development easier and faster especially for the 16 bit environment, and to aid in particular the design of the screen to be used on different environments. It means that the principles so hard developed and won with the first MINLIB will now be inherited by the new PROLIB.

AIDING DEVELOPMENT

It is important to appreciate that the Library actually serves two functions; as well as addressing the issue of portability through its 'rules' and the library for each host machine, it is a blueprint for the development of modular and readable programs. Not only does it encourage modularity through its structure, it also encourages the programmers to think carefully of the total framework of the code and break each component part down into self-contained parts. This is important for the legibility of function of the code for a variety of people, and for the saving of space, which is always a problem particularly in the 8 bit, 32K environment. But it also means that the inevitable changes of direction in the design of the unit, or the frequent addition of extra components, can be achieved with minimum disruption to the logic of the program. Different members of the team can, and do, get moved across to work on each other's programs. Using the MINLIB structure, they can do this with relative ease.

The developers who are working as part of a CAL team face a task that is harder than in many commercial environments. There they would receive a clear detailed specification for implementation in one particular environment. But in the CIC model not only are they asked to work in a variety of hardware environments, but also to work from relatively hazy specifications as the really valuable educational idea generally emerges as part of the development process. This means that the initial code is highly vulnerable and will be prey to many modifications. Much work with regard to rewriting can be saved if the code is as structured as possible. If it is, the coder can, on the whole, feel more than confident that the modifications to the unit will not have to necessarily cause a fundamental re-jigging of the code. This means, therefore, that such modifications that have to take place will not necessarily result in gross distortions or failures of the logic. The Library of Subroutines is aimed at providing such a framework. It acts now, in a sense, as a training manual for new programmers/developers who join the team.

TRANSFER SOFTWARE

The language standard and Library of Subroutines both define the software environment in which the programmer/developer works. In order to achieve the principle of transportability however, a third 'branch' is necessary — that is, the software that gets the machines 'talking' to one another. Although this task was not large, the ability to transfer electronically the code of the main section of a program, resident, for example, in a 380Z, to a BBC machine, and to then have the BBC subroutine library merged with it has always been a key part of the plan. The transfer software written in-house which is currently in use, can enable the RML to be host to either the BBC or Apple, but will not allow the BBC to transfer direct to the Apple. As other machines, particular the 16 bit generation have emerged, further transfer software was written from, for instance, the RML 480Z to the RML Nimbus, or the IBM PC. At the same time, commercial software has emerged that has enabled the Project to discard its own versions of some of the transfer routines.

DE-BUGGING TOOLS

It is inevitable that with large pieces of code various bugs and errors will slip in during development which may not necessarily emerge during the running of the programs. These need to be systematically searched for; it is also important to try and secure a double check to ensure that the language and Library Standards have been adhered to. If they have not, an unnecessary amount of time can be lost during the transfer process while the programmer tries to identify the source of a problem which is causing a transfer failure. Accordingly a variety of small, but heavily used, de-bugging tools have been developed in-house.

LINREF and VARREF speak for themselves – they are line number and variable cross-referencing programs. TROUBLE looks for a possible misuse of variables, while CONDENSE squashes programs so that they can run on target machines which only have a small amount of memory. This latter program was developed during a critical period in 1983. The Project had 'gambled' in 1981 that 56K of memory would be the standard to which it could work on its new phase of development. With the production of the 32K BBC machine by Acorn, and the announcement that the Department of Trade and Industry (DTI) sponsored machine recommended to secondary schools was the 32K and not 56K version of the RML 380Z, the question of memory became acute. The Project desperately began to squash programs, by means of removing spaces and creating multi-statement lines. This just solved the problem and enabled us to transfer to the BBC 32K model with all the limitations of size that imposed. It is still used for RML and Apple micro versions, but has been superseded for the BBC by commercial utilities, and the use of overlaying, which have since emerged.

The development of these de-bugging tools has fluctuated according to the demands and the contrasts between the various host machines. Their coding, in-house, and use is an indication of the seriousness with which those in the team who have been associated with the principles of transportability and design, have taken their responsibilities. Although these responsibilities have principally rested in the hands of the Chief Programmer and Chief Systems Programmer, the Software Support Manager and all the other programmers/developers in the team have regularly contributed to these developments. They are continually having to anticipate and be aware of changes in the environment within which they are working, and use such commercial software there is that can possibly aid their task. Where it has not been available, it has had to be developed in-house.

IMAGES

Pixel images, the graphics that makes working in the microcomputer environment so interesting for CAL work, are also non-portable. This has meant that another whole new suite of decisions has had to be taken, and tools developed, to handle the problem if CIC was to maintain the principle in which it had invested so much between 1980 and 1983. During this period programs were developed which included graph drawing and simple images. This was clearly not enough, as more complex graphical representation, a greater emphasis on the screen design and the increased use of icons, clearly demanded a comprehensive image policy.

STORAGE

Since the method of storage of pictures is unique to each machine, it was first decided to develop programs which would encode pictures in a common format. *Run length encoding* was the format chosen as being particularly relevant for 8 bit micros. This means that although the pictures are developed in the machine's particular method, by storing them in a common format, they can be transferred between machines. They are then, of course, decoded to the specific format of the second machine.

These picture files obviously lie 'outside' both the main program and the Library of Subroutines. They are stored as picture files on disk, and called up as and when required and loaded into the relevant picture memory of the host machine.

STANDARD

As with BASIC, there is a standard for drawing pictures which is based around the weakest machine currently supported, which is the Apple II series high resolution graphics screen. This can cause problems as indicated earlier; but there are some programs that have been allowed to be developed outside the Apple minimum requirement, as the development was becoming too influenced by this constraint. Problems can also be caused because the software itself is, through its content matter, unlikely to travel beyond UK boundaries. This, however tends to be the exception rather than the rule; 90 per cent of the programs to have been developed run with picture images on the Apple.

It is important to appreciate another aspect of transportability – that of uniformity. The Apple, RML and BBC versions of the programs must run in the same way to all intents and purposes to the user. The printed accompanying notes must cover whichever machine version the user happens to be working from. Different pictures, or indeed methods of user response, in different machine versions of the same unit are neither acceptable nor practical. Where they have been used (e.g. DMS) it has caused innumerable headaches. Thus the picture developed on one machine acts as the standard that must appear in all machine versions.

FRONT PAGE GENERATOR

It became a policy in 1984 to try to present a clear visual front page to the user as the first screen they see when they use the program. This meant designing a picture which related closely to the content of the unit; indeed a picture that occurs elsewhere in the unit was often used. This also appeared on the front cover of the notes, so that there was a clear connecting image between the notes, and the software; in this way a total unit was created. In the case of the Windmill Location Game (MILL), for instance, a windmill itself was chosen, and an appropriate picture drawn.

At the same time, a total design to the front page was required, into which the picture could be incorporated. During the design, the author and developer may decide to change the location of the picture within the graphics screen, as they juggled with the location of title pages, icons and frames. Re-coding the picture for a new location was wasteful of time.

During the third major publishing phase of the Project, 1985–6, there were over fifty CAL packages that were completing development and needing front pages. Accordingly a front-page generator was developed to run on the BBC machine to aid the design – by providing a facility for choosing size of typeface, drawing and locating various boxes, and by locating various images once they had been drawn initially. This was completely designed around the principle of run-length encoding and enable the front page, once developed, to be transferred across to all other host machines.

MACINTOSH IMAGE TRANSFER

The arrival of the Apple Macintosh sent clear waves of excitement through the development team, for a variety of reasons that emerge throughout this section. One of the key aspects was the facility to draw with the mouse in great detail in a large scale, and so produce good pictures. Freehand drawing and then laborious coding is not a task much loved by programmers, especially those with little artistic leaning. Here we had a machine that enabled pictures to emerge using the pencil and rubber principle, and for the code to then be stored. This was too good a tool to be confined to the Apple Macs.

A protocol for defining bit images and software including machine code sub-routines for displaying, encoding and decoding such images has been developed. A program has been written to take images from the Apple Mac to any of the other host machines using the protocol. This speeds enormously the time taken in physically designing and drawing pictures for the screen.

A VARIETY OF OTHER TOOLS

PROTOCOLS

Some parts of the total program, as indicated earlier need to go outside the standards and library. Protocols for doing this are carefully laid down to prevent a sound program having the ten per cent of hotch-potch added to it that causes unnecessary confusion at the transfer process. The machine dependent parts of any program are confined to a central group of line numbers; all programmers know that all 'extras' will be located there. These routines also have to be written, as much as is possible, to make them compatible with the library. In the past this has often resulted in an extension of the library itself, as a new routine has been incorporated. For instance, on the RML you use a routine to clear the screen before new text emerges. On the BBC you may want to plot on top – so it is now accepted that you simply remove the library part of CLEAR for the BBC version.

The long life of programs developed in this way demands not just adherence to standards and structure, but also rigorous documentation, certainly much more than would usually be the case.

Such documentation ensures the survival of the program on the various host machines, it enables efficient software support to be offered, and it leaves the way clear for future transfer to other machines some five or six years after the initial coding, when the original programmer may no longer be part of the team. Note that all these standards can be found to be embedded in the principle that an interesting educational idea that is translated into a successful CAL unit should not have a life of only one or two years.

PRINTER ROUTINES

In order to keep us on our toes, a major problem arose over being able to produce hard copy. There was no problem, of course, in the days of mainframes – the actual output was produced line by line on a printer-terminal. The problems arose firstly with graphics, and secondly with the variety of printer configurations that could be addressed by each microcomputer.

During the initial stages of development on micros, the role of printers was pushed rather to the back of the list of issues to be tackled. As time progressed however, it became apparent that using printers to keep a record of what has been happening was an important part of the educational operation, at least in some programs. Pressure was being asserted on the team by both authors and the trials feedback; accordingly a print dump routine was developed. This however presupposed that the user had set up and correctly configured, their printer before they started to run the program.

Consequently, a printer configuration routine was written so as to enable the novice user to choose whether they wanted to use a printer with the program, and if so, to set it up accordingly at the beginning of the program, rather than choose a print option half way through a run only to find the printer not working.

NETWORKING

A major issue currently being tackled by the team is that of networks. The provision of networks in schools causes a variety of headaches for the programmer. In order to ensure that the internal files on any program are secure, they obviously have to be given unique names; such software can be used as a stand alone program on a network configuration. But the network manager is quite likely to load a multiplicity of programs onto the same disk. A system needs to be devised to ensure that the internal files to one program remain unique to it, and cannot be called by 'accident' from another program. It was first decided to ensure that each Project unit had a unique initial two letter combination for the program name and its internal files, to avoid muddles. It was then discovered that the Project already had many programs with the same combination – e.g. ARABIS and ARCHEO (both History), and CIRFLOW and CIRCUIT. These were all carefully changed. Much of this had to happen even at very late stages in development in order to avoid confusion by the users of our software in this new hardware environment of networks.

The Project cannot always readily adjust its existing material, and that currently under development, in the light of new environments. It can only ensure that new developments, yet to be started, take them into consideration. Multi-user CAL units for networks is a classic case. All the CIC units, through careful checking of issues such as file names outlined above, can run on the current networks in UK schools, that is RML 480Z link and BBC Econet 2, as long as the software is used as if it was stand alone at one station. Such software cannot readily be used in a multiple access mode – the file handling operations have simply not been designed to accommodate this. One of the problems the Project has faced is, the assumption that because we have been so careful to try to ensure portability of our software across environments, that this can happen in all environments. This is simply not the case.

OTHERS

A variety of commercial tools are available which also aid the development process. Indeed it is to be welcomed that an increasing number of tools of quality are emerging, particularly in the 16 bit environment, that will possibly shift the whole emphasis of effort required in this area. The use and dependence on commercial versus in-house tools is an area of currently hot debate in the development team, a debate that will not lessen over the next few years.

In the meantime a great variety of commercially available tools, from small to large, are an everyday part of the total working environment. TXED and WORDSTAR are used both in program development and as a word processor for the writing of documentation. PASCAL has been used as a development language for some algorithms where BASIC was proving too impracticable. Macpaint and Macwrite are both used by developers. Apple public domain software, such as character definitions, are used, as are multifonts. Assemblers are increasingly being used, and there is always experimentation with input devices such as the Graf pad, Koala pad, trackball and AMX mouse. The BASED chip on the BBC is now used to edit and squash programs, and the overlay technique is often used. Note that these are all used for specific reasons to help programmers during the development process.

PATCH

Obviously these various standards and tools have emerged and changed over time. All the programmers working in the tean, both those located centrally at Chelsea (King's College) as well as those in various locations around the country, need to be informed and kept up-to-date on what is happening. Each programmer has a link programmer nominated who is located centrally. But most importantly, PATCH appears regularly. This itemizes the latest routines or solutions to problems that have recently emerged.

IMPLICATIONS OF TRANSPORTABILITY PRINCIPLE

The CIC is extremely fortunate in having key members of the programming team who have spent many years building up this principle and their expertise in its execution.

Investment in these practical manifestations of the principle of transportability is not trivial. It requires expertise to be incorporated into the team that can reflect the attributes of various machine versions of BASIC, as well as expertise in the architecture and performance of the hardware. Both of these need to be supported by a rigorous application of the standard by each programmer/developer in the team. Such rigour however can and does pay dividends handsomely. Within six months of the arrival of the BBC Model B system, some thirty programs, hitherto running on the RML 380Z and Apple II, and even on the Commodore PET 3000 and 4000 series, were running on this new machine. Currently in 1986, it is anticipated that the majority of the current library of developed CIC and CSSP programs, that is over eighty published CAL units, will be able to be transferred to the new RML Nimbus and the IBM PC. The converse also holds. There is a minimum configuration that is required of any machine before it can be the host to the subroutine library. The Sinclair Spectrum and Commodore 64 fall below the required configurations. If these standards were not maintained, the coders would have to work to too low a common denominator to make the principle acceptable.

There is one major disadvantage to this scheme of portability that has to be considered seriously. Programs developed in this manner may not be developed to use the entire range of features of a particular machine. Were they to do so, they would be tied so tightly to the original host machine as to make them not transferable without a complete rewrite. This means for instance that the library standard does not allow for use of more than a four colour mode (which includes black and white). Location of the graphics area in the RML in the first 20 lines of screen means that all programs must address this graphics area and use the bottom four lines for textual messages only. Programs are certainly slower in their execution than they would be if written in their machine version of BASIC, or indeed in machine code.

Working to this 'lowest common denominator' of the spread of machine characteristics means that some useful and imaginative features of particular machines are taboo to the developer. There is no doubt that many developers have felt that the continued inclusion of the Apple II series has been a severe limitation on the scope of the library and thus the design of units. On the other hand, the Apple II series is still a machine found commonly in educational environments in many parts of the world. Adhering to this machine has meant that CIC and CSSP software has been able to travel well beyond the boundaries of the UK. The value of our continued commitment to Apple has been reinforced by the fact of working in an academic environment in which it is important and valuable for us to share and discuss the role and implications of CAL in the international community of educators.

It must not be assumed that the implementation of methods designed to achieve this principle are fixed and inflexible. It can be seen that discussions are always underway about the appropriateness of tools and languages, as well as about the hardware environment for implementation. There is no doubt, however, that having an over riding principle of transportability, where appropriate and possible, has provided an essential framework within which the team has worked. This framework forced the team at an early stage to consider the team's need for development tools to aid the indiviudal programmers and provide cross-comparability and fertility of ideas.

PLANNING THE PROGRAM

There is no doubt that many programs do not necessarily emerge as structured as these guidelines would suggest. It is also hard to keep up documentation when pressure is immense to complete coding tasks. Nevertheless the use of all these standards, both those developed in-house as well as commercially, obviously has had a significant impact on the way the coder plans out the program from the first.

The careful planning of programs saves time by:
● identifying requirements for programs;
● reducing the problems faced by programmers which they cannot solve; and
● avoiding the need to recode programs for technical reasons at a late stage in development.
Recoding may be necessary for educational purposes; sometimes so many additions to the code have been made as the ideas have developed that the only sensible thing to do is to start again. Later chapters in this book provide some examples. The following rules are a synopsis of a CIC in-house publication (Millwood, Sellman and Creasey, 1984).

A FLOW DIAGRAM

The flow diagram in Figure 7.2 illustrates the nature of the tasks a programmer must achieve. It should be viewed in conjunction with Figure 5.1 in the chapter on 'Stages in the Development of a Unit'.

Some of the key tasks indicated in this plan are outlined below:
● *Specify in outline*: The author(s) write down an outline (the OPU) of the topic, classroom use, computer role, style of interaction, screen and paper presentation, underlying model and hardware requirements to implement the idea as a CAL unit.
● *Is it worthwhile?*: This decision is made by the development group and central team on both educational criteria and the resource required to develop the idea.
● *Specify in detail*: The authors now specify the program and paper based materials in some detail (i.e. the COMIC STRIP). Advice is provided by the programmers, as this will

Program plan

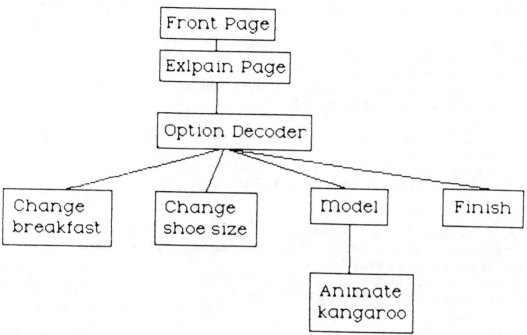

FIGURE 7.2   A program flow diagram

include screen layouts, options or choices, the model, all text in the program and the target machines.

● *Plan draft program*: The programmer prepares a plan based on the detailed specification. This includes a description of the flow of control, the major subroutines in the program, the variables, the data structure used, and the use of any special techniques.

● *Is the plan sufficient?*: This decision is taken by the senior programmer in the central team. If the plan is not sufficient, it may be referred back to the coder or to the authors if the specification is incomplete.

● *Code draft program*: Programmer implements the plan.

● *Program Plan*: Before starting any coding on a new program or amending a program, a plan should be worked out and written down (this may take up to three days to complete). Once this has been done, the plan must be discussed with the senior programmer, and the decisions taken justified. This helps to sort out any weaknesses in the plan, or specification, before coding begins.

PROGRAM PLAN

The plan should be written under the following headings; the examples below relate to a theoretical BASIC program.

Flow of control:
Draw a diagram, using a box for each major subroutine. Put the name in the box with which you intend to REM the subroutine. State at this point if it is possible to split the program into parts (which may involve file handling skills) and if so what parameters will need to be passed between the parts. Figure 7.3 provides a simple illustration.

Data:
1. Define clearly exactly what data is needed.
2. Decide how you intend to structure the data.
3. State how you intend to implement the data structure.
4. State how the data will be utilized.
For example:
   1. *What Breakfast data*: Name of food and calorie content.
   2. *Structure*: Array structure.
   3. *Implementation*: Direct access file, 2 fields per record.
   4. *Initialized*: From program with DATA statements.

Variables
List all the global variables you intend to use, giving:
1. The name – not necessarily a unique 2 character name at this point.
2. The purpose of the variable.
3. The type – real, integer, string. . .
4. The range of the variable or length of string.
For example:
   Name: shoe size.
   Purpose: Size of shoe.
   Type: integer.
   Range: 1 to 12.

Subroutines
Write out each subroutine:
1. Its line number and name, to be used in REM.
2. What it will do.
3. What are the parameters which affect it.
4. What values it returns.
For example:
   1. 4000 model.
   2. Calculates the length of a kangaroo hop.
   3. Needs amount of breakfast and shoe size.
   4. Returns the length of a hop in metres.

Techniques
List any techniques that are used outside the library standard. For instance, animation of hopping kangaroo with user defined characters.

Documents
Ensure that the following CIC internal documents have been referred to (where necessary):

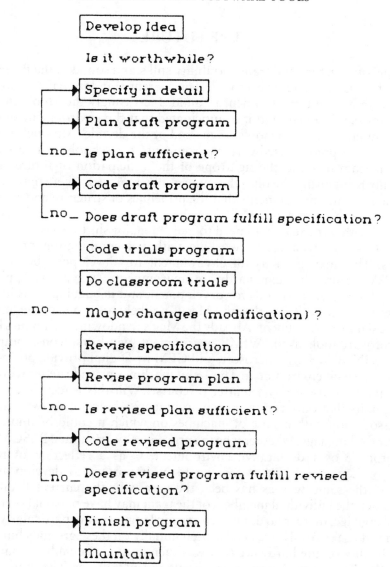

FIGURE 7.3   A program plan

1. Subroutine Library Manual.
2. Guidelines to Effective Screen Design.
3. Stages in the Development of a CAL unit – programming aspects.
4. Stages in the Development of a CAL unit – development sequence.
5. Finalization document.
6. BASIC standard (incorporated into new Library Manual).
7. Documentation Document (!).
8. Option Decoder.
9. Notes on moving sub-files within a program.

THE FUTURE

The principle of structure and transportability still stand sound in the Project; but their implementation is reaching a threshold. The current standards and routines were all developed with an 8 bit environment in mind. Increasingly the 16 bit environment is being used for development and it is anticipated that the environment should become relatively common-place in schools by the end of the decade. Although it is both hard and dangerous to predict hardware environments for schools, it is important for a development team to tread the tightrope of the anticipation of future environments whilst equally recognising the ones that may not be replaced. There may even be such a radical change in the environments that the principles of structure and transportability will simply have to be re-examined.

It is probable that the team will need to make a major shift into working with *mixed environments* – for instance, to working within a combination of compilers and interpreters. This may be a useful environment for developers, but is it the most practical? We are already seeing hardware environments, such as the Apple Macintosh which provides a total set of aids for development and debugging tools in its PASCAL implementation. Yet we know that the Mac is unlikely to be one of the main machines found in the school environment. Already the Mac's windowing techniques have become standard software tools in the WIMP environment (windows, icons, mouse and pointers). Both WINDOWS, by Microsoft, and GEM by Digital provide powerful tools for working in the 16 bit environment. The 16 bit machines provide better word-processing and file handling software as a matter of course. Will this lead to the temptation of developing units that only run in one environment? Choice of software tools must be made in association with a suite of machines on which it could be implemented.

Whatever the language, whether it be the procedurally orientated PASCAL, PROLOG with its promise of a declarative environment, C as a reflection of the windows technique, or Logo, or LISP, it is going to be important to develop and maintain standards in the same way as has been the case with the current BASIC standard. However much the individual members of the team may have personal preferences for a particular language, there is no doubt that certain languages are particularly appropriate for certain tasks. Yet BASIC was not chosen initially on these grounds but rather on its ready availability on the hardware that was then in-use, originally in mainframes and then in the first 8 bit microcomputers in schools and institutions. The choice of languages will be determined largely by the availability of that language in association with the host machine in schools.

There is no sensible way in which a Project team can expect its programmers to become efficient in a wide variety of languages, as well as familiar with the constraints of various hardware environments, and capable of interfacing the code with various software design tools. The strength of the team in the past has been based on its commonality of experience, so that the problems of BASIC are shared and understood by the majority. Work that is already progressing in PASCAL on a new CAL unit specifically designed for a 16 bit WIMP environment is illustrating the dangers of isolation. The programmer/developer needs to be able to talk, explore and share common issues with others in the team. A team composed of a variety of different specialists each working in their particular language on a particular piece of hardware loses the advantages so hard won over the last five years. On the other hand, as the systems become more complex, and the variety of commercially available software tools becomes greater, certain specialization by individuals will be essential if the team is to keep abreast of developments. Consequently hot debate must continue, and hard decisions have to be taken if fragmentation is to be prevented. All teams working in these new environments must face these same issues and resolve them in the light of the purpose of the particular team itself.

It is important that these teams share their experience. What may be seen initially as fragmentation may in the long run actually be a strength, as long as there is regular communication between teams. CIC has been involved in maintaining a dialogue with others in the software development field. All CAL development teams will need to resolve the same issues that CIC has had to face; naturally their solutions will reflect both their own philosophy and their environment.

8
SCREEN DESIGN

The importance of screen design to the development of CAL has emerged as a result of two closely related issues. Firstly, current microcomputer technology with the dynamic visual display rather than the older, typed scrolled output from a teletype printer terminal, has opened up opportunities which have very greatly affected the way in which the user can actually interact with the program – the implications of this point are discussed in more detail in the next chapter. Secondly the problems of handling images requires methods of defining very clearly particular areas of the screen and the drawing of graphs on them. The first set of guidelines within CIC emerged with Project Paper 20 (Lewis and Want, 1980b). This Project Paper addressed emerging aspects of 'Screen Design' and the 'Control of a Program'. This was inextricably linked with a style of designing and code, and was related to the Option Decoder. The paper explored the implications of a Library of Subroutines that would provide a framework whereby the programmers could handle these issues. The fundamental thinking behind this approach led to the subsequent completion of MINLIB and the *Library of Subroutines Manual*. The guidelines were based on the clear location of windows, and subset windows within them, to cover the first 20 lines of the screen. The plotting and scaling of graphs within these windows were all handled by the library. The option decoder system was introduced, so that screens could be designed with a keyword interface.

Unfortunately, this resulted in a distinct uniformity of presentation in a variety of units to such an extent the CAL units of different content and context looked disturbingly similar, if not almost identical, on glancing at the screen. This is one of the dangers that can be overlooked when providing framework software for development purposes.

After a few years of development it has become apparent that the screen is not just a dynamic replacement of the rolling paper, line by line output, of the teletype; it is now a key part of the way the user perceives the program and interacts with it. Effective screen design facilitates such interaction by way of informing and directing the user through the environment generated by the software.

PLANNING THE SCREEN DISPLAY

Since the effectiveness of the computer as a learning aid is being influenced by the design of the screen, far more attention needed to be given to the planning, design and execution of screen displays. Initial units were very much a reflection of the structure of the code and its associated rules, this, in some cases, actually obscured the educational purpose of the unit itself. After much internal debate in the team and trial and error during development, a three day workshop was held specifically to address the issue.

During the workshop in November 1983, four guest speakers addressed the team on issues of screen design, and there is no doubt that their understanding of design, whether on a computer screen or not, influenced the outcome. They were: Peter Bratt, (Producer, BBC Schools Television), Fred Daly (Director, Homerton Curriculum Development Project) Dr Jeremy Foster (Principal Lecturer in Psychology, Manchester Polytechnic), and Dr Steve Scrivener, (Head of Graphics, Human–Computer Interface Research Unit, Leicester Polytechnic). Members of other CAL development units, with which the Project has maintained a regular dialogue, were also present – such as Rod Mulvey representing Netherhall School Software, Derek Esterson representing ILECC (Inner London Educational Computing Centre) and Rosemary Fraser representing ITMA.

The workshop acted as a catalyst for ideas that reflected both programming and educational concerns. This combination of expertise gave us new general insights into the issues:

● The graphics area should not be solely associated with graphs, but rather with pictures, or with pictorial images. Pictures should be used to replace words.

● There is a limit to the amount that the user can take-in, on the screen, at any one time. The role of movement and of the best location on the screen to attract the eye must be considered.

● Even though the screen is two-dimensional, various stratagems used by artists over the centuries could be used to provide a sense of depth and related importance.

● Excessive and inappropriate use of colour could do more damage to the eye through confusion as to which colour to focus on, than a design in black and white.

● Space itself is an important component of any picture; use space effectively by considering its positive benefits.

● Eliminate screen clutter; the rules that have been devised with regards to graphs and artwork on paper, for instance the use of a key or scale, are luxuries that may need to be dispensed with on screen.

● Messages to drive the program do not need to be separated from the graphics area, but can be incorporated within.

The Library of Software Routines, referred to in Chapter 7, was produced over a series of years by the processes of internal debate, trial and error and prototyping, as described in the preceding section. It is true to say (and it was most appropriate) that the majority of these discussions and decisions took place amongst the professional programmers. Those on the CAL authorship side of the team were not qualified to discuss details of coding or structure, and indeed did not necessarily understand the implications of the decisions reached due to their relative technical ignorance. There will always be the problem, in teams such as these, of the balance of expertise – technical and educational – and of the level of awareness of each other's skills and concerns. This has been commented on as being particularly relevant to the development process. But, it is even more relevant during the production of guidelines.

The synthesis of ideas that emerged from the Screen Design Workshop included perceptions from the full range of expertise within the team. It became apparent that they needed to be written down formally to avoid their becoming blurred and lost over time. Accordingly, a CIC *Guide to Effective Screen Design* was produced (Alderson and DeWolfe, 1984). The guidelines identified below are a synopsis of the key points in this publication by the Project.

GUIDELINES FOR EFFECTIVE SCREEN DESIGN

There is an underlying assumption that these guidelines are to be applied to a unit whose educational context, aims, target users and environment are clearly defined and understood. The type of learning activity envisaged by the authors will inevitably influence the design – thus a program aimed at presenting factual information sequentially will not look the same as one encouraging discovery learning and decision-making. This means that screen design cannot be considered in isolation from the user interface with which it is inextricably linked. Both need to be tailored to suit the age, ability and experience of the user.

PRESENTATION

- Designs should be kept as simple as possible; a complicated display is only justified if the system it explains is equally complex, or if the display is built up gradually to expose the complexity.
- The gradual build up of information on the screen, bit by bit, as the user interacts with the program may end up looking cluttered, however a valuable educational exercise will have been taking place during the build up.
- In those cases in which there is some doubt as to whether or not more information should be displayed, consider giving the user the choice of calling up that information.
- Clarity of definition of small images is difficult to achieve on many microcomputers, and so they should be avoided.
- Programs intended for large group use should not contain as much display detail per screen as that for use by a small group gathered round a well-adjusted monitor.
- Avoid presenting more than one idea at a time. The users will not know which of the two or more new pieces of information they should focus on, and in which order.
- Consider designing for the user who is swapping between two displays in order to divide and clarify the information. Dividing the screen into different windows with framing can be a useful method of separating types of information on one screen. Think of each frame as a subscreen, but avoid losing unity of the whole display.

THE MEDIUM

- It is important that developers appreciate that they are dealing with a unique medium which should not be confused with other more familiar forms. The computer screen is not the same as a printed sheet of text, nor a film or television.

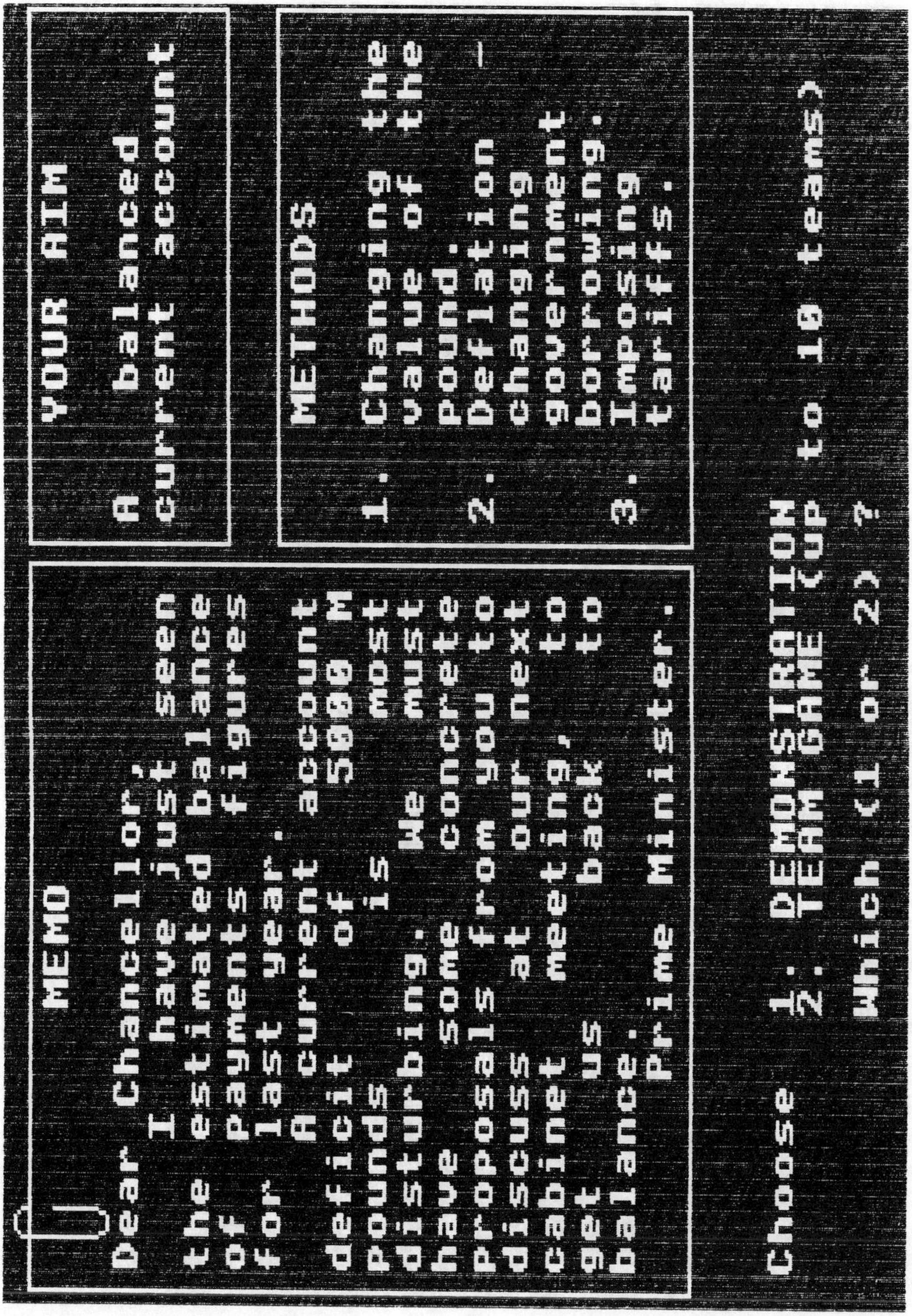

YOUR AIM

A balanced current account

METHODS

1. Changing the value of the pound.
2. Deflation changing government borrowing.
3. Imposing tariffs.

MEMO

Dear Chancellor, I have just seen the estimated balance of payments figures for last year. A current account deficit of 5000 M pounds is most disturbing. We must have some concrete proposals from you to discuss at our next cabinet meeting, to get us back to balance. Prime Minister.

Choose 1: DEMONSTRATION
2: TEAM GAME (up to 10 teams)
Which (1 or 2) ?

FIGURE 8.1   Text boxed to indicate 3 different sections – DEFCIT

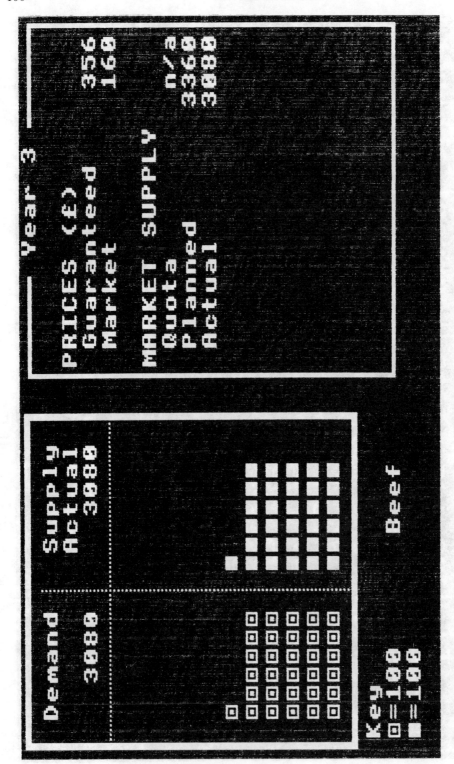

FIGURE 8.2   Two separate parts of the screen, the table and the list boxed to keep them clear – AGCOM

● Each medium has its strengths and appropriate uses. Developers should not attempt to use the computer screen where it is not the best method of presenting information. An example of this was the vogue for putting all the material relevant to a CAL unit on the screen rather than in print. Indeed CIC was castigated for continuing to produce sheets of A4 printed materials of courseware in association with the software, rather than incorporating all background information and instructions on the screen. Attempts by the Project in the early 1980s to produce comprehensive help screens, in association with keywords, produced screens with such a density of text that we should now be most ashamed to have produced. One well designed A4 sheet of a teachers' guide can contain 300 words with space for diagrams and layout. One 40 character by 24 line screen can display less than 200 words in dense closely packed text.

● Two important assets of the micro are that it can be dynamic and interactive. These characteristics make the comparison between educational television which is watched passively and educational software spurious. Current developments in interactive video will reinforce and combine the uniqueness of the two media in the future.

● Always remember that the CAL unit can draw on the other media which it accompanies. Currently this includes paper, television series, and radio, and in the future interactive video disks will also be included.

FOCUSING ATTENTION

● The dynamic display is an excellent medium for focusing attention on key aspects of the educational message. Images can be highlighted (or flash) and made to stand out and thus be reinforced.

● It is very tempting to overdo this aspect using too many eye-catching methods which can cause more confusion, or even worse, focus attention on a less significant part of the program, weighting it unduly for the user.

● It is important to try to give the screens, particularly when they change, some visual continuity, without linking disparate elements in a spurious way.

● Since most western people read from left to right and top to bottom, it is sensible to place all headings or titles at the top, and all prompts, such as 'Enter your choice' or 'Press return' at the bottom.

● Always clear existing information before replacing it with new. This not only attracts attention to the cleared part in anticipation of the new, but it prevents the new from being muddled with the old.

● Avoid allowing visual continuity across frames from suggesting false links between elements where this is not the case.

● An alternative technique is to overlay information and so reveal layers, or titles, in a sequence.

● Create an impression of depth by using shadow, colour or perspective.

● Overlays are a useful method of giving the illusion of depth. Draw boxes around, or highlight the dominant image. The less significant image can be left 'fuzzy' till called to the fore.

● Animation can direct the eye towards the area of the screen that is currently most significant. However excessive movement causes confusion.

TEXT

● Visual display units are simply not suited to large amounts of text – these should only appear when absolutely essential. Most text resides more happily in the accompanying notes.

● When text does have to be presented, it must be laid out in such a way as to help the reader.

● Text should be divided into small paragraphs of not more than three or four short sentences. Space should be left between each paragraph. If necessary use more than one page of screen, rather than cram it all in.

● Text should be set in upper and lower case characters.

● Do not right justify blocks of text – the spacing is usually too crude.

● Avoid scrolling text; preferably expose the text on screen at once, or paragraph by paragraph, but not word by word, unless it is a deliberate part of the design as for instance when emulating a Telex message.

● Take care to avoid breaking up words which would interfere with comprehension, for instance, 'to decide', or 'in case'. Move to a new line if necessary, and avoid hyphenation at the end of lines.

● Keep grammatical structures consistent. There really is no excuse for the debased forms of language that are used despite the severe limitations on screen size.

GRAPHICS

● Wherever possible, use graphics rather than text, for this is what the computer screen is best suited to.

● Stylized drawings have to be used, as the technology cannot emulate the reality of photographs or complex artwork.

● Icons are a positive advantage, but it is important that the icon clearly and simply reflects only the aspect, or matter, which it represents.

● Keep drawings simple. Over elaborate detail may distract the eye, thereby emphasizing points that are unimportant. More significantly, they will make the drawing slower in appearing.

ANIMATION

● Use animation sparingly; it is not easy to achieve and time spent on it may be more effectively spent on other aspects of the program.

● The illusion of movement is another powerful feature that can focus attention dynamically; it can often be related to the very processes of change which the program is illustrating, for example, the rise and fall of a graph during an experiment.

● Too often animation is used inappropriately which causes the user confusion either through its excesses, or by its highlighting a part of the total screen of lesser significance.

LEGIBILITY

● All components of the display, both text and graphs, must be able to be read clearly and easily. The golden rule is 'as simple and large as possible' for images.

● The positive use of spacing around text and images to aid clarity.

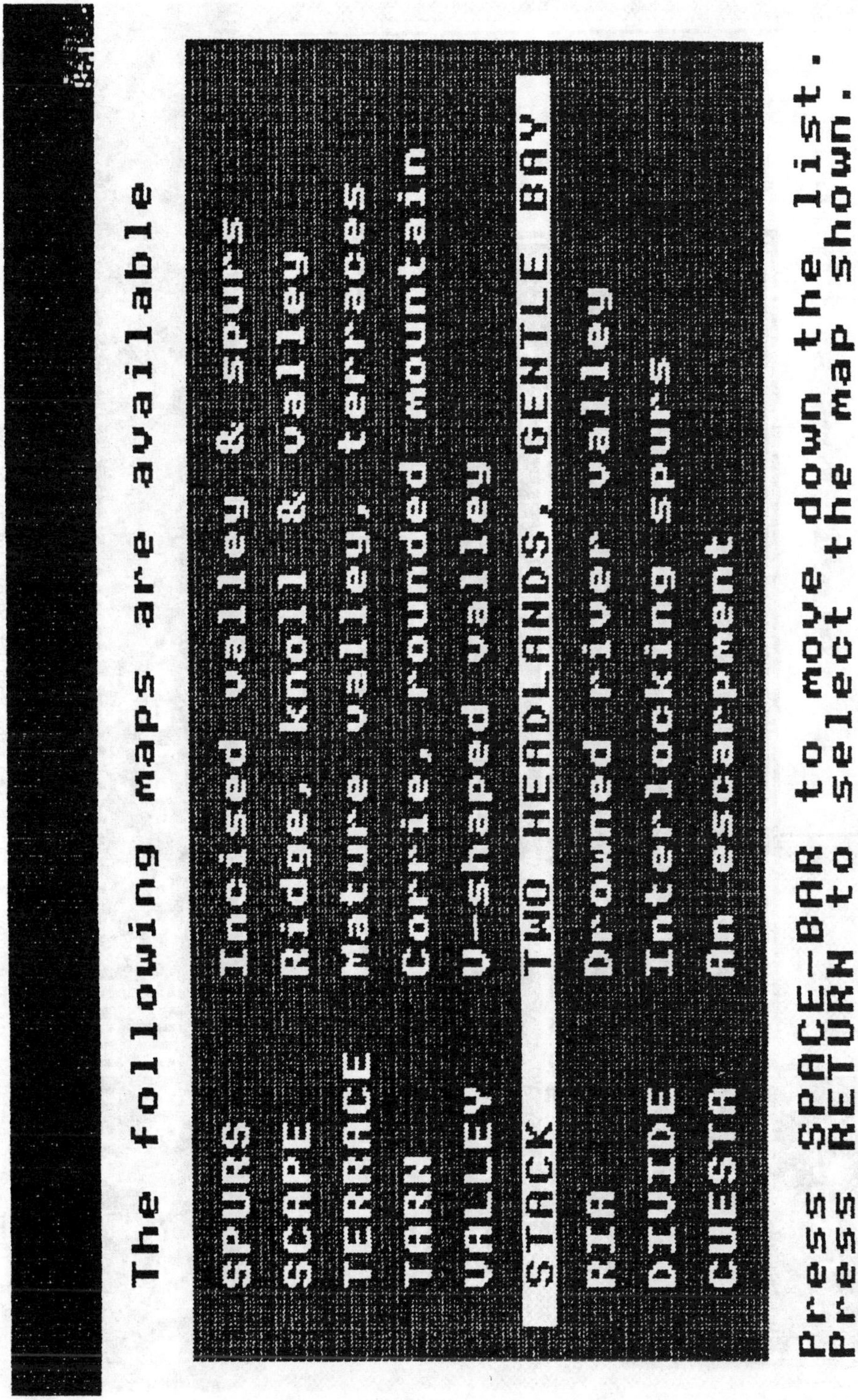

The following maps are available

SPURS	Incised valley & spurs
SCAPE	Ridge, knoll & valley
TERRACE	Mature valley, terraces
TARN	Corrie, rounded mountain
VALLEY	V-shaped valley
STACK	TWO HEADLANDS, GENTLE BAY
RIA	Drowned river valley
DIVIDE	Interlocking spurs
CUESTA	An escarpment

Press SPACE-BAR to move down the list.
Press RETURN to select the map shown.

FIGURE 8.3   Selection by highlighting over the chosen option – LAND

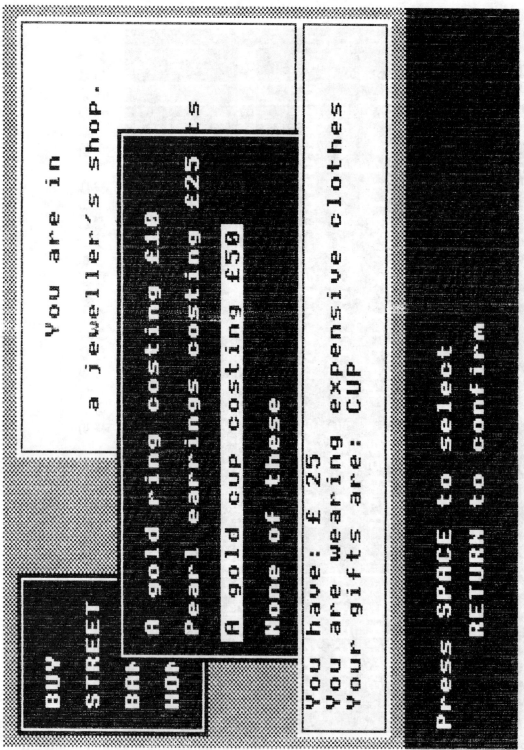

You are in
a jeweller's shop.

BUY
STREET
BA
HON

A gold ring costing £10
Pearl earrings costing £25
A gold cup costing £50
None of these

You have: £ 25
You are wearing expensive clothes
Your gifts are: CUP

Press SPACE to select
RETURN to confirm

FIGURE 8.4   Overlaying the latest box, the choice of purchase in the jewellers shop, on top of previous windows – COURT

Qu'est-ce qu'il a?

Press RETURN to continue

FIGURE 8.5 A single clear picture for use in a classroom demonstration – ACCDNT

● Space itself is a positive part of the screen – not just an empty area that automatically needs filling.

COLOUR

● Colour is possibly the most misused asset of the current generation of micros. Because machines have the capability to place eight or more garish colours together on the same screen at the same time, there appears to be an overwhelming temptation to use them all. This is often the result of a muddle between the concepts underlying arcade games and those underlying educational software.

● A restrained use of two or four colours focuses attention on the appropriate parts of

Brightness	Colour
Highest	White
	Yellow
	Cyan
Medium	Green
	Magenta
Lowest	Red
	Blue
	Black

FIGURE 8.6   Colour brightness

the screen. Constraints due to problems of memory size or availability of colours can, in reality, lead to a more carefully considered product.

● The range of colours on microcomputers is not a reflection of those available in reality; so they should not be used as if they were. However, colour can help to create an impression or mood.

● Many of the colours distract and give undue weight and prominence to the words or image with which they are used.

● Colour can add information to the display without taking up extra space. In this sense, it is a bonus for the designer.

● Elements of the display which appear in the same colour appear to be related; those in different colours, separate. This 'coding' can be used, quite deliberately, for educational purposes.

● Keep the use of colour consistent throughout the program.

● Use colour for emphasis. Keep to the minimum number of colours if possible, and select ones that provide both good contrast and legibility. Colours may be ordered on a scale of relative perceived brightness. Legibility will be best achieved by selecting two colours of contrasting brightness, for instance, black on cyan, or white on blue.

● Placing two bright colours together simply causes confusion to the user who does not know on which colour to place the greater emphasis. Figure 8.7 gives a recommended table of colour pairing.

● Avoid large solid areas of white or yellow – they give an irritating flicker.

● Few users will be sitting in front of well-defined colour monitors, most users will view CAL units on monochrome monitors or on television. Blue on black may be acceptable on a colour monitor, but it will be almost illegible on the majority of monochrome screens. Always, therefore, wherever possible design with the monochrome user in mind. I have often had reason to bless this rule when giving a demonstration to a large audience with the mixture of colour monitors and monochrome televisions at my disposal.

Foreground Colour

Background Colour \ Foreground	White	Yellow	Cyan	Green	Magenta	Red	Blue	Black
White	#	#	#			/	/	/
Yellow	#	#	#	#		/	/	/
Cyan	#	#	#	#			/	/
Green			#	#	#			
Magenta				#	#	#		
Red	/					#	#	#
Blue	/	/					#	#	#
Black	/	/	/	/			#	#

/   **Recommended pairings**

Pairings to Avoid

FIGURE 8.7   Colour pairings

TIMING

● The timing at which changes occur on the screen is often important to the learning process.

● Changes of display that result from a user input should be clearly visible, and preferably appear soon after the input.

● The changes should not be so fast that they occur while the user is still looking at the keyboard during the input.

● If possible it is best to design in user control when changes to the screen take place, as this can accommodate different levels of ability, and indeed long pauses while groups of pupils may discuss their decisions before making an input.

● Capitalize on the inherent 'patience' of the machine.

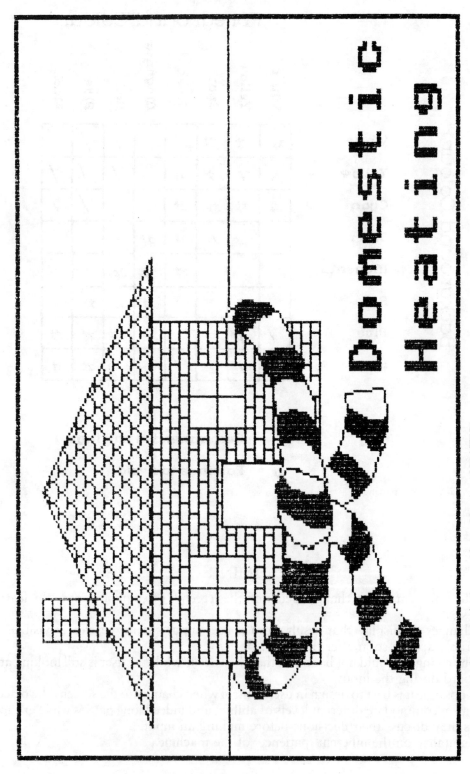

FIGURE 8.8   A linking visual image – Home Heating (HEATER)

SOUND

● Many programs can now be accompanied by appropriate sounds – either whizzes and bangs of the 'arcade games' varieties, or tones to reflect success or failure, or sometimes even appropriate ditties that relate to the content.

● Let the user determine both whether they wish to have sound, and at what volume. This should be determined preferably at the beginning of the use of the program.

● The use of music is an interesting issue producing a wide range of personal responses by teachers and pupils, so flexibility is required, to ensure that it enhances rather than detracts from the educational aim.

LINKING DESIGN WITH NOTES

The careful consideration of screen design can make a significant difference to the impact of a CAL unit. It is important to link the design with the accompanying notes – this creates a sense of the unity of identity for the whole package (see Figure 8.8). This can be achieved by choosing a particular pictorial image and a title that are not only used on the front page of the software and title cover of the booklets, but which can be readily associated in the user's minds with the unique content of that particular unit.

The aim of all these guidelines is to make the process of creating effective screens less arduous, more imaginative and more efficient. They, therefore, ease the task of development for the programmers and authors by providing framework for design. Inevitably as new hardware and software tools emerge, some of these guidelines will become redundant. Developers however will always have to deliberately select quite what is to appear on the screen in order to develop software that will focus the users' attention on the particular tasks in hand.

9
USER INTERFACE

During earlier work on CAL development attention focussed on finding an appropriate topic, verifying a model, and writing the code. Over the years, and increasingly with the introduction of the sophisticated graphical capabilities of microcomputers, more attention has been paid to both how ideas may be translated into screen design, and to the associated problems of designing for a dynamic screen.

At the same time growing attention has been paid to the third part of the issue, namely what is known as the user interface. This phrase had little meaning in the seventies – and indeed some large purpose-built pieces of commercial software are still designed with the barest minimum of attention paid to how the user interacts with the actual software. Nevertheless, the 'front end' of a piece of systems software, or *the style of user interface to a CAL unit will contribute significantly to the effectiveness of the material.*

The Project held a second workshop conference on the 'User Interface' in October 1984 to explore the issues. Present to help us in our deliberations were: Bill Tagg (AUCBE), Professor Hugh Burkhardt (ITMA), John Laycock (Royal Aircraft Establishment – Farnborough), Derek Ball (Leicester University) and Fred Daly (Homerton College). During the course of the workshop, six published CIC programs were explored with a view to analysing how effective their interface was, and how we would wish to change it. It emerged that, possibly even more than with screen design, there was a clear historical perception of the way a user interface may work, which in part was influenced by the changing attributes of the machines. The advent of the arrow cursor keys, and more recently the mouse are two clear examples.

DIALOGUE

The 'dialogue method' was ideally suited to the teletype terminals, with its line by line output and response. A clear question was asked, such as 'Do you wish to change the temperature?', to which the user responded. This could often be in the form of a YES/NO answer. Indeed, I remember great and heated discussion on whether it was acceptable to allow 'Y' or 'N', or whether the whole words must be typed. For a long time, I felt that so much to do with computers was impoverishing our language, so that it was important to keep whole words as much as possible. This, however, ran counter to programmers sensibilities at the neatness with which one could allow 'Y' or 'YES', 'N' or 'NO' in code. Would that design problems were as simple as this today!

DEFINED RANGE OF RESPONSES

Many more questions than those requiring a YES/NO answer could be and were asked. For example:

From what date would you like to start the projection?

What variable would you like to change next?

What course do you wish to sail?

All of these questions would expect answers within a range of the possibilities, i.e. 1990–1995 – or any number between 1970 and 2070 in five year intervals; oxygen; or any eight points of the compass. In design terms, therefore, it was just as easy to make a range of answers available, each of which would trigger a particular response, as it was to provide only the two routes stemming from YES/NO.

How would the user know the range of answers allowed to a single question? The first method is to ensure that this is covered in the accompanying notes. But it does become rather cumbersome to have to refer to the notes every time you are asked a question. So increasingly, the range would be displayed at the same time as the question on the screen (wherever this is possible).

For example:

● What date do you wish to start at (between 1970 and 2070)?

● Which course do you want to sail (N,NE,E,SE,S,SW,W,NW)?

This works if the range can be condensed sufficiently to be manageable within brackets in association with the question. But it is clearly not possible if the range of variables were to be: oxygen, temperature, carbon dioxide, limestone or iron. One method is to use symbols wherever possible, but this can result in the use of an excess of symbols which may not be clearly understood. Thus, the pupil/user is actually concentrating on what the symbol stands for, rather than upon which actual variable they want to change.

An alternative method to placing the range in brackets is to leave the question unadorned: however, if the user fails either to read the notes and or to choose an appropriate reply, then the first error message will state the range. For example to the question:

'Which course?',

should the pupil respond.

'SSW',

then the error message will say

'Only 8 points of the compass possible.

Try again!'

There are serious misgivings at using this method because it encourages the user to make responses at random and not necessarily think beforehand.

Another way is to ask the question only after a sentence which outlines the range of variables open in the operation. Whilst this is highly satisfactory in some circumstances – for instance in the question of variables – it may not be satisfactory in others where the same choice across the same range is going to occur frequently. There the sentence may appear the first time, but not at subsequent questions. For example:

You may only sail in 8 compass directions; thus SSW or NNE is not possible. Which course?

CONDITIONS TO RANGES

Many questions of this type will have not only a range from within which a reply is required, but possibly a condition within the range. In the question of dates, the range is between 1970 and 2070, but with the condition of only five year intervals. Thus 2075 is unacceptable because it is out of range; 1974 is also unacceptable because it is not within the condition; while 1968 is unacceptable for both reasons. There are, as well as the method of making ranges clear in the notes, certain decisions to be taken. You will need three error messages to accommodate the three possible incorrect responses. Do you put both conditions beforehand in brackets, or in a complete sentence before the question 'which year?' is asked. Both of these latter solutions demand more space on the screen – and there is not much space in 40 characters × 24 lines in which to place all these messages without seriously interrupting the overall design. But there is another more fundamental problem.

To what extent should the hand of the user be held during the learning operation? Should you expect the user to be able to work within a range clearly identified for them, or do you need to hedge every entry so as to ensure they are never at a loss. This will be looked at further in this chapter under the section entitled 'HELP'. But the concern that has led to such a detailed consideration has been led in part by responses of people when looking at software quickly in demonstrations. The views of adults in the educational or publishing world at commercial exhibitions and conferences should not necessarily colour design issues for software that has been developed for use in the classroom within a curriculum context.

RELEVANCE OF DIALOGUE

With the increasing variety of methods of user interface possible today, let us not forget the humbler 'dialogue style'. When used appropriately it can draw the user along a path in a friendly fashion. Thus when a path is wanted, and help is requested through the use of pointed questions, the dialogue style may be the most appropriate method to use. It is still pertinent in a variety of role-playing exercises.

CHOOSING THE ROUTE – OPTIONS

By the early 1980s more attention was being given to the way the user perceived his or her route through the learning operation. One of the great justifications of simulations is that the user could choose a variety of paths through the operation. A dialogue style tends towards a linear route, a sequence of which had to be completed before a second route could be chosen. Developers were now looking for a method of placing more control in the hands of the user. Thus instead of posing a question, 'Which variable do you want to change?' – which suggests that changing the variable is the next logical thing to do in a sequence – the design should be forcing the onus of thinking back onto the pupils. Should they next change a variable, or the time period, or the speed of operation? What do they want to do next, and more importantly, in what order? Thus instead of posing suggestive questions, a method was needed that enabled the user to choose their own option in the sequence. Thus the keyword or command style emerged.

KEYWORDS

In essence, the option style operates through a series of defined *keywords* (Want, 1982). Rather than respond to a question, the user is given an open-ended prompt Option? In response they may choose from a list of keywords, for instance, TEMPERATURE, DURATION, RAINFALL, SEASON. The user decides which aspect of an environment they wish to explore next. If it is RAINFALL, they input that keyword, and then choose between the related conditions, e.g. light, drizzle, heavy, storm, none. They can then see the implication of that change, or decide to make two changes at the same time. So they may also opt to change the SEASON, and so choose which season in particular – spring, summer, autumn or winter.

After using their selection of route by identifying keywords, they then have to select a keyword that drives the program on, such as GO, START, or CONTINUE. Lists of keywords therefore contain two types of instruction for the user, those that select content and those that drive the program forwards. This, in itself, can cause confusion; care needs to be given to designing ways of distinguishing between the two functions.

DIFFERENT TYPES OF OPTION

What is interesting is that different CAL development groups came to very similar conclusions in the early 1980s. The Advisory Unit in Hertfordshire (AUCBE) under the direction of Bill Tagg developed a *Command* structure (Tagg, 1980). The appearance of a colon acts as a prompt for the user to use a command word to lead into a section of the program. The choice of the word 'command' is interesting as it indicates that the control of the program is clearly in the hands of the user; CIC's word 'option?' would suggest more a choice through the learning environment.

Another group, the ITMA (Investigations into Teaching using Micros as an Aid) collaboration, under the direction of Rosemary Fraser and Hugh Burkhardt, went for *Drive Charts*. (Fraser, 1983). This was a more complex method of options. Letters rather than words are used; the user knows which letter they want by reference to a 'Drive chart' in the notes. This chart shows clearly the pattern of routes and results that are possible within the structure of the program. Thus the chart provides a whole scenario, at one glance, of the way the code itself is structured, and the user drives through the software by single keystrokes.

HELP

For the individual(s) sitting at the screen, the word 'Option?', or simply a colon, means that there is not only the freedom of choice, but also less of that element of help that had been forthcoming through the dialogue method. This places the role of the accompanying 'courseware' into greater focus.

Unfortunately the introduction of keywords coincided with very serious attempts to reduce the paper that accompanied software to the very barest minimum. There were two distinct pressures trying to reduce the paper based materials related to software.

Firstly, there was the lobby that saw the value of software in the means of electronic delivery. Why go to the bother of distributing cassettes or disks containing the code, when you should be able to download it yourself? Currently, some software can be downloaded by electronic mail networks.

Secondly, there can be no doubt that producing accompanying notes to a good publishable standard is expensive. They take time to develop, and increase the total cost of the software unit to the end-user. Accordingly there was pressure to put as much information, particularly help messages, onto the screen.

Attention has to be paid to the plight of the user, who when faced with 'Option?', is not sure as to what to do next. In CIC material, one keyword is always HELP. Using this word enables the pupil to call up a list of all the keywords that are relevant in the program, such as TIME, LENGTH, OXYGEN, CARBOHYDRATE. These words by themselves are not enough, so a brief phrase is added to explain their role. This is incorporated into all the keyboard style programs. If there were many keywords, the list could fill a whole screen, and on rare occasions has even required a second screen. Calling up the help screen has meant that a graphics screen, on which the user is working, has had to be cleared. A further message – 'this will clear your screen, do you still want HELP?' – has been devised. Use of screens for HELP, not paper, clearly causes some problems. One of the things that a HELP option can not do is help the pupils decide what to do next, or to choose an appropriate path. Thus it does not necessarily provide that hand-holding which we associate, in normal English usage, with the word 'help'.

Another aspect of providing help has been devised. The open-structure of simulations driven by option keywords means that the user does not necessarily get a clear picture of the totality of the possibilities of the unit against which to make their choice. Thus another two keywords, DEMO and EXAMPLE has been introduced, which give a sample run through the program. Often the front pages of information recommend that the user chooses this option first in order to sample the flavour of the unit. The DEMO option has all the variables present in order to show how the simulation will progress and to display appropriate results.

SECONDARY KEYWORDS

A teacher may want the facility to illustrate an aspect of the simulation without setting up each of the conditions laboriously in front of the class. Programs written with a keyword structure in mind, and thus using the Option Decoder, have the facility to enable the user to set up secondary keywords. Thus they can define the TEMPERATURE, RAINFALL, DURATION, SEASON with each separate condition pertaining to those keywords, and set it up as a new keyword, e.g. CLASS. Then at the lesson itself they can use CLASS as their keyword and their predefined sequence runs.

Two aspects devolve from this. Firstly, secondary keywords are an attempt to give the teacher control over how they choose to use the material – thus they could customize the simulation for their specific classes. Many of the programs devised with secondary keywords gave a clear indication in the notes as to how the teacher could also list the program, go to the data files, and change these with data relevant to their specific requirements. This aspect of customizing the software seems important. Yet there is little evidence to suggest that teachers have used this secondary keyword facility or incorporated their own data into the data files.

The aspect of customizing the data was a precursor to attempting to design framework software. CIC has developed a suite of English programs whereby the users, both teacher and pupil, can build up their own files without having to list the code or set up secondary keywords (ACROSS, CBLUFF, and BSTORY). There is evidence to suggest that this method of customizing, by providing files specially designed for user input, is more successful. It is this approach that CIC will use for future framework developments.

But more importantly the need for teachers to devise specific routes, reflected by teacher groups, which led to the development of secondary keywords, was in part a reflection of concern at the totally open-ended nature of simulations that were structured around keywords.

KEYWORD LIMITATIONS

Keywords while providing a useful freedom to the user are not necessarily the most appropriate method of the user controlling the flow of their interaction with the program. While almost ideal for some environments – science simulations, for instance – humanities authors, in particular, while struggling with this new standard of design associated with the development of the Library of Subroutines, found they were forced to plan around a keyword structure. This simply did not work with some role-playing games or simulations. Here a form of modified dialogue was maintained as essential to the nature of the tasks.

This indicated a problem. The keyword style had a specific relationship with the logic of the program design that was a recommended standard. This does not mean that all educational paths can be fitted into such standards. Working on unity will constrain uncomfortably the freedom of educational design. Within CIC the period of development of the Library of Subroutines and the associated option structure caused severe problems for some members of the team. CIC would be most cautious before allowing any one standard that was appropriate for one area, but not necessarily for others, interfere with educational design again. The problems of uniformity associated with keywords emerged with the design of the screen.

The main problem with such a rigorous approach to design and user interface is that it obscures the uniqueness and thus the individual curriculum message of the software. The design of the typeface, font, layout of a page in a textbook, is not uniform across the whole suite of individual texts. They tend to be uniform only across a series, whose link is that they cover the same or a related theme. CIC made the mistake of making the link with the fact that the software all has to be written in the same style. However laudable the latter's aim, by crossing the boundary of code and influencing the screen presentation, it had an unwelcome influence on the message itself.

One still hears desperate cries for a uniformity of user interface; but the interface should always reflect the CAL topic itself and the way the learner is learning, rather than the way the machine is being driven. Keywords were in danger of being used inappropriately, while the design associated with the option decoder was forcing a uniformity of interface that was in danger of obscuring the purpose and character of the unit. The idea behind 'Options?' still fundamentally, forms the basis of how the user drives through a program. However, the presentation and selection of the choice has now been changed by the use of cursors and menus.

CURSORS

Dissatisfaction with the constraints of keywords and the dangers of screen similarities coincided with the growing realization that we had barely begun to exploit the dynamic nature of the screen for user input. Most dialogue questions, or 'Option?' appeared in the bottom left of the display. We were also still affected by our consideration of the use of the qwerty keyboard. Two factors influenced a subsequent shift in our thinking. Firstly, a range of peripheral devices appeared on the market, in particular alternative keyboards, which others, but not ourselves, had begun to explore. And secondly, the generation of micros that began to appear in 1982/83 in the UK – that is the Acorn BBC and the RML 480Z – had arrow cursor keys as part of their keyboards.

The problem with designing software in which a joystick or concept keyboard are an integral part, is that unless you can be confident that the audience for your software has all these peripherals, your units are going to be available to only a limited group, and then will die when that peripheral is succeeded by another. But the emergence of arrow cursors as a matter of course on all the newer machines meant that we could consider incorporating them into the software quite seriously. The question was how?

One way is to use the cursor to locate a particular part of the screen, for instance for inputting numbers. Hitherto the way of changing the temperature on a graph in response to the question 'How high is the temperature?' would be by inputing 17°C on the bottom line, which would be followed by the temperature on the screen moving up to the new level. Now a block representing the temperature could flash, the user move the cursor by means of the arrows over to the temperature part of the screen, input 17°C, and that part would change. So there is a more direct relationship between what you enter and its area on the screen. Thus the attention of the user is focused as closely as possible on the fact that the temperature had to change. The cursors also became useful, particularly in Geography, when moving objects through locations, for instance, when siting windmills or blast furnaces. Use of the cursor in this way is making the user interface directly related to the flow of the work.

But, as with all new approaches, there are limitations. Because, for years, man has needed to be able to locate areas and exact points on a wider flat plane, a convention for the use of co-ordinates has been developed, and used to some significant degree in Mathematics and Geography. Using cursors to point and locate yourself on the screen means you no longer, in this particular medium, need to get for instance, your map grid references right. Yet having previously had to input four figures in the correct sequence in software as a means of accurate pinpointing on a map has been a useful method of reinforcing pupils' competence in grids without it in any way being the main aim of the exercise. Using cursors means you lose that other reinforcement – and it is important to remember that conventions which are used across media must not be ignored simply because they may not be necessary in this particular one.

If there are no arrow keys, you can use Up (U), Down (D), Left (L) or Right (R). But how easily?

MENUS

Moving the cursor across the screen means that it is easy to have menus of options on the screen itself, through which the cursor can run to select the option. So the principle of design shifted from the user typing in an option, to his or her selecting it from a menu that can take up part of the main screen. The cursor could be used to highlight which of a menu of options was available. This choice would then be confirmed by pressing Return at which point the program moves into the new phase.

One method of executing this idea is for the screen to contain an arrow which would move, as the cursor was moved, to point to the selection chosen. Another is to highlight the actual selection itself. This can be done by boxing the choice, changing the colours when the cursor rests within the box, or changing the text from lower to upper case. All of these show the user where their cursor selection is currently located. Pressing the return button is then used for confirmation of choice, at which point the screen changes accordingly. Using cursors and menus reduces the amount of typing needed significantly.

An interesting development, that has occurred while using these methods of selection through a menu, is that the role of the actual arrow keys has been taken over and simplified by means of the Space Bar. One tap of the space bar moves the selection down one. Thus the user can 'space through the selection'. When the highlighted selection reaches the bottom of the list, it can either return to the top and start again, or bounce back up the list rather like a yoyo.

Selection through menus provides that aspect of 'help' that was missing on the dynamic screen with 'Options' in that the possible routes for the user to take are made clear. Thus menus, as a method, lie somewhere between Dialogue and Keywords. Menus are methods of applying better design to the flexibility of driving power offered by keywords. The choice made by the user is the same as a keyword choice, but the choice is selected by them from the variety presented on the screen. Phrases can represent the choice rather than a single word, as long as it can be highlighted and selected efficiently.

A LIST

Locating the various options that can be selected within a list can pose interesting issues. The list provides a synopsis of the scenario of what is possible. A list suggests a sequence or order. Looking at some option programs now can be quite amusing. On using the keyword HELP, the list of keywords available often had FINISH – to end the program runs – at the top of the list. This was because at the time many users were not sure about how exactly to END, and would use the HELP option in those circumstances. We have of course tried to standardize such general words, but we have never really resolved the relative merits of GO and START, DEMO and EXAMPLE, or FINISH and END. Lists, themselves, can be useful ways of indicating a useful route through the program, notably, the sort of route that is forced by a dialogue style.

However, lists can have drawbacks. Numbering lists, from one to five for example, can suggest a spurious ranking. This can be avoided partially by use of letters. In dialogue or keyword selection, choices are often indicated by typing a letter which indicates one of a series of possibilities. A complete alternative is to avoid using lists at all, and instead placing the options in a circular menu. Here, each space bar or cursor stroke moves an arrow around the choices, possibly highlighting each box in a circle in turn – usually travelling clockwise. This method is particularly appropriate when you actively do not want the user to place a spurious importance to the location of an item in the list.

Unlike the earlier use and execution of option keywords, there is emerging a greater variety of styles of main menu selection and cursor use. This is partly a reflection of the fear of uniformity prompted by previous experience, and partly because each method is chosen principally to reflect the content of the software itself. In other words, the design of the user interface is becoming more related to the learning operation with which the user is involved. If the user has to think about how they drive through the program, then their attention is being regularly diverted from the educational content, concept and/or process that the unit is aiming at. The ideal is, therefore, to produce both an interface, and a design that produces the minimum barrier between the user and the message.

MOUSE

The appearance of a mouse as a method of driving through menus, and in particular, in association with Windows and Icons is a welcome extension to using cursors and menus. As an almost uniform 16 bit standard, new CAL currently under development can incorporate them as a matter of course.

RELATED ISSUES

'User interface' has been used here, to cover in particular, the relationship between the user and the changing dynamic screen. There are certain other aspects of control that also need addressing.

WORDS

There are some words in the English Language which now have a specific meaning with respect to micros, such as disk, file, transfer, list, data. These words have all been used in other contexts already. There is no justification for assuming that when used on a micro screen, the user must automatically associate them with the internal processes of the micro rather than the subject or educational context in which they have been chosen by the author. Historians were processing and interrogating data long before computers appeared. Thus 'data processing' is not a term unique to the machine, rather, electronic data processing is a means that the historians have not had available to them in their endeavours hitherto. On the other hand, living language is always adjusting to accommodate the meanings words are given at the current time. Increasingly society will come to associate some words with a computer environment.

This does mean that terms which have different associated meanings according to their environment must be used with care on the screen. Either their use must be associated clearly with their function, or they should not be used at all. This can cause interesting problems. Indeed the current challenge is to ensure that the words that reflect logic in programming terms, such as IF and THEN, are used either only in such strictly defined terms on the screen, or that their looser meaning is made very clear to the user. It is a question of either matching the logic and the words used to express it, or clearly avoiding the conflict. It is arrogant to assume that words with a specific computerate meaning must now have dominance over earlier meanings, or interpretations, simply because the environment in which the words now appear happens to be a computer one.

CONSISTENCY

It is important, as an aid to clarity, to be as consistent as possible within a program and preferably across a batch of related units. Because there is no accepted general standard for 'driving through' programs, the user is currently faced with a multiplicity of methods. If pressing the return key is needed to confirm the last input, it should always be used. Pressing Return in the unit in order to move onto the next page is therefore giving it two functions. For this reason, CIC began recommending using pressing space to move on to the next page, and return only to confirm entry. With some entries however, especially where they are single stroke, the flow becomes very disrupted by having to press return each time – so the program is coded to confirm and respond on single key strokes. In menus, though, pressing return to confirm selection is usefully similar to pressing return to confirm input.

Clearly different methods can be justified according to each program and the personal preferences of the author. Examples are given in Chapter 15. But uniformity really aids the users' tasks significantly. What causes confusion is the lack of distinction between methods of driving programs generally, and methods that relate to the content specific aspect of a particular unit.

ERROR MESSAGES

Developing CAL demands a large amount of memory, not because the actual model or algorithm lying at the core of the code is large – indeed it often takes barely 1 or 2K of memory. What adds significantly to the size is the large amount of hand-holding that is required for educational software compared with other varieties. This investment in hand-holding is exemplified, typically, in the use of error messages.

Error messages have already been referred to in the context of outlining the possible range for an answer to a dialogue style of question. Indeed the very term 'error message' is unfortunate – it is after all a term taken from the systems side of the business to refer to a situation when the user is attempting to do something that is inappropriate for that particular system in its current configuration and implementation.

Within the style of CAL, I have been describing, error messages are in fact used to indicate that an inappropriate input has been used in the current circumstances. The obvious one is when the user inputs a number, when a character (letter) is expected, or vice versa. The first rule is never to use the normal system error message. 'Invalid input' does not help the user to know why that input was invalid and what should be tried next time. 'Invalid', itself, is an unfortunate and rather harsh term – after all, that input was only invalid in those particular circumstances. At least a direct translation is needed – so 'enter a number only' or 'numbers only accepted'. Partly through dictates of space, these messages still tend to be rather curt and often adopt the imperative style.

With a bit of care, a more personal direct style can be used, such as 'you need to enter a number here', or 'you can only chose between 1770–1970'. This reflects what the user has entered rather than how the system has been designed. Since the system has been designed to cope with entries of numbers only, there is, therefore, a condition in the code that when anything other than a number is entered, it is to be ignored and an error message printed. The systems error message, 'invalid input', reflects directly on the logic of the code; the more personal message 'you can only enter a number here' reflects directly on the user interaction. Unless the structure of the code is directly relevant to educational content and its aims, it should not intrude upon the user's operation of the software.

Each time error messages are extended, they take up that much more space in an already crowded piece of code. Compromise has to be reached on the number and type of error messages in the light of each piece of software. But the principle of thinking of how the user is going to respond to these harsh imperative statements is important. To a programmer designing a code, or someone familiar with software, these phrases are commonplace and often go barely noticed. To an insecure novice user of the machine, whether learner or teacher, it can confirm their belief that the machine is rather more in control than they are. When the machine refuses to accept an entry and the cursor blinks while it waits for the correct one with no error message, the sense of confusion and even anger in the user can be enormous.

Attention to detail with respect to the style of language overall in which the user is addressed, whether in general instruction or in simple error messages pays dividends in terms of the user friendliness of the environment generated by the software.

THE USER IN CONTROL

The term user friendliness is something I do not particularly like – it appears to give a somewhat patronizing gloss to the real nature of the program. Neither the user nor the software has to be overtly or falsely friendly; silly messages and patronizing statements can be a significant turn-off for some, as much as they are a turn-on for others. It is important that the interface between the user and the software on any system should be as clear as possible yet unobtrusive, be simple without unnecessary simplicity, and as unambiguous as possible. The interface should help and guide the user in as unobtrusive a way as possible through the curriculum content of the software.

The task of designing an appropriate screen and associated user interface is made harder by the fact that the end-users, the teachers and pupils, are composed of a combination of individuals who will have their own idiosyncracies and preferences of how to view a program. Tagg reminded the Project of this when in discussion during the User Interface workshop, he noted that some people work through images while others prefer words. Some work comfortably with a range of both words and pictures. Designs must allow for these preferences and not assume that everyone is most at home with icons and single keystroke entry. Burkhardt at the same time contrasted this by stating that it was not good enough for CIC to think of design for a general amorphous group, but we should try and be quite specific about the group and indeed the subset of the group, for which a unit is being designed. Does one therefore design for a specific audience with a known, or perceived, preference or style, or does one design with a general audience to be made up of a combination of perceived preferences or styles? This question will be resolved by each design team for each unit in the light of their own ideas until evidence of the acceptability of various designs and interfaces emerges.

10
ACCOMPANYING NOTES

The educational notes, sometimes referred to as courseware, that accompany the software and thus make up the total CAL unit, are just as important as the program itself. Yet paradoxically little is said about them. Presumably this is because the medium with which we are dealing here, that is the printed word on paper, is thoroughly known and familiar to all.

Despite this, getting the notes written is almost as hard as getting the last part of the program finished, debugged and checked. This is partly because the authors themselves often lack confidence in their ability to put their ideas onto paper. Here they are, teachers from the classroom or lecturers who have become CAL author/developers, they have overcome their initial concerns or scepticism and have taken a central active role in the development. The core of the idea around which the unit has been developed has been theirs. What causes the problem?

Most authors have not been authors before, in the sense in which they perceive it. They have certainly often written notes for use by their own pupils in their own classrooms. They are usually articulate. They place the published written word in a different category to that of their own notes. This means that their first attempts are often fraught with a stiffness and formality of language that they feel appropriate to a public document. In this case they mirror the same problem that English teachers work so hard to bridge – the sense by pupils that there are two forms of language, the colloquial in which they talk and write happily amongst themselves, and the more official language of adult or public life.

Thus I believe, it is the lack of confidence many teachers have in their own writing, that causes them problems when writing the notes. The co-ordinators' role, here, is to inspire them with confidence in their own abilities while acting also as an editor. The co-ordinator will polish up notes in an actively editorial way; but they must have the basic material from the author/developers.

There are certain key questions you can ask authors to consider, to act as a focal point to their task.
● What is the unit rationale; why has it been developed?

- What pre-requisite knowledge of the student has been assumed?
- What teaching strategy, or strategies, does it relate to?
- In what teaching context can it sit?
- How could it be adapted to suit a variety of circumstances?
- What tasks would you pose a student to place their work at the keyboard in a context.
- How do you drive through the program? Are there any essential keywords?

By answering these questions, the basic content of the notes emerge. These will then need to be ordered into an appropriate contents list.

FRONTPIECES

All written material should include information on who has developed the material and under what auspices, in the same way that any other printed material does. Prefaces, Acknowledgements and a Contents list all provide the reader with general information so that he or she can place the material within an appropriate context.

TEACHERS' NOTES

The browser wants to be able to see at a glance what the unit is about and particularly how it relates to their task as a teacher. Thus the notes must:
- Clearly state the topic area and age and rough ability level of pupils for whom it has been developed.
- Outline the style of unit, in other words the way the topic is handled. Thus, 'this unit provides a drill and practice exercise in French verbs', or 'this is a role-playing simulation whereby the pupils adopt the role of the Chancellor of the Exchequer whose aim is to balance the economy.'

THE EDUCATIONAL AIM

There has been much internal debate over the words, 'aims', 'objectives' and 'rationale'. In essence the reason why the unit has been developed must be clearly articulated.
- Which area of the curriculum does it cover in detail?
- Why has it been developed?
- What advantages might it have over other methods of teaching or learning the same topic?
- What pre-requisite knowledge is expected of the pupil, if any?
- What new approach to a topic does it provide that was not hitherto available?
- What style or styles of learning is it designed to encourage?
- What therefore is the overall educational context into which the user can locate this unit?

The content in this section will relate to general aims within a specific syllabus, as well as the more specific aims for the topic covered. Thus in the Economics material the section on Objectives for the unit 'Workers and Machines' covered the following under the headings – key ideas, skills, issues, values and attitudes.

'The following list of objectives will not be relevant to every circumstance, but it is hoped that many teachers will find it a useful guide to the educational possibilities of the unit.

Key Ideas
● In order to achieve maximum production with the minimum average costs, resources must be allocated effectively
● As more labour is used for a particular process, output increases at a progressively slower rate, and may eventually fall. This is an example of the Law of Diminishing Returns.
● New technology will raise output, but may change the pattern of demand for labour.
● Production processes can more easily adjust to change when labour is mobile between jobs.

Skills
● Decisions must be made about the use of labour in response to production and cost data.
● Graphical data on production levels, the use of labour costs per unit and output per worker must be interpreted.

Issues, Values and Attitudes
This unit may be used to stimulate thought and discussion and to explore feelings on such issues as:
● The costs and benefit to society of new technology.
● The causes and effects of industrial disruption.
● The advantages and disadvantages of division of labour by process.'

UNDERLYING MODEL

Any underlying model must be clearly and thoroughly exposed in the notes.
● Often models have had to be simplified from larger ones or else developed where none had existed in mathematical expression before. The model may be unknown to the teacher.
● Stating the model provides an important resource for the teacher. Not only will it explain why certain variables will behave in certain ways, and the limits which have been placed upon them, but also it can provide the basis for a clear discussion of the appropriateness of the model with the class. Some CAL units, RICE and MALTHUS, for instance, have been specifically designed for this purpose.
● There should be no mystique about the way the 'computer gets its results', nor should these results be taken as 'gospel'. The results produced are there because of a formula that has been designed for that purpose. There are assumptions and limits to every model.
● In education, as in society in general, it is important to recognise the distinctions between facts and relationships which are known and indisputable, and relationships that are theoretical or which represent certain views on the interplay of certain variables.

PROGRAM DESCRIPTION

● All notes should have sample runs which give a flavour of the output and the routes which can be used through the software. This sample run must give a clear idea to a teacher who may be browsing through the notes but not standing next to a micro.

● Examples of the screen displays must be included through the use of photographs or screen dumps.

● Examples of the user interface, through sample dialogues or menu routes must be given so the user has a clear idea of how to drive through the software.

● Where necessary, for instance for keywords, a simple reference chart should be provided that can comfortably be kept by the machine during use.

CLASSROOM USE

A good teaching resource should include a section on how it could be actually used in the classroom. This is no less true of a CAL unit. The content of this section can be drawn partly from the trials experience. This section should:

● Consider the appropriateness of classroom organisation, for instance the use of one micro with large monitors as an electronic blackboard, compared with the value of small group or individual work, for this particular unit.

● Outline various strategies of appropriateness of use within the syllabus, whether for the introduction to a topic, or reinforcement of existing knowledge.

● Address the various teacher and learning strategies that could be adopted, and why the CAL unit provides advantages over other approaches.

● With such an open-ended, interactive resource, teachers need more help to show them how they can use the unit within the class. Notes need to itemize a variety of ways in which it can be used to illustrate its flexibility, but more importantly so that a particular teacher with a particular style and strategy can see how this resource can dovetail into their own personal methodology.

● Suggestions for use should include a clear list of any prior knowledge that is assumed, and also the answers to any questions posed in the Students' Leaflets. Asking teachers to adopt and use this new resource places great demands upon them, both of an organis-ational as well as a methodological nature. Teachers will rarely have had enough, if any, in-service experience or training to provide them with strategies to cover these issues. Without help in defining strategies and an indication of the flexibility of this resource, the software will not be purchased, or even if it is acquired, will tend to stay on the stock cupboard shelf. Thus the section on Classroom Use is most important.

● Refer in detail to the aspects of curriculum outlined in the previous section and interrelate this to their teaching context.

REFERENCES

This may seem to be a somewhat academic approach, but wherever possible a biblio-graphy or references should be given in the notes.

● The model, and the assumptions behind it, must be clarified. The underlying facts, theories or general ideas behind every piece of educational software ought to be justified by reference to some of the literature as would any other educational resource. It all adds to the professional approach that should be adopted for CAL as well as anything else.

● References provide a wider basis of information for the teacher to follow should they so want. This can include information on other relevant teaching resources, such as film. Teachers are very busy and lead lives that do not make it necessarily easy for them to find out about appropriate references around topics. The more information that is collated together for them in one area, the better.

STUDENTS' MATERIAL

Writing material for students themselves to use while working on the CAL unit provides a variety of functions that reinforce the points made in the Teachers' Notes.
● They should be very deliberately written in a style and language that is appropriate for the age and ability level of student for whom the unit is designed.
● They should provide introductory material both to the topic and to the unit.
● A sample run ought to be included, with reference to how to drive through the software.
● The provision of questions to be answered before, during or after the use of the software, places the unit within a learning context for the student.
● Record sheets to be filled in with results that the students acquire during their work, are useful.
● They should wherever possible be attractively laid out with plenty of associated artwork.

The primary function of the students' material is to create a sequence of questions or tasks that act as prompts for the student (Lewis and Want, 1980a). Teachers may wish to alter or vary the sequence, and for this reason each part of the students material should have a unity of its own. The questions, interspersed with information or discussion have three characteristics:
1. easy questions that revise knowledge or refer students to previous work;
2. questions that refer the student directly to the program and designed to aid the work during the use of the software; and
3. questions that are more open-ended, to be answered once the student has been through the unit. These questions will be designed to blend the elements of the experience gained from the CAL unit with other learning experiences gained from the laboratory, field, or other environments.

A secondary function of this sample material is to provide an indication for the teacher as to how they may use the unit. They can use some, all, or none of these notes, as they choose. What has become apparent over time is that the teachers often look at the students material first, in order to give themselves an idea of what the unit is about. This could mean a variety of things:
– that the investment in writing in a clear and straightforward way for pupils has paid off;
– that the teachers need even more hand-holding than was thought; or
– that these notes are usually more attractively laid out.
Notes for students provide a way of repeating some of the same information in the Teachers' Notes but in a different style. They act as useful reinforcement, therefore, and contribute to the training aspect of these notes overall in the use of this new resource.

TECHNICAL NOTES

● Most software, and particularly that written for use on a variety of machines, needs technical notes accompanying the whole pack for information such as which machines, operating environment, style of printer, can be used.
● Such technical information, such as which BASIC needs to be used with an RML 380Z, or what printer configurations are possible, must be written in the simplest and clearest of language.
● This type of information should not be muddled with the user instructions for driving the software.
● This information should *not* be the first thing the teacher reads, yet it must be clearly available in separate leaflets or booklets.

PACK UNITY

It is very easy for a CAL unit to seem to be made up of many distinctly different parts – that is the disk, the technical running notes, the teachers notes and the students notes. Yet they should all form a combined whole; the obvious way to do this is through some unity of design. It recently became apparent to CIC that the first impression of their software was amazingly boring. The software once loaded came up with a title page, giving name of unit, software, authors and the copyright. However interesting or visually exciting the package was, this was not indicated in the first impression. So it was decided that the first frame should always be highly visual, preferably reproducing a graphical image that was going to be used elsewhere in the program. Where this was not feasible, a new graphic was drawn specially for the front page to represent the topic.

This provided the opportunity for producing a design that aided the unity of the pack by using the same graphics on the front of the notes. Thus there is seen to be a direct and close relationship between the notes and software.

THE ROLE OF THE EDITOR

Writing the notes for one unit is the task of the author/developer of the individual unit. For a project the size of CIC there needed to be some consistency across the material. Consistency across all units was thankfully impossible to achieve. After a few attempts it became clear that this was as undesirable as consistency of screen design.

Nevertheless it has been possible to produce a certain consistency across subjects, so that a suite of units in, for instance physics or economics, that represent the work of a particular phase have a similar 'feel' to them. This has been the task of the CAL co-ordinator who often becomes a single subject editor. The title 'editor' can be misconstrued. It actually demands some writing as well as the more usual correcting of text and developing consistency of style.

The reason for this is related to the phasing and timing of the development process. As has been indicated elsewhere, the involvement of the author/developers often diminishes after the unit has been trialled. The editor is often the one who picks up the notes, incorporating the information gained in trials and polishes them, accordingly, to the pre-requisite standard.

One of the biggest problems when drawing a unit to completion is that the two halves of the development team are often waiting for each other. The author/editor will claim that they cannot possibly finish the notes till they have a complete working program to work with. Yet the minute they get this program, they think of new little extras they want incorporated, for instance, changing the phraseology or adding a new section. 'Wouldn't it be nice if' tends to be said so often. It is not just the authors who are tempted. Programmers in these last stages have been known to decide that they wish to redesign the internal code, frame some sections more elegantly, develop a new printer-dump routine, and so on. This may take up to three months, by which time the editor is very frustrated, has lost interest, or worse, says 'well if you are really re-writing, you could now incorporate this aspect. . .'. Sometimes rather than work in a chicken and egg environment, with the CAL developer/director never knowing whether the notes and program will both be finished, the programmer and author/editor together embark upon a whole new 'closet' phase of development.

Despite all protestations from programmers and authors that they are dying to see the back of the unit, they are actually often reluctant to let go of a really good idea. This is a management task for the CAL developer/director, who is often a series editor, and who has to keep a relatively firm control of the final stages. Brutal though you may have to be, CAL units must be *finished*. It is the overall series editor, the CAL developer/director, who may not have been too closely involved in the detailed development, who now assumes responsibility for the final flow of the unit to completion. This final flow invariably happens not in the writing group location, where it has been developed, but within the central team.

This final part begins with the successfully wrenching of notes and program respectively from the author and editor and the programmer. Having done so, two sorts of checks are instigated before the text is completed as a manuscript and the program is mastered so that both are ready for the publisher. Firstly, the series editor goes through all the material with a fine toothcomb whilst sitting at the machine itself. Surprising inconsistencies can be spotted at this late stage. The model or variables may not have clearly explained; too many assumptions may have been made. This is inevitable. The author and even the group co-ordinator/editor may have become so familiar with the material that they have not been able to step back from it to analyse it afresh. The notes say 'teams' but how many can you have? What does this word mean, it is not explained in the notes?

At the same time, a programmer other than the one who has developed the software, runs through it, checking and testing it to its limits. Any faults or problems that occur are thrown wherever possible back to the original programer to solve. References made to the program documentation. Remember this checking has to happen on all machine versions of the software.

Once this editing, checking and cross-referencing has occurred, the final screen dumps can be safely taken to accompany the manuscript to the publisher. This checking has to be done whether the CAL development team published in-house, or whether it has a contract with an external publisher.

11
TRIALS

All the CIC materials have undergone some form of evaluation during the development process; the trials process is an integral part of the development scheme and contributes to the time involved in development.

WHY EVALUATE?

Even though the CIC model involves practising teachers in the whole development process, it is extremely important to test out the whole unit, both the software and accompanying written notes, in the classrooms for which they have been designed. This provides a useful pause in the development process; it is a time for those actively involved in the development to step back and reflect on the idea and how effectively it has been executed. This follows a pattern initiated by other Schools Council projects and reported in Tawney (1973).

More importantly it enables us to test the reality of the idea, both technical and educational, within the classroom. Do teachers who have had nothing to do with its development find it useful? Is it manageable within the constraints of lesson periods? Is it understandable to the user? Does it provide an appropriate learning environment? Is this CAL unit an effective learning aid for teachers to use? The answers to such questions when set against the writing group's own criteria for analysis enables the materials to be refined before publication.

Authors and developers who have been closely involved with a unit can become inevitably somewhat blinkered. After the initial brainstorming and the subsequent intense peer group review, the unit is adopted emotionally by the group during its development. This is often important as a motivator for continuing to work away at the development, but it can blunt the critical faculties. They may not themselves be able to take a 'cool and careful evaluation of their product' (Sparrow, 1973). So units must be trialled independently, and not just in those schools whose teachers are part of the writing team.

TYPE OF EVALUATION

This formative type of trialling provides feedback that influences the completion of the material, by contributing insights directly culled from the classroom. In order to do this, those who undertake the trial need to be aware of the purpose of the unit and the philosophy within the Project that relates to it. Thus the Project's philosophy of CAL must be made apparent to this user.

With one exception that will be described later, the Project has never had an independent evaluator associated with it and responsible for organising the trials. This has been partly a matter of funding, and partly of priorities. It has to be accepted, therefore, that trials conducted by the development team may not be as rigorous as an outside evaluator, although Sparrow (1973) also acknowledges that such an evaluator often acts as a 'critical friend' to the project. Nevertheless, trials have always been seen as an important staging post in development. Units have been dropped in the light of trials responses.

THE SIZE AND SCALE OF TRIALS

The aim of the trial is to provide definite responses to the material that will influence its further development. Thus the trial has to be of manageable proportions otherwise the responses cannot be adequately collated and used by the development team. This indicates a small qualitative exercise rather than a large quantitative one. The purpose of the trial is not to arrive at large scale generalities, but rather to elicit detailed informed opinions. Thus material is ideally trialled in anything between six and fifteen schools, which should contain a useful cross-section of types of school, while having as its principal aim the fact that for a particular subject the school is willing and able to provide classes in the age range required, and the appropriate hardware.

LENGTH OF TRIAL

This is a real problem area. For the trial to be of greatest relevance, the unit should be trialled at the time when the teacher is tackling that particular part of the curriculum. Thus a unit on 'Third World Farming' or on 'Chemical Bonding' needs to be available for trial at the time when the geography and chemistry teachers normally plan to teach these topics. This is the only true indication of how well the resource can be integrated into the normal curriculum.

There are flaws in this scheme. Firstly, not all teachers cover areas of the syllabus at the same time of year. Indeed part of the richness and variety to be found in schools in the UK is determined by each subject teacher's and each department's own curriculum plans which they execute in their own schools. It is obviously unrealistic for the Project to send a unit on 'Rice Farming' to trial in one school in one LEA in the Autumn, but to another in the Spring. These units are increasingly designed to be flexible resources with respect to the age range and curriculum area they can address. Thus one unit could be used by the third year in November, but by sixth formers in May. Although it is difficult to arrange, it is important that the trials are not squashed into an end of term 'game' activity simply because of a lack of time to integrate them more realistically into the relevant part of the year.

THE STYLE OF TRIALS

QUESTIONNAIRES

The first phase trials were based around two feedback forms: one for the teacher and another for the students both of which are reproduced below. *Note* that throughout there is reference to the terminal – these forms were used before the appearance of microcomputers.

Computers in the curriculum – Teachers' feedback form

Your opinions are a valuable aid to us in designing and modifying our packages. Please help us by completing and returning this form to:
I used the package during the .... Term 197........
Number of students? .... Average age of students?........
Timetable subject ....
Examination course... (CSE/O/A/none)

A   TEACHING TECHNIQUES
1. Do you usually teach the topic at this level?...
2. Please outline briefly the methods you use to teach this topic.
3. Do you consider this to be a difficult topic to teach? If 'YES', why?
4. How does this computer-based package compare with other ways of teaching the same topic?
5. How well did the package fit into your course? Was it flexible enough?

B   STUDENTS' NOTES
1. Did you follow the sequence of work given in the Students' Notes?
   If 'NO' please outline briefly the sequence of selection of work that you did follow.
2. Please comment on content, clarity and presentation of the Students' Notes, and mention any errors or inconsistencies.

C   TEACHERS' GUIDE
1. How useful was the Teachers' Guide as an aid to using the package?
2. Please comment on the content, clarity and presentation of the Teachers' Guide, and mention and errors or inconsistencies. Can you suggest any improvements?

D   COMPUTER PROGRAM
1. How long did each student or group of students spend at the computer terminal?
   ....minutes.
2. Are your students familiar with using the computer terminal? ....
3. Have your students used computer packages before? ....
4. How long was the total time that your class spent at the computer terminal?
   ....minutes.
5. Was the computer output clear and meaningful? ....
6. In what ways might the computer output be improved?

7. Please mention any errors or inconsistencies encountered whilst running the program, or enclose the output.
8. Would you have preferred to use this program by the batch method of analysis? (i.e. Your students send their data to a computer centre and receive the results of their enquiries 2 or 3 days later).

E   ADDITIONAL ACTIVITIES
1. How much discussion and further work was undertaken after using the computer program?
2. Are you likely to re-use the package?
3. Are you and your students enthusiastic about using other packages?
Space for further comments overleaf. Thank you for your help.

Computers in the curriculum – student feedback form

Please return completed form to your teacher. Use one of the five numbers as a response to the questions.
1–Strongly agreed, 2–Agreed, 3–Not sure, 4–Disagreed, 5–Strongly disagreed.
   1. I found the Students' Notes easy to understand.
   2. I spent a lot more than half an hour studying the Students' Notes before using the terminal.
   3. The amount of time I spent on the Students' Notes was wasted.
   4. The Students' Notes are not essential.
   5. I was enthusiastic about using the package.
   6. My teacher was enthusiastic about using the package.
   7. My teacher needed to explain some of the questions in the program.
   8. I'm interested in finding out how the computer program works.
   9. We spent a great deal of time in discussion after running the program.
10. The results were clearly set out.
11. I got many meaningless results.
12. I got bored while at the terminal.
13. I needed more time at the terminal.
14. I have gained a good understanding of this topic through using the package.
15. How long did you spend running the program as:
       (a) an individual ....
       (b) a small group..
       (c) a class demonstration ....
Please use the back of this form to add any other comments you would like to make.
Thank You.

The feedback gained from the Students' forms was disappointing. We found that we did not actually learn very much from the pupils' responses. When we looked in some detail at, for instance, a fairly universal response to, Question 5 or 10, we could not be too sure how influential the teacher has been in conditioning their responses. We found we were able to extract more generalities than anything else. This was possibly partly to do with the style of form with its five conditions of response. It was therefore decided from 1979 onwards to concentrate on *Teacher Evaluation*.

Accordingly a new form was produced in 1980 in preparation for the second phase of materials that were currently undergoing development.

EVALUATION CHECKLIST

A detailed letter outlining the purpose of the trials was sent; the central paragraph of which is quoted below:

> The Project believes that a small amount of in-depth feedback will prove to be of much greater value than a multiplicity of superficial reports. It is appreciated that the provision of good feedback does place rather an onerous burden on those involved, but the Project hopes that you will appreciate the importance of this and be able to devote the necessary time. In the case of some of the questions listed it would seem necessary to read right through the material with that single question in mind in order to be able to answer it adequately and then to go back through the material again in detail looking for some other aspect. For example, it is not clear to what extent one could answer the question about pre-requisite knowledge at the same time as considering the use of language in the student material. It is hoped that in cases where it is really necessary teachers providing feedback will be prepared to take the trouble to go through the material in this way.
>
> (Lewis, 1981)

After outlining the purpose of the trial, the teacher would reply indicating their willingness, and most importantly by now, which machine they had available for trials purposes. We had moved from supplying punched paper tapes in the 1970s to the nearest computer centre to a position whereby we could send out material in 1980 for the RML 380Z, the Commodore Pet 3000 and 4000 Series, and the Apple II. Within a few years, with the advent of the UK Government's Department of Trade and Industry (DTI) scheme for microcomputer purchase in schools, this was rationalized for trials purposes to the RML 380Z or BBC Model B.

The teacher then received with the software and notes an Outline of Proposed Unit (the OPU), and the main questionnaire shown below. This questionnaire still acts as the basis for the schools trials in the mid 1980s, but as will be seen later in this chapter, it has been customized in the light of further demands from the subject groups. Note that the checklist demands an open-ended response now, rather than constrain the teacher to use the five grades of 'strongly agreed, agreed, not sure, disagreed, strongly disagreed'.

Formative evaluation check list

Below is a check list of points helpful in assessing how well a CAL unit has been designed and written. Your reactions to these points are important to authors in editing a unit prior to publication.

The answers to questions such as those in the check list are in fact very important to us but what would also be extremely valuable would be suggestions for alternative ways of expressing a particular idea so that, for example, in question S3, the identification of current shortcomings and proposals for alternatives would be most valuable.
PLEASE MAKE COMMENTS ON THIS FORM AND ON A COPY OF THE UNIT

B:BACKGROUND DATA (where appropriate)
B1.   Unit used by students – number
                                – age
                                – exam/other course
B2.   Average time devoted to the unit by a student.
B3.   It would be helpful if we could identify you. If you have no objection please give
      your name.

S:STUDENT MATERIAL
S1.   Do the questions provide an adequate framework for students' activities not
      involving the program?
S2.   Do the questions provide an adequate framework for students' use of the program?
S3.   Is the pre-requisite knowledge of the questions adequately covered:
      – in the printed material itself
      – deducible from the program
      – otherwise?
S4.   Is the language used appropriate to the age/ability of target student?
S5.   Are the illustrations adequate?
S6.   Could the layout be improved?
S7.   Are there particular points of difficulty/confusion?

T:TEACHERS' MATERIAL – DOES THIS ADEQUATELY PROVIDE:
T1.   a statement of objectives?
T2.   a statement of the level and pre-requisite knowledge?
T3.   a statement of the rationale for the unit, its scope and limitations?
T4.   useful suggestions re use of material in class, classroom organisation etc.?
T5.   warnings of places likely to give student difficulty?
T6.   warnings about program limitations?
T7.   a statement of the computer model and assumptions made?
T8.   references to other sources etc.?
T9.   hints or comments on questions in the student material?
T10. suggestions for extensions or increased flexibility?

P:PROGRAM
P1.   What, if any, failure occured?
P2.   Are there unhelpful/misleading messages?
P3.   Does the program have a structure which makes it easy/convenient to use?
P4.   Are students puzzled by the display or uncertain what is expected of them?
P5.   Could the display of information be improved?
P6.   Is essential information lost from the display at any time?
P7.   Do changes in the display happen too quickly or too slowly?
P8.   Was the program used by students or as a class demonstration?

GENERAL
Your free ranging comments on the value of the unit would be valuable. Why would you
use it again (or not)? Also, it would be valuable to know of any data you may have on
students' performance linked to their use of the material. Anecdotal evidence e.g.
students' comments, your own observations, are always valuable.
PLEASE RETURN THIS FORM WITH AN ANNOTATED COPY OF THE UNIT –
THANK YOU.

CUSTOMIZING TRIALS

As work progressed on new materials in the 1980s it became apparent to some subject groups that they wanted feedback on particular areas of concern that related to either their subject in particular or to the style and unit they had deliberately developed. No group kept the OPU or fiche at the beginning of the form, that had been an incorporated part of the earlier questionnaires. By now it was recognised that the OPU may no longer relate directly to the trials unit. More importantly, the information about the style and purpose of the unit was usually properly embedded in the accompanying notes.

AN ENGLISH TRIAL

Some subject groups modified the proforma by adding a specific set of questions to the end. For instance an English group was particularly concerned that their material should generate discussion amongst the pupils while at the keyboard (Watson, 1985). Thus the following five questions were added in a further Section entitled 'English Considerations'.

D1.   Did the program generate discussions while it was running?
D2.   Are the general aims of the program consistent with good English teaching?
D3.   Did the program act as a stimulus for further work?
D4.   Does the program fit easily into a lesson format?
D5.   What are the main strengths and weaknesses of the program?

A HISTORY TRIAL

The history group decided to rewrite their proforma questions in 1983 and use it for all eight subsequent units. The one for 'Elizabethan Court' is reproduced below. Notice how they felt they needed more feedback on the relationship between the preparatory work, specific cases of the unit, as well as the more detailed questions relating to the user interface and screen design. To counterbalance the length of this, many of the questions have a simple YES/NO answer. In some ways this is a more directed type of form. The role and value of this approach has been described by the Project Co-ordinator (Blow, 1986a) as a fundamental part of the development process.

Trials questionnaire : Elizabethan Court

USE OF THE PROGRAM
   1.   Was the program used with: a whole class?
                                                            small groups?
                                                            a single pupil?
   2.   Number(s) in the class/group(s)
   3.   Age of pupils
   4.   Ability range of pupils: more able
                                                  average
                                                  less able
                                                  mixed ability

5. Total number of teaching sessions in which the program was used.
6. Average time per session given to the program.
7. Did you use: the whole program?
                    part(s) of the program?
    Please give details.
8. Was the program run through with each class/group: once?
                                              more than once?
9. For what purpose(s) did you use the program:
      as an introduction to a topic?   yes/no
      to teach a specific point?   yes/no
      for revision?   yes/no
      other?   yes/no
    Please give details.
10. How did you organise the pupils/class? Please give full details.
11. Was there any preparatory work prior to the class-group seeing the
    program?   yes/no
    If yes, please give details.
12. Was there any follow-up work after the program?   yes/no
    If yes, please give details.
13. Which part of the program did you find most helpful? Please give reasons.
14. Are the statements/instructions in the program clear and umabiguous?   yes/no
    If no, please give details.
15. Is the use of menus (i.e. contents lists from which you select) a convenient
    way of running the program?   yes/no
    If no, please give details.
16. Are menus easier to use than simple questions?   yes/no
    If no, please give reasons.
17. Is it useful to have menus overlaid, with previous menus still visible on the
    screen?   yes/no
    If yes, please give reasons.
18. Is the screen display always easy to read?   yes/no
    If no, please give details.
19. Does the program structure make it easy to use?   yes/no
    If no, please give reasons.
20. Does the screen display change: too quickly?
                                    too slowly?
                                    at the right speed?
    Please give details if necessary.

TEACHERS' GUIDE

1. Are the stated objectives relevant to your history course?   yes/no
2. Are the stated objectives appropriate to the ability level of your pupils?   yes/no
3. Are the stated objectives sufficiently detailed to be useful? If no to any of
    the above, please give details.   yes/no
4. Does the guide adequately provide a statement of the level of pre-requisite
    knowledge?   yes/no
    If no, please give details.
5. Does the guide adequately describe the scope and limitations of the program? yes/no
    If no, please give details.

6. Does the guide adequately provide useful suggestions re use of material in the class?   yes/no
    If no, please give details.
7. Does this guide adequately provide references to other sources?
    If no, please give details.   yes/no

STUDENT MATERIAL
1. Are the student leaflets: useful?
                             necessary?
                             unnecessary?
    Please give details.
2. Was the student material provided: sufficient?
                                       insufficient?
                                       excessive?
    Please give details.
3. Could the layout be improved   yes/no
    If yes, please give details.
4. Was the language in the student material   too difficult
                        the computer program   too simple
                                                                         appropriate

BUGS   Did the program fail to operate properly at any point? yes/no
Please give full details if yes.
Previous experience of CAL: Please describe your use of any software prior to using this unit.
ANY OTHER COMMENTS
Your free-ranging comments on the value of this program would be welcomed.

SCIENCE SOFTWARE AND TV

In order to evaluate software that was written to be used in conjunction with a BBC television schools series on science topics, a particular form was devised and used in 1984/5. Notice that this not only asks questions naturally on the use of the television as well as the software, but that it includes two other aspects. First, a sense of time is given — part to be filled up during the use of software, and part to be completed after using it. There is also again, for the first time since the mid-70s, a pupil sheet to be completed.

Evaluation report – science topics software and TV

COMPUTERS IN THE CURRICULUM/BBC PROJECT
[After the usual data on the school, name of the unit, come the following sections.]

A   TO FILL IN *BEFORE* USING THE MATERIAL
Details of class and context.
Size of class .... Age range ....
Mixed or single sex... Ability range.....................
(G or B)   streamed, mixed ....
Date of lesson .... Time of day ....
What computer and television facilities will be available for the lesson?
Describe how you intend using the material with the class, e.g. the class organisation,
whether part or all of the software and/or TV are to be used, in what order, etc.
Length of lesson..........Approx time any one pupil will use
                        (a) software
                        (b) TV
How easy was it to prepare to use the material with the class?

B   TO BE FILLED IN DURING (OR IMMEDIATELY AFTER) THE USE OF SOFT-WARE – PLEASE GIVE AS MUCH INFORMATION AS POSSIBLE
How easy is it to use the software and the television in the same lesson? Have any
unexpected problems arisen?
Is there anything you find particularly useful/unsatisfactory in either the software or the
television?
Are pupils more interested in either the software or the television or both/neither
equally?
Are any words/ideas from the television being used by pupils in their use of the software?
Do any occasions arise when it would be useful to refer back to either the software or
television?
Please check before the end of the lesson
Number of pupils in school who have
(a) used a computer today ....this week........
(b) watched television or a film today...this week........

C   TO BE FILLED IN *AFTER* USING THE SOFTWARE
1. Class organisation
Did the use of the material create any special problems for you in:
(a) class organisation
(b) in terms of the context in which it was used, topic, ability range?
2. Educational aims
With what ideas/areas of knowledge did
(a) the software
(b) the television

(c) both the software and television
help the pupils?
3. Further use
Would you use the material again in the same way. If not what would you do differently?
If you had not used this material how would you have taught the topic?

PUPILS QUESTIONNAIRE
What do you think of the software?
What do you think of the television programme?
What have you learnt from using the software?
Did you learn anything different from using the software that you did not find out from
the television programme?
Which do you think is the easiest way to learn:
1. Watching a film or television
2. Using a computer
3. 1 and 2 together
4. None of these
Do you use software in other lessons in school?
Do you watch television in other lessons in school?
Do you use a computer at home or at a friend's house.

   Also, as with the history questionnaire, the phraseology of the questions is less formal
and more directly addressed to the teacher.

A MATHEMATICAL TRIAL

A mathematics unit, TFORM, was trialled in 1985. The questions asked were similar to
these others, but this time the particular innovation was the inclusion of a trials diary,
described below. The authors have reported that this diary provided a most useful form
of feedback.

TFORM *trials diary*

The diary consists of blank spaces to be filled in every time the unit is used, under the following
headings:

Date:	Time:	Teacher:	Use (Who & How):	Comments.
Examples				
June 4	*30 min*	*AKP*	*Teacher review*	*Nil*
June 7	*1—20*	*TJ*	*5 groups of 3 mixed ability 10 year olds exploring translations using pupil leaflet*	*Needed help loading program. Pupils not motivated by this work*

(Alderson and Blakeley, 1986)

ANALYSING THE FEEDBACK

As each group has moved towards their own particular type of trials questionnaire, so have they handled the responses differently. Some groups, in particular the *Secondary Science group* in association with the Association of Science Education (ASE) Secondary Science Curriculum Review, decided not to use a detailed proforma at all, but to rely upon close contact with the trials teachers and to extract their responses at meetings, where they all discussed the unit frankly. This trials process has been described by McCormick (1986)

> Trials schools are usually chosen within the same area as the development group to promote as much discussion between trials teachers and the authors as possible. In this case six local schools were using several trials programs including DEFT. The programs were demonstrated by the authors at an introductory meeting and some weeks later a further discussion meeting highlighted issues that had arisen when the programs were used with pupils. This gave teachers an opportunity to discuss frankly their opinions and to provide the type of feedback that was not always readily committed to paper. Brief written comments however were also obtained but teachers were not expected to fill in detailed formative evaluation checklists. This type of feedback has proved more useful when it is the educational value and classroom use of the program in question rather than simply its robustness.
>
> The team group mode of development with regular discussions on programs ensures that a good deal of in-house assessment and evaluation has occurred before a program ever reaches a trials stage. Often development programs are used by members of the group with their pupils at various stages. The introduction of a group of teachers outside of this development process provides a new range of comments and criticisms. The program was in addition sent to several middle (8–13) and high (11–18) schools in Leeds and general comments received through the Leeds development team.
>
> (McCormick, 1986)

She goes on to itemize eight key issues that this trials procedure exposed with relation to the program DEFT, and how this affected subsequent modification.

The use of the *mathematics* questionnaire and proforma by fifteen schools in London and the West Midlands has been described by the authors Alderson and Blakeley (1986) with regard to TFORM.

> Schools were encouraged to use the program as freely as they wished and to provide feedback on a number of specific points. They were asked that the trials diary be filled in every time the program was used, indicating the time taken, who used it, what they did and any relevant comments. The trials questionnaire concentrated on difficulties encountered when using the program and the documentation and requested suggestions for improvements. It also asked for suggestions for new ways of using TFORM. Two of the schools were visited by members of the project and additional observations made.
>
> Eleven of the schools supplied the information requested. One or two of these returns were rather sketchy but the majority of schools had gone to great lengths to be as informative and helpful as possible and thanks must go to the teachers who gave up their time in this way.

The most informative feedback came from the trials diaries. The diary was a sheet of paper stapled to the flap of the folder in which the documents and disk were sent out. The 'Comments' section of this proved especially informative and gave feedback not covered in the questionnaire.

Completed diaries were returned by three secondary and six middle/junior schools.
– The shortest total usage by a school was 40 mins and the maximum 595 mins.
– 54 sessions totalling 2435 mins (over 40 hours) are recorded, with a mean time of 45 mins per session.
– The age range covered 8 to 14 with the majority in the 11 to 14 group.
– Eleven of the sessions were for 'teacher reviews' of the program (mean time 32 mins).
– Six sessions were used for class demonstration (two in Physics using reflections).
– The vast majority of sessions were with small groups of pupils, usually of two (15 sessions) of four (16). On only one session was the program used by an individual pupil and once the group size was three. Thirteen sessions did not have the group size recorded.

(Alderson and Blakeley, 1986)

They then itemized in detail the difficulties these trials teachers had in operating or understanding the program, and also the improvements that were suggested and the problems they encountered.

For the *history* group, the co-ordinator firstly analysed all the responses in detail and prepared a report. This was then discussed in some detail at the next group meeting. By the end of the meeting, suggestions had been made as to how to respond to the feedback and the suggested alterations either noted immediately, or the author was detailed to develop them further with the programmers.

The essential common element in these methods is a *feedback meeting* at which all the working group attend, and at which the questionnaire responses are given. The process of listening to and responding to feedback is another important aspect of the peer review principle upon which the writing group operates. The group co-ordinator and the teacher authors, the programmer and the overall CAL developer all have some quite detailed discussions. It is in the light of these discussions that modification decisions are taken.

RESPONDING TO THE FEEDBACK

It is important to remember, nevertheless, that receiving the feedback and responding to it, are two different aspects. Some feedback may indicate that the teacher has failed to understand some fundamental aspect of the program. Other comments may demand change which would run counter to the general philosophy of the program. How the group responds to the feedback therefore must be seen in the light of the experience of the writing group.

This is a difficult area. Some responses may suggest that the trials teachers were reluctant to accept a 'new' approach to teaching the topic, or even an emphasis on process skills rather than content. Does this mean that the writing group has moved too far away from the perception of the teachers to make the unit credible? Can we gamble that in a year or so, the climate of opinion will have changed sufficiently for the unit now to be seen in its true colours? Is this not to be expected when using teachers at the forward edge of their subject and curriculum concerns? This style of curriculum concern, especially when the units are being developed in association with new curriculum projects, and by people who are curriculum 'thinkers' can result in rather odd guessing games of the same variety that the programmers have to make about the hardware environment likely to be available in two or three years time. There are no guidelines to be offered here apart from the exercise of professional judgement, which is reflected again by McCormick (1986).

There can be little doubt, however, that every unit has been modified in the light of the trials feedback. To this is added the feedback from the group members who have themselves used the unit in their classrooms. The trial period itself provides for the development team a fruitful time of reflection. Trials are not used as a reinforcement of what we already think – a simple independent yes. They are integral to the actual development, and the post trials modification stage can take as long as the development stage.

AN INDEPENDENT FORMATIVE EVALUATION

A unique opportunity presented itself during the development of one batch of units. The other curriculum development project in the group had used an independent evaluator for its paper-based materials. Arrangements were made for this process to be applied to the first six units produced by the group which went out for trials in 1983.

This was useful in two main ways. Firstly, the CAL units were to be evaluated in the same way as the paper-based materials. This would provide useful data on the relationship between CAL units and other materials as perceived by the triallers. Secondly, it enabled us to have for the first time an independent reviewer organising the trials. The evaluator and his team worked closely with the co-ordinators from both projects.

The evaluation has been written up in a report by Smith (1983). Fourteen schools that were already pilots for the Curriculum Project were invited to trial CAL units. They attended a one day induction course in which the range of contexts in which they could use the materials was indicated. Data was collected as to the range of topic lessons to which the teachers anticipated they would use the materials with their related themes. A questionnaire similar to others used by CIC, was sent to all schools but with the addition of a section entitled 'Outcomes' which is reproduced below. There was also a Unit Report Form completed by the teachers each time the program was used, in which such information as sex and composition of the class, and length of the lesson is trapped.

OUTCOMES
1. Could you illustrate the particular *key ideas and area of knowledge* which you believe the work on the unit helped among your pupils (equally areas where you feel the unit failed to meet its objectives)?
2. Could you illustrate the *range of skills* (or particular skills) which you believe the unit helped develop among your pupils (equally areas where you feel the unit failed to meet its objectives)?
3. Could you record some of the attitudes displayed by the pupils *towards the ideas* represented in the unit?

4. Could you record some of the responses made by the pupils to the processes of *working the unit*, e.g. towards group work, discussion, research tasks, role play, etc.
5. Did the use of the unit create any problems *in terms of the context in which it was used*, e.g. in relation to the examination syllabus, ability of pupils, time and resources available, subject discipline within which it was used, teacher expertise?

OTHER CONTEXTS
1. Could you indicate other age ranges and/or subject areas *for which you have responsibility* in which you would be prepared to use the unit?
2. Are there other areas of the curriculum where you think your colleagues might use the unit? If yes, please indicate which.

The units trialled in this way were Estate Agent (ESTATE), Teddy Tales (TEDDYT), Break Even (EVEN), Workers and Machines (WORKER), Stockmarket Portfolio (STOCK), Stock Market Role Play (MARKET), Locate Game (LOCATE) Balance of Payments (DEFCIT) and A Business Game (SUCKER). The 'other contexts' sections relates to the attempt to develop units that are not seen to belong to just one subject boundary.

As well as the questionnaire and report forms, the evaluators made two visits a term to each of the schools and carried out interviews with teachers and pupils. Issues that had been raised in teacher's questionnaire returns were raised and discussed in detail, and additional general questions were asked. The evaluators also observed lessons in which the CAL units were used. Specific questions on the user interface and screen design were included.

The report contains the detailed breakdown of the data together with the evaluators qualitative analysis in the light of the teacher and pupil responses. This was all used in the subsequent feedback meeting of the group to decide how to respond to the evaluation report and put in hand the appropriate modifications. As a methodology it was clearly more rigorous than other forms of trials. It is not necessarily clear though as to how much more this rigour influenced the subsequent response and modifications compared with other trials.

In another vein however, it has been most helpful to have a document that outlines and details this evaulation. The Project has failed through pressures of time to write up enough of its feedback. It is true that this evaluation has been undertaken in order to influence the development. For an actual trials report to be produced would not necessarily influence the development of the particular units, but it certainly influences credibility in general, and is a way of transferring information within the team more effectively.

This is, however, another example of the problem of time. Nearly all the development team works under significant pressure; stopping to write-up stages, guidelines and progress reports, beyond those which are essential, means that other development work simply does not get done. There has always been a pragmatic emphasis on *the doing* in the Project (Lewis and Want, 1979, Lewis, 1983). Increasingly, however, the team is recognising that time spent in writing-up reports and guidelines is in the long term extremely valuable both within and beyond the Team.

POST-PUBLICATION EVALUATION

There is no doubt that a CAL development project would benefit from some further studies of CIC units once they have been published. This would provide a truly independent form of evaluation, and to a depth that would hopefully provide insights into methodological, organisational and pedagogic issues that using CAL raises. Increasingly CAL developers and authors want reference to material that can support or alter their pragmatic understanding of the 'state of the art'. The lack of such an evaluation is dire: it is needed badly. The CIC Project members keep a wary eye open for studies in this field; they are becoming involved increasingly in research in it themselves. The lack of reference to independent evaluation studies is not because the Project would not respond, but simply because of their absence. Future developments will be richer when they can be undertaken in an environment where the research and literature is richer.

12
ONE WRITING GROUP

Chapter 4 describes the model for the development of writing groups. This chapter explores the theoretical and actual establishment of one writing group and traces through the path it followed over a period of years. This provides an example of both the operation of a group in reality together with the associated resource and management issues that are raised.

NEGOTIATIONS STAGE

This work is undertaken by a CAL developer who is also a Project Director.
● Identifying a potential area of the curriculum as a focus.
● Making contact with curriculum development group in particular discipline.
● Making contact with Local Education Authority adviser in the appropriate subject and where possible the computing adviser.
● Identifying a key 'local co-ordinator' around whom the scheme hinges.
In essence it is the identification and interest of this individual which usually acts as a focus for the other contacts.
● Negotiating with a local institutional base, usually the home of the co-ordinator, to act as a potential centre for the work.
● Submitting funding proposals outlining the purpose of the scheme.

PLANNING

● Local advisor identifies key teachers in the area and negotiates their release for some time from school. Thil can vary from two days a term to attend meetings, to one day a week secondment for a term or even year.
● CAL developer negotiate part-time secondment for local co-ordinator with host institution, with plans for a two to three year period.
● CAL developer and co-ordinator arranges to aquire hardware for the group to use to be based in host institution. In the early 1980s this was essential as many polytechnics

and colleges of education simply did not have hardware that matched that of schools. Today (mid 1980s) the situation is quite different.

● Employs a programmer to work locally, or persuade one to move from the central team to the host writing group. Allocating program resources to each writing group has proved one of the hardest problems. Programmers tend to be in regular contact with the teachers and co-ordinator, who as the work progresses take a most important role. Yet it is also important for them to be in regular contact with the central team and to be aware of the latest techniques and software tools that are being developed so as to overcome problems. This has been resolved by identifying a 'link' person whose job it is in the central team to act as a bridge between them and that group.

● CAL developer and the co-ordinator negotiate balance of secretarial work between Chelsea and local base.

● They also negotiate a home base or room in which the programmer can work. If funding allows, the search can begin for the second programmer.

Following the successful completion of these two stages, the work should progress along the stages indicated in Chapter 5.

THE TIMETABLE FOR ONE GROUP

All plans go awry. At any one stage within a year a combination of activities are taking place that are very hard to juggle, as nearly all participants are in reality doing more than one job, both within or outside the Project and often fulfilling different roles accordingly. The co-ordinator is trying to maintain a pattern of work, and is attempting to cure problems from two sides, both that of the writing group's perception, and that of the central team. Thus the co-ordinator, while acting as a bridge between the writing group and central team will have conflicting demands loaded on him. The teachers will not understand why coding takes longer than they thought. There may have been no progress on one unit while a programmer has now produced modifications or new machine versions on another. The actual timetable for one group serves to expose these problems:

1980–81

● Director interested in planning further development in relation to curriculum projects to overcome the 'random pecking' problem.

● Author associated with one existing working party explains his involvement in a new curriculum development project. His area is to ensure that one of the Local Education Authorities is to become an active participant in the Project.

● Discuss possibility within directorate of setting up combined working party drawing on this second project.

● Approach the LEA adviser, the curriculum development project director, and the local polytechnic which is the home base of the author. Favourable responses as long as CIC organises and funds the scheme.

● Initial informal discussions suggest it may be favourably viewed.

● Write budget and planning proposal to potential funders.

● Teachers to form working groups in next academic year negotiated by LEA and heads of schools. Project negotiates to pay LEA a flat sum to cover their occasional

secondment on working party meetings for two years.
● Advisory group constitution discussed.
● Funding turned down. Director concerned as so much potential commitment already in place.
● Funding proposal placed before a new body.
● Secondment agreed for local group co-ordinator; 50 per cent of his time from local polytechnic. This is a major budgetary item.
● Funds agreed. Relief all round.
● Machine acquired on long term loan from manufacturers for location at host institution within the LEA.

1981–82

● Sept–Dec, Group meets six times for CAL awareness organised by the chief programmer in central team.
● *Note* none of teachers familiar with CAL – except the co-ordinator who is member of a previous CIC working party. One, however, is an experienced writer of text books in his subject. All are also part of the LEA's other curriculum development project initiative.
● Programmer in central team identified as 'link' and attends awareness meetings.
● There is a programmer based in another location working for CIC for a few months on a very short-term contract. Asked if he would consider move to location of home group. This programmer is a graduate who did part of the PGCE course and then decided to learn programming.
● Programmer salary arrangements negotiated between host institute and central team. Host institution able to pick up part of his duties under an *ad hoc* arrangement. Programmer, though based in the institution will work to a Chelsea College contract.
● Curriculum developer, as project curriculum and managerial link, attends some meetings. Advisory group meets for first time.
● Programmer begins at institution base in January.
● Initial ideas lead to specifications being drawn up by February. Primary authors or pairs of authors emerge.
● Second machine loan arranged from manufacturer; this one matches the type currently available in that LEA's schools.
● Early coding on two to three units looks promising.
● Need for another programmer highlighted.
● Central programmer not able to give as much coding time as needed due to other tasks.
● Advisory committee meets to review progress.
● Initial two units demonstrated at national one day conference in July.

1982–83

● Programmer living relatively nearby employed part-time to work with project. Already experienced at writing CAL and found through Project contacts.
● Authors begin to write up notes for trials of first batch of units. Eight are emerging as hopeful.

- Further discussion of new ideas begins due to success of initial work. Over twenty-three potential ideas emerge.
- Plans afoot to have notes and software ready for trials by independent evaluation.
- Negotiations between two Projects over purposes of evaluation. It is agreed to dovetail trials in with the evaluation of the paper-based materials from the other curriculum development project.
- Co-ordinators meet to draw up appropriate questionnaire and framework with evaluator.
- Authors produce next set of ideas.
- Authors want software for trials available on machines for their own schools; this is not the machine most commonly used in UK (at that stage) nor the one used mainly for the development.
- Time taken ensuring transfer OK for two machines.
- Time spent by programmers familiarizing themselves with transfer routines and issues from central team.
- Graphics debate with central team over map for one unit.
- Debate with specialists for a different subject over aims of another unit, which is cross-disciplinary.
- Units go to trials.
- Coding progresses on part second set of ideas. Group decides which are the better ideas; primary authors emerge.
- A third year negotiated with the host institution and LEA for continuation of the writing group.

1983–84

- Evaluation feedback meeting to decide which units to move forward to completion and publication. All of first six succeed.
- Modifications debated.
- Coding begins on modifications.
- Coding progresses on second set of six units.
- Development of third set of ideas; these are to cover 14–18 range, not just 14–16. Teachers moving away from the strict philosophy of the curriculum project. Agreed that new set is separate from first two.
- Debate over role of business studies software.
- Some authors get disillusioned and fail to attend meetings. Group noticeably smaller and made up of those who have become associated with one named unit.
- Negotiation with funders over publishers.
- Publishers nominated; style and format meetings between them and the co-ordinators of the two projects.
- Timetable agreed over texts.
- Significant time spent by co-ordinator in editing and producing texts for the modified first six units. This interferes with timetable for development of the third set of ideas.
- Second set of units sent for trials in schools. Not associated with the formal evaluation; more of a 'dabble' in organisation.
- The other curriculum project withdraws with completion of original six units to publication stage.

- Final manuscripts checked against trial program versions of first six units.
- Texts, screen dumps, and artwork sent to publisher.
- Artwork for screen front page discussed with publisher and developed for six units.
- Six units prepared for finalization at central team, transferred finally to all machines.
- Galleys checked.

1984–5

- Pages checked.
- Post-trials modification meeting to second set. Two units dropped.
- Co-ordinator finds increasingly that he has to act as author as well as editor on the modifications in design and notes of the second set.
- Group no longer meets formally, individual authors meet in institution to discuss modifications and further development of the third set. Two dropped as no progress possible with no time for authors. Programmers too stretched with current commitments.
- Third batch sent for trials.
- Group has dwindled to key authors who have seen one or more units through. These are now very experienced.
- Two authors approached by Project to be involved with separate cross-disciplinary unit in the light of their CAL experience.
- One unit in second batch subject of discussion to do with expanding it to include a general data file-handling routine.
- Co-ordinator's time taken increasingly on lecturing about CAL and its relation with the subject curriculum project, especially now there is some product to display in terms of finished units.
- First six units published. An enormous boost to morale.
- Trials feedback for third batch. Two dropped.
- Modifications agreed to remaining two of third batch. Editorial work on second set well behind schedule.
- Cut off point agreed for August 1985. Urgent planning meeting to agree flow of work for the remaining (batch 2 + 3 combined) six units.
- Co-ordinator's secondment (which has run for four years) will cease in August.
- The same two programmers still working and will continue into 1986 as long as funds permit.

1985–6

- Director reviews the position. Six units published, six in various stages of re-design and re-writing at the modification stage.
- The individual authors of these six units and the editor meet when possible to agree modifications. No more group meetings.
- Programmers modify when tasks available. In the meantime they have been sent other urgent tasks by the central team.
- Part-time programmer moves to new location. Complete as much of tasks as is feasible. Two units will, as a result, have to be versioned by the central team.
- Text for three units agreed, checked, front pages designed and manuscript sent to publisher.

● Programmer leaves at Easter to take up new post. Leaves programs near complete as possible to be taken up and finalized by central team.
● Text for remaining three arrive at end of year and processed.
● Galleys and pages will have to be checked and the programs finalized in late 1986 at Chelsea (King's College).

Over a five year period the group has been responsible for producing twelve units, each running on three different machines.

RESOURCE

The writing team has cost the following man-years of resource to run. Please note that these divide into two — direct costs and related, often hidden costs.

Direct and notional costs	*Man/years*
50% of co-ordinator × 4 years (Sept 81–Aug 85)	2.00
60% of programmer × 4.25 years (Jan 82–Apr 86)	2.80
40% of programmer × 3.75 years (Sept 82–June 86)	1.50
Fixed sum equivalent of 75% of 1 teacher × 1 year	0.75
(For secondment costs. Extra time and supply cover over and above this sum borne by LEA)	
10% of CAL developer × 5 years	0.50
10% of chief programmer × 4 years	0.40
Expenses for teachers to attend meetings over 3 years	0.20
Expenses for travel between central team and writing groups, over 5 years	0.40
Secretarial support 10% for 5 years	0.50
Other material support to institution	0.25
Nominal sum for independent valuation	0.10
TOTAL	9.40

This adds up to roughly 9.40 man years of endeavour, stretched over a five year period to produce twelve units.

Putting real figures to this depends on salary levels and local conditions. The project has to pay not just the salary levels, but National Insurance and Pension Contributions. Averaging salary levels of programmes and teachers at 1985 will result roughly in a total, including overheads, for one man/year of about £15,000. 9.40 man years would therefore cost in 1985 £141,000 for twleve units.

There are a variety of related costs that cannot be ignored. These figures depend upon a large team being in existence from which small percentages of expertise, and therefore time, can be drawn. This makes it economical for a large project, but the figures for one writing group are not transferable to an independent team.

On the other hand, for rough costing and budgeting purposes, CIC has worked for some time on an average cost rate per unit. In 1982 this was £10,000, in 1985 it was £15,000 and in 1987 it looks as if it will be £20,000. Twelve units in 1985 at these costings all amount to the not inconsiderable sum of £180,000.

Note that all the participants are on salary levels and do not receive extra payments for their contributions. The teachers who are seconded by their authorities do not receive a payment. There is no doubt that many of the authors and co-ordinators work extremely hard well into their 'own time' for no monetary return at all. This is not necessarily satisfactory and CIC has regularly explored using an honoraria, albeit fairly nominal, as a method of easing the situation.

Whichever way a CAL unit is costed, it is clearly an expensive operation when using this model.

SPECIFIC ISSUES

THE TEACHERS

The teachers felt a significant sense of involvement in the work in the first two years of development. As a group they met regularly in that time and the brainstorming was a co-ordinated group activity. The programmers would travel to individual authors in their schools to show draft versions during development. They were most interested in the trials stage and produced plenty of ideas for further units to develop.

By the third year their interest has begun to wane. There were no quickly produced draft programs for the second batch of ideas, because the programmers were by now also occupied with the modifications to the first batch. Meetings were held in which there was little progress to report on the new programs, because the finer detail of the first batch were being reviewed. Only the specific authors of each unit were really involved in this finer detail. By the end of year three, with the second set at trials and the third set under development, the group met together for the last time. There were various levels of frustration – some were concerned at the seemingly endless time it took between agreeing to the unit modifications needed post-trials, and a publication date. Some were no longer as interested in the developments as they had never been a primary author, or because their unit had been scrapped. However, a few badly wanted to continue and develop new ideas, particularly in areas outside the remit of the curriculum development group. These were frustrated because no resource could be given to those ideas until the existing ones has been completed. All, however, has given very positive reports to both the group co-ordinator and CAL developer about what they had gained through their involvement.

THE LEA

The LEA via both the subject adviser and the computing adviser were most supportive throughout. As development progressed it was clear that the in-service aspects of the work with respect to enhancing and broadening the skills of the team were becoming apparent. On the other hand, there was natural frustration that the end-product, to be sold by a publisher nominated by the funder, should not be freely available to the host authority who had after all contributed to the development. Special purchasing arrangements were made but this aspect leaves LEA's cautious of further involvement. This LEA is however one of the key LEA's that has emerged in the UK with respect to educational computing, with an active centre and an evaluation team. It really is not possible to assess the contribution this working group may have made to this.

THE PROGRAMMERS

The main programmer worked with the group from within the first three months. He also worked for the local host institution and so had a sense of identity with an academic (not the computing) department. A close and successful working relationship developed between him and the group co-ordinator, the second programmer and all the author teachers. He regularly travelled to Chelsea but was in some sense isolated from some of the main team developments. He seemed generally fairly satisfied with the work and arrangements.

The second programmer fitted into this team well. This group of three individuals formed the core of the writing group to whom the teacher/authors related. The programmers both needed regular contact with others in the team and found the project workshops in particular useful as a way of freshening up their ideas. Both programmers contributed towards central programming ideas and tools. There was a two way flow of information via the chief programmer who was the groups programmer link person with the central team.

THE CURRICULUM DEVELOPMENT PROJECT

A member of the other curriculum project was a bridge between the working party and that curriculum development project, its philosophy, aims and current ideas. This worked well, as most of the teacher authors were also Project members who were trying out these other curriculum materials in the classroom.

Problems did arise however with a sense of identity or ownership of the work. The restraints of funding meant that the initiating and funding Project, namely the CIC, was responsible for the arrangements for publication. It became apparent that the detailed implications of the co-operation between the two projects had not been discussed and agreed in sufficient detail at the planning stage, and the curriculum development project felt that there was an inbalance in the nature of the partnership and a lack of clarity over the nature of the co-operative work. This problem is difficult to resolve as long as one project takes on the responsibility for setting up a co-operative venture and it is run within the framework of the host project. A solution is to set up an entirely new project with the one specific aim for the joint development and with a totally separate structure. This would be more cumbersome and costly but may avoid conflict. The issues are: who is in overall responsibility, who, therefore, takes the final decisions, and where does ownership reside?

THE GROUP CO-ORDINATOR

The group co-ordinator was an experienced CAL developer having been involved with CIC in earlier writing groups. He was an integral part of the negotiations and planning stage, as it was around his expertise in CAL and an interest and involvement in the new curriculum development initiative, that the new working group was built. In this sense he fulfilled the dictum of the Nuffield Foundation who encouaged projects to find people and build around them. CIC has become increasingly aware of the value of building upon the expertise of individuals gained through involvement in the project. The next generation of work can then take a short-cut in the development cycle.

The group, both the teachers and programmers related to him well. He acted as group leader and drew together a tight team with a sense of purpose. This job became much harder in the second half of the four year span.

During the post trials modifications stage, with issues relating style of publication, copyright and decision-making, the co-ordinator found himself torn between two conflicting groups, that is the two curriculum development projects. He was a member of both, yet for the purposes of this writing group was a CIC member. This put him in the uneasy middle position. This very 'middle' position then served to emphasize the fact that key decisions were being taken, and influenced by factors beyond his control (but not influence) about *his* material and *his* writing group. This naturally chaffed him and the writing group, and for a period caused an uneasy working relationship with the CAL developer/director.

Any model that uses a combination of centres of work, however it is structured and however well intentioned its individuals, will be prey to problems of this sort. This has already been mentioned in Chapter 4. The CIC team works rather like an octopus with lots of legs with large nodes on the end. The nodes, the writing groups, are responsible for much innovative work and are at the core of the CAL development model. It is inevitable that the nodes should want to break away and become autonomous. The hidden benefits of the lifeline along the leg to the main core are less obvious than the restrictions to individuality and autonomy that the leg creates. These hidden benefits include taking the funding initiative, organising the negotiations, providing cross-fertilisation with other developers, other programmers, that is the breadth of expertise provided by a large team. There are disadvantages for a working group, which feels constrained when decisions have to be taken with respect to the project as a whole, rather than the one working group in particular. This is compounded when the flow of work at the central base intrudes upon the simpler programming or editing flow of work within the writing group.

THE CAL DEVELOPER/DIRECTOR

Having taken the initiative, seen a likely opening, identified individuals, and set up the group, the CAL developer finds the first few years provide an interesting tension. He is, by now, well experienced in CAL development and will have clear perceptions of what is possible and desirable. Yet, it is extremely important that these perceptions do not intrude unduly on the highly creative first part of the operation. The group co-ordinator will also have clear ideas and the teachers need the freedom to explore a variety of avenues. This exploration must be allowed to progress without any excessive direction, otherwise the ideas will not emerge. They will be the echo ideas from the experienced developer. This will narrow the work, so the professional CAL developer must step back and be wary of contributing to discussions. This can be hard, but the whole purpose of setting up writing groups is to let them have their heads. The CAL developer must simply promote a stimulus for ideas if that becomes necessary.

Where the group then does draw upon the experience of the CAL developer is once the initial ideas have been bounced around and draft programs developed. After twelve to eighteen months work, the group members have been closely involved with the idea – the unit is now their baby. The CAL developer however does not view it in this light and is able to comment on the program and its development drawing upon their previous experience. What seems obvious to the group can be incomprehensible to the CAL developer. Thus basic flaws, as well as more sophisticated consideration of the unit, can emerge. The role of the developer here is to probe — probe the software, probe the intentions of the developer, expose strengths and weaknesses, and therefore ensure the security of the idea.

It is easier to do this if the CAL developer is seen to be only a more distant part of the writing group. But criticism is always hard to take, and especially if it comes from an individual who only comes to some of the meetings. Finding a balance for constructive criticism is the key to a successful relationship between the CAL developer and his writing teams.

The CAL developer also has a managerial role and represents to the group the whole CIC philosophy and perspective, and how this is currently interpreted. He is their main link with the Chelsea team. While in the first half of the group's life, the group co-ordinator spends the bulk of the time with the teachers; whereas in the second half, the co-ordinator spends less time with them as the team disperses, and as more of the modifications and editing of the Notes devolves upon him. His working relationship with the CAL developer and others in the central team, then becomes more regular as all the final modifications and issues are resolved and the units progress towards publication. Much slog work is undertaken by both parties at this stage, each of whom probably feels a certain moral pressure to get these units finished – both of whom privately think of them as *my* units.

CENTRE/PERIPHERY

Ideally the 'node' of each working party should be in a position to disperse and return at the end of the defined period of work, or to build upon expertise thus gained and so begin new initiatives. The local group that wishes to continue will have a choice – to either remain part of the large team and so integrate into new proposals and directions that the team is planning and discussing. Conversely they can form a new independent group, seek funds and proceed with further work in the field independent of the main central team.

All three solutions provide useful routes. In the first the expertise in the group is fed back into the classroom and in-service institutions concerned. In the second, the main project is able to build upon the intuitive understanding the individuals have for the second round of CAL. In the third, the team had spawned a new smaller team to expand and take work in new directions.

The second route may not always be possible. New directions and shifts are often required, so the central team is often not in the position, even when it wants to, to continue with a group after its three to four year funding period. And as has been seen, the majority of a writing team will have lost their impetus after this period of time. However individuals who have emerged in the team are highly likely to act as a focus for planning new initiatives. New writing teams are more likely to relate to areas of general curriculum concern, e.g. modelling, rather than a subject-specific focus.

A NEW TYPE OF TEAM

CIC has now been working this model for long enough to want to explore shifts. One shift is currently in operation, because it satisfied a combination of requirements.

1. An interdisciplinary team was wanted.
2. A suite of related units were planned, the first of which had to be produced relatively quickly.
3. There was not enough time or funding to set up a new naïve writing team from scratch.

Accordingly a new team was set up. This consisted of named individuals in the specific subject areas involved – that is physics, geography, mathematics and economics. These individuals were made up of two groups – experienced CAL developers and co-ordinators, and a couple of lecturers who were involved in maths or computers and physics education but had not previously been CAL developers. A programmer was nominated to work with the team, and also the chief programmer. The team is based in the Centre at Chelsea (King's College), where it meets.

The natural concommitant of such a group is that it positively exudes experience and ideas. The need to use such a group is because the type of work envisaged includes looking beyond a straightforwrd CAL simulation into a carefully structured inter-disciplinary suite of interconnected programs. It may indeed become a large program with interrelated modules. To tackle such an idea satisfactorily demands an understanding of the participants well beyond that of first base. As a result, the nature of the production of the specification and draft program become very different. The participants are all aware through experience of the various CIC guidelines and stages of development; more detailed concrete planning can take place on paper before any coding has begun. The style of software environment can be envisaged at an early stage and any preparation with respect to familiarization of new software tools or languages can take place automatically. The latest ideas in screen design and user interface can be incorporated at the planning stage.

This seems an ideal configuration. Two things must be remembered. Firstly, it is only possible because there is now, within the team for the first time, a variety and depth of experience in CAL development that the previous years have brought about. Secondly, it is a model that may be excellent for developing leading-edge software, but how do we ensure it does not move too far from the practical and real issues of today's classrooms and curriculum? An examination of how this and other similar writing groups actually work in practice will influence the further development of this model, just as the operation over many years of the earlier style of group has enabled us to identify and expose weaknesses to be resolved.

13
SHALLOW HILL – ARCHEO

THE WRITING GROUP

The group that developed this unit was made up of ten History teachers drawn from two urban Local Education Authorities in the industrial north east of England, with the active assistance of the two History Advisers in those authorities. The team was directly associated with Schools History 13–16 Project, based at the institutional project home and co-ordinated by a member of that history project team. The co-ordinator had already been a member of an earlier CIC History working party that had looked at History decision-making games and worked on a large data analysis package [CHOICE, CAMPAIGN, and CENSUS ANALYSIS]. The History teachers first met in January 1981. Few had seen or had any experience of computers at all. After an initial term of familiarization with both microcomputers, some CAL, and the CIC ground rules by a CIC programmer resident in Leeds, they had begun work on two ideas. These two ideas, their development into specifications and draft programs took all their energies in the first year. It was not until 1982 that they began to discuss a second batch of ideas.

DIG

THE GERM OF AN IDEA

Ideas are generated usually through discussions, although often the particular point may have come from an individual who has been mulling over the idea for some time. The two units that this group had been working on for a year, VILLAGE and SUFFRAGETTES were both out on trial. At a meeting in the summer of 1982 they looked at some other CAL units under development from geography and languages groups. They were at this stage at a low point in their morale – they were already dissatisfied with VILLAGE and SUFFRAGETTES for a combination of reasons: excessive use of text, attempts to tutor the user, not enough user interaction. This dissatisfaction became more pronounced as they viewed the other software under development. They had also taken over a year to develop; progress seemed very slow. During the September meeting a brainstorming session took place which was very different from the one held the year before. The limitations of the micro now meant something to the authors in real terms; they all appreciated that developing CAL was not the same activity as writing other paper-based units – you had to avoid turning it into a teaching pack that reflected your current method of tackling the whole topic. Essentially, they had to accept the loss of control – the fact that they were using a resource that was not ideal for a planned direct teaching route. It was inappropriate when using the medium in the CIC style to try to determine the pace and exact path of the learner.

With this in mind, they began covering, in discussion, areas of their syllabus and in particular the areas that from their experience are difficult to teach. From my notes of the meeting, I have a record of a discussion that related to 'Picturing the Past'. This is a key part of the philosophy of the History 13–16 Project which aims to give pupils a real understanding and flavour of the nature of history, by concentrating on issues such as evidence, conflicting or counterfactual evidence, and on the historian's methodology.

- 'Pupils have great difficulty with chronology'.
- 'It's hard for them to realise that some evidence comes from different times'.
- 'The density/layering of evidence can be confusing'.
- 'This problem relates to interpreting evidence'.
- 'Can we devise a unit that actually works through time layers? But what period?'
- 'We could perhaps use an archaelogical dig as an example of this problem'.

This last idea was attractive, and discussions then centred on aspects of its potential. One teacher was charged with the task of drawing up a specification to outline the ideas that had been expressed by the whole group. Note that the work of the archaeologist, or the specific time periods, do not come into their syllabus; it was the aspect of historical work and thought that made them consider an archaeological dig as a starting point.

INITIAL SPECIFICATION

The teacher took away an OPU, outlined in Chapter 6, to act as a basis for the specification. This was then to be brought back to the whole group to work on. The OPU is intended to act more as a framework to cover the salient points, rather than a rigid document. The specification produced is given below. This was presented at the group in the following January. The program was initially called DIG.

Archaeological dig program – OPU

AIMS
1. To introduce the idea that the historian obtains information from sources other than documentary ones:
Viz. (a) the landscape,
     (b) artefacts,
     (c) marks/indentations in the earth.
2. To discuss some of the problems encountered in handling such evidence:
Viz. (a) information might be incomplete

(b) obtained randomly

(c) supported by written materials

(d) has to be interpreted in a chronological structure that is perceived working from the present backwards – or downwards.

3. The program therefore is not intended to be a reconstruction of a real archaeological dig.

4. And the program is not overly concerned with the techniques of the archaeologist's method – more with interpreting the evidence the archaeologist obtains.

Some aspects of an archaeological investigation that might be incorporated are:

● the last landscape may not nessarily correlate with the present;

● information will be in the form of artefacts or soil markings/post holes;

● information is incomplete:some materials do not last/some environments are hostile;

● interpretation of information will be dependent on the:

depth ⎫
position and ⎪
relationships to ⎬ of artefact/markings
other materials ⎪
on the site ⎭

● artefacts might get displaced by ploughing;

● concern with the life of the common man not a rich ruler;

● the historian is working from the present back to the past;

● an explanation of the site requires an ability to synthesize the data and provide a consistent interpretation.

The CAL Unit:

1. aim to reconstruct an Iron Age Site

2. time unit is a feature of the program: a multi-storey car park is scheduled for the site. Excavation must be completed within x number of days and hidden weighting might be attached to certain activities.

3. Structure:

(a) Screen display: grid to identify sites to dig – choice of square.

(b) Selection of type of excavation: test pit, trenches, grid or open.

(c) If teacher chooses: full site revealed.

The group spent some time discussing that outline. The level of thought about the educational aims was excellent. Both the group co-ordinator and the CAL developer wanted the teachers to feel confident of the idea, and then to have it expressed in an appropriate form for the actual unit. How the unit might progess through the selection of excavation was then sketched out throughout the day. The identified author then took it away to write up as a 'flowchart' to send down to the programmer who was now based at Chelsea. This is reproduced in Figure 13.1. The general schema was approved by the whole group, and in particular the fact that the pupils had to attempt to categorise each find as it emerged, but that they would have to reclassify them in the light of subsequent finds. But two further aspects were immediately needed by the programmer. First, a drawn outline of the site itself, and secondly more ideas in detail about what the 'Interpretation' grid would contain.

SHALLOW HILL

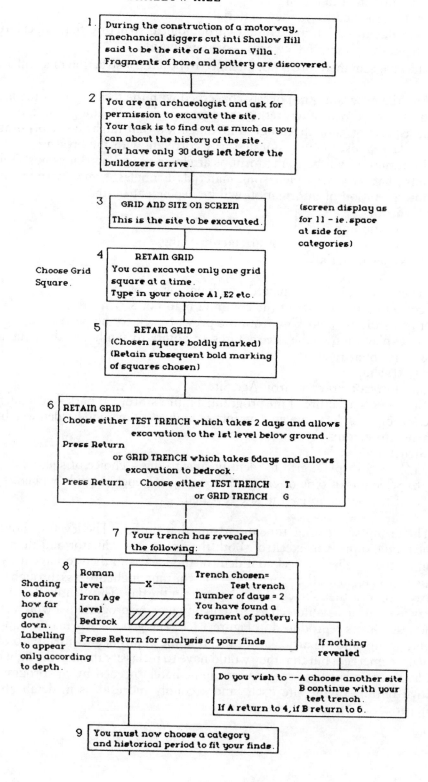

1. During the construction of a motorway, mechanical diggers cut inti Shallow Hill said to be the site of a Roman Villa. Fragments of bone and pottery are discovered.

2. You are an archaeologist and ask for permission to excavate the site. Your task is to find out as much as you can about the history of the site. You have only 30 days left before the bulldozers arrive.

3. GRID AND SITE ON SCREEN
   This is the site to be excavated.

   (screen display as for 11 – ie. space at side for categories)

4. Choose Grid Square.

   RETAIN GRID
   You can excavate only one grid square at a time.
   Type in your choice A1, E2 etc.

5. RETAIN GRID
   (Chosen square boldly marked)
   (Retain subsequent bold marking of squares chosen)

6. RETAIN GRID
   Choose either TEST TRENCH which takes 2 days and allows
       excavation to the 1st level below ground.
   Press Return
       or GRID TRENCH which takes 6days and allows
           excavation to bedrock.
   Press Return   Choose either TEST TRENCH   T
                       or GRID TRENCH   G

7. Your trench has revealed the following:

8. Shading to show how far gone down. Labelling to appear only according to depth.

Roman level	— X —
Iron Age level	
Bedrock	////

   Trench chosen=
       Test trench
   Number of days = 2
   You have found a fragment of pottery.

   Press Return for analysis of your finds

   If nothing revealed

   Do you wish to --A choose another site
                 B continue with your
                    test trench.
   If A return to 4, if B return to 6.

9. You must now choose a category and historical period to fit your finds.

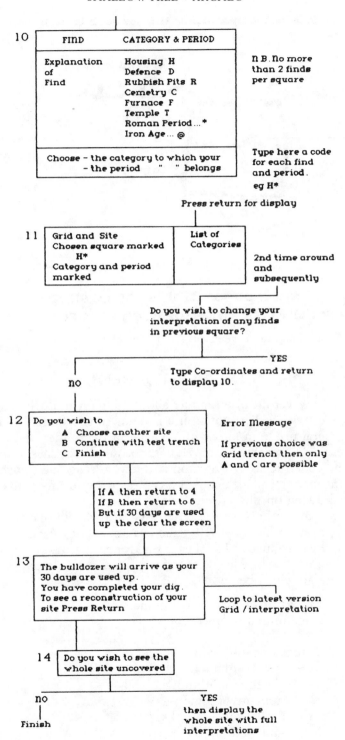

10
FIND	CATEGORY & PERIOD
Explanation of Find	Housing H Defence D Rubbish Pits R Cemetry C Furnace F Temple T Roman Period ... * Iron Age ... @

n B. no more
than 2 finds
per square

Choose – the category to which your
— the period   "   " belongs

Type here a code
for each find
and period.
eg H*

Press return for display

11
Grid and Site Chosen square marked H* Category and period marked	List of Categories

2nd time around
and
subsequently

Do you wish to change your
interpretation of any finds
in previous square?

—— YES

Type Co-ordinates and return
to display 10.

no

12
Do you wish to
A Choose another site
B Continue with test trench
C Finish

Error Message

If previous choice was
Grid trench then only
A and C are possible

If A then return to 4
If B then return to 6
But if 30 days are used
up the clear the screen

13
The bulldozer will arrive as your
30 days are used up.
You have completed your dig.
To see a reconstruction of your
site Press Return

Loop to latest version
Grid / interpretation

14
Do you wish to see the
whole site uncovered

no   YES

Finish

then display the
whole site with full
interpretations

FIGURE 13.1   Program flow – OPU for Shallow Hill

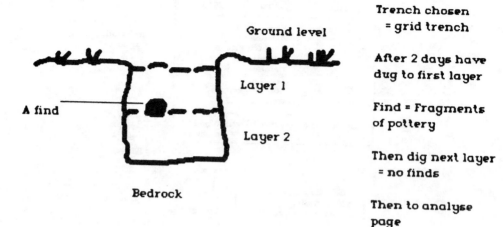

"......" days left (can we show this for each trench?)

There were 12 such pages in this comic strip, each representing the finds for each square.

FIGURE 13.2 Part of comic strip requirements for Shallow Hill

THE DEVELOPMENT

In the meantime, however the programmer allocated to the unit who had attended both the discussion meetings began work on an initial screen design of the trench, and discussed the general program idea with the chief programmer.

A month later the 'Comic Strip' arrived with the initial sketches of the site, shown in Figure 13.2. The coder began to work on two key screens, the trench screen and the production of the map. He made detailed sketches on a grid square in order to help the plotting of the drawing on the screen.

In the meantime, the authors were asked to give more details of exactly what wording they were going to need in Screen 10 – the evaluation of their find. The group and principal author then produced a list of each find for each grid square, and where it was to be located in the trench. This was accompanied by a description of each find. Examples of these are given below.

Cemetary	Collection of bones, some human,
Description 1	some animal and pieces of pottery.
Find D2	
Temple	Three stone walls which appear to
Description 1	form a section of buildings lying N–S
Find B2	across the square. Within the walls
	are the remains of some pillars.
Ramparts	Two parallel lines of marks at
Description 1	regular intervals following contours
Find D1	but broken with a gap of two metres in
	NE corner. Marks are 16 cm in diameter.
	Fragments of wood are embedded in some marks.

The programmer meanwhile had had to find enough symbols to represent the various finds, for instance a fragment of pottery, and the two age periods. Once the main framework for the description of the finds was worked out, the number of words for each description had to be drastically reduced to fit the available space.

The initial framework to the program was coded and displayed to the group in May. This was by now nine months after the initial idea was discussed. Firstly, some immediate problems had to be solved. A third 'age', i.e. Bronze Age was introduced, to make it both more realistic and to avoid an 'either/or' random choice between only two. Some trenches revealed three items, some only one. It was agreed that no trench would reveal more than two finds. This avoided some cross-level confusion. In order to do this, location of many of the objects in the site were shifted to either new locations or layers.

This all resulted in some major additions to the coding. At the same time the user interface was polished, for instance, the use of the Press Return message was rationalized. Then suddenly, just before trials, it was noticed that the trench levels were actually labelled Bronze Age, Iron Age and Roman, on the screen, thus giving the pupils the very information that they had to deduce from the finds! This ruined the whole purpose of the exercise. When this was noticed, incidentally at a meeting, the group was amazed that they had not noticed this before. These changes were incorporated and the notes were written. In March 1984, the unit was sent to trial.

TRAILS

It was sent for trials to fifteen schools across the country, and also used by the development team in their own schools – or rather as many as had access to the necessary equipment. All the initial coding and design has taken place on the RML 380Z. It was not available for trial on the BBC. The CAL developer did not want the coder to develop this second machine version until after the trails has taken place. We needed to feel confident that we were on the right lines this time, and to incorporate modifications onto one machine version, before transferring to a second.

The trials questionnaire was similar to the one used by this group for the triallir 'l
their material. As well as answering a straightforward question, such as 'Is t⌐
material sufficient, insufficient, or excessive', there would be room for th⌐
to expand their replies with a comment. Some of their trials prof⌐
questions about the history in the unit. Some extracts are given f⌐
that was collated by the co-ordinator in July 1984.

1. *Use of program* : Whole class – 4, Sm⌐
2. *Numbers in class/group*: Ranged ⌐
3. *Age of classes* 11   12

More able	
Average	2
Less able	
Mixed ability	

4. *No. of teaching sessions for which program used.* 1:3; 2:2; 3:3; 4:1; 7:1.

5. *Average time for each session.* 30–40 mins : 2; 45 : 1; 60 : 4; 70 : 2; 80 : 1.

6. *Use of whole program* – 10; Run program once – 9; More than once – 3.

7. *For what purpose did you use the program?*

Introduction to topic – 2; Teach specific point – 5; Revision – 4; Other – 4.

'Part of a course on variety of evidence and local historians.'

'To teach layers of evidence; incompleteness of evidence'.

'To test the program and see how pupils would respond to it with no prior introduction.'

'Program used to revise previous 2 terms work and revise ideas on evidence.'

'All pupils studying the work of an archaeologist and this is part of the course.'

'As an interesting add-on for archaeology students.'

'Class in studying aspects of Roman Britain and this formed the centre theme for Evidence of the Romans.'

'Used to show pupils what computer programs are being developed.'

'Introducing remedial pupils to computers.'

8. *Was there any preparatory work?*

Yes – 6 with descriptions; No – 5 with descriptions.

9. *Follow up work given?*

Yes – 7 with descriptions; No – 4 mainly because of lack of time given constraints of the syllabus.

10. *Are the instructions unambiguous*

Yes – 9; No – 4.

'Once into the program, no instruction to Press Return after entry'.

'If you press Return after 30 days you are unable to use the RESULT facility'.

'The up/down instruction for categorising finds is not clear until you get the hang of it.'

11. *Is screen always easy to read?*

Yes – 10; No – 1.

'Symbols difficult to understand on plan of site. Pupils suggested a table of finds and analysis would be easier to understand.'

12. *Was the screen display of the plan of site and the cross section easy to understand?*

Yes – 10; No – 1.

'Rather closer together – needed explanation.'

13. *Does the program structure make it easy to read?*

Yes – 11.

'Were particularly relieved to find you could return to a square where they dug only one layer to later dig further.'

14. *Does the screen display too quickly, slowly, at right speed?*

Too slowly – 1.

'More able found screen change too slow.'

15. *Are stated aims in Teachers' Guide relevant to your course?*

9; No – 1.

lessons on archaeology in 2nd year.'

relevant to ability level of your pupils?'

iled to be useful?

18. *Does the Guide adequately provide a statement of the level of the amount of prerequisite knowledge?*
Yes – 9; No – 1.
'The major problem as I see it is that the program falls between 2 stools. For 6th form use it is too simple and lacks information which they wanted. For those without archaeological training I think the stratigraphy and archaeological processes needs a lot of explaining.'
'Information on artefacts is not enough.'
19. *Does the Guide adequately provide suggestions as to class use?*
Yes – 8.
'Basically quite good but I would have liked to see suggestions of follow up work.'
20. *Are the Students' Leaflets* useful? – 5; necessary? – 7; unnecessary? – 1.
'The leaflets are useful but I feel pupils will gain most from this piece of software after they have studied the relevant periods, e.g. Stone Age in detail. The leaflets are no substitute for this.'
'Absolutely crucial. It was most rewarding to find the pupils coming to terms in using a reference source to enable them to come to scientifically based findings.'
'Leaflets useful but on the whole pupils relied on collective knowledge rather than the examples provides.'
'Plan was of vital importance since display on screen did not show grid lines.'
21. *Is the student material sufficient?* – 5; *insufficient?* – 4.
'Necessary to provide more usual information on finds.'
'I devised a table on which pupils could describe finds.'
'Wording of leaflets with reference to readability and reading levels needs attention.'
'Less able pupils found the leaflets too hard – print too small and vocabulary too hard.'
'More pictures of finds please.'
'Pictures of similar finds wanted.'
22. *Could layout be improved?*
No – 3; Yes – 6.
'As program is aimed at 13 + years, it would be helpful if graphics were used more, e.g. bulldozers on site.'
'Larger print needed on screen and more illustrations.'
'Yes – bring the graphics up to commercial publication levels.'
'Pupils did not like having to confirm that they had made their choice – Y/N, all the time.'
'Some pupils commented on the lack of sound.'
'More visual material on finds.'
23. *Any bugs?*
No – 6; Yes – 0.
'Program ran perfectly till the end but then it took us a while to work out how to re-run it.'
'Problem of getting RESULT put in.'
'Problem of getting RESULT put in especially once bulldozers have arrived.'
   All the teachers fitted in a section on their previous experience of CAL, and also gave several overall comments.

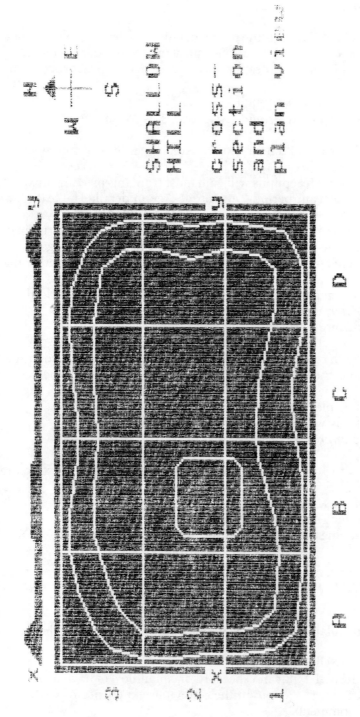

FIGURE 13.3   Front page of Archeo – no digging yet

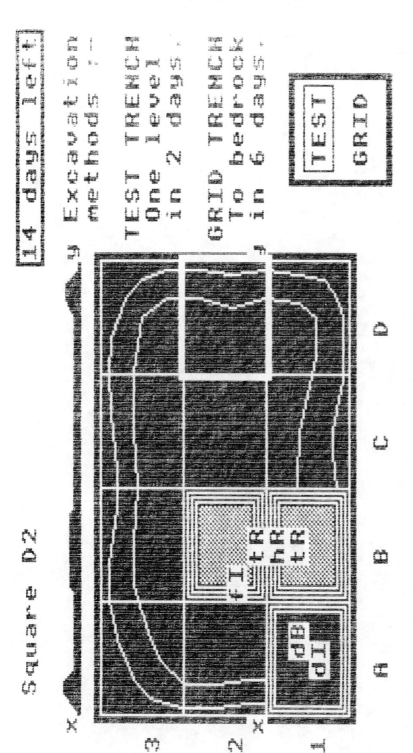

FIGURE 13.4   14 days left – choosing a test trench for square D2

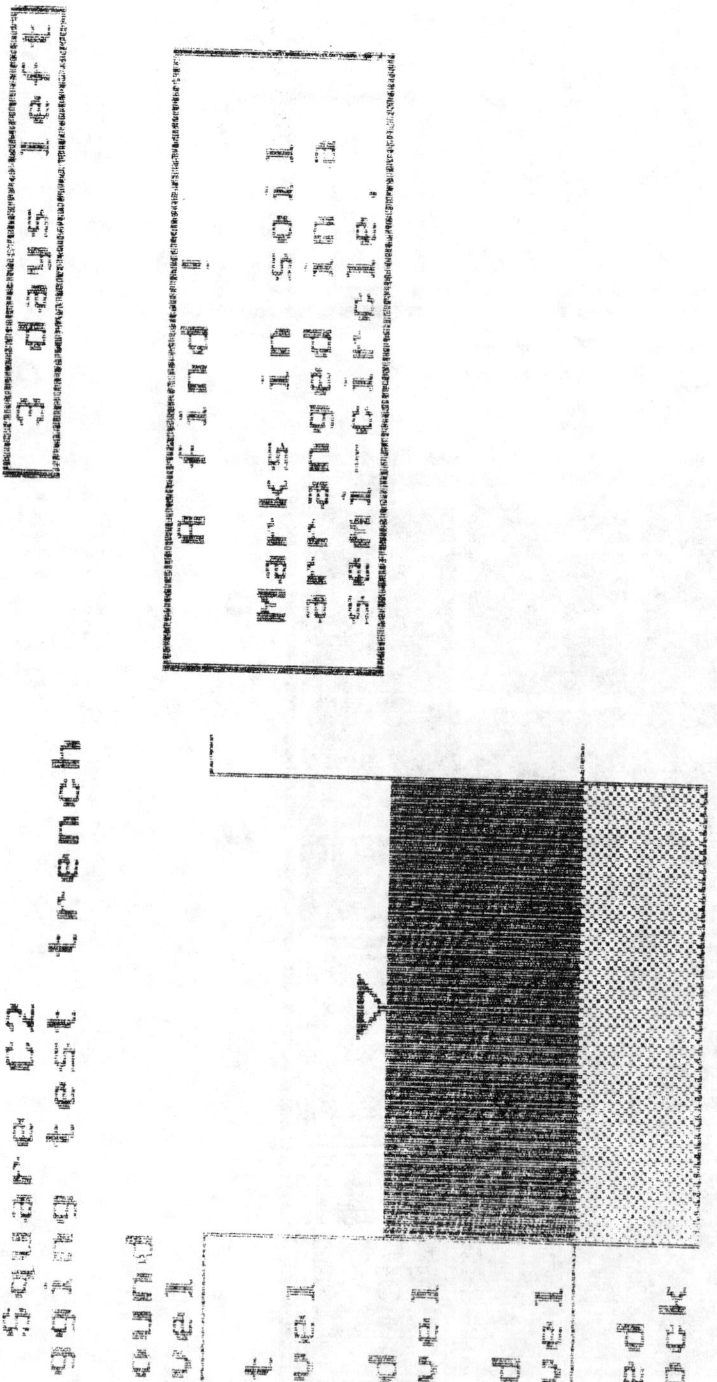

FIGURE 13.5 A find

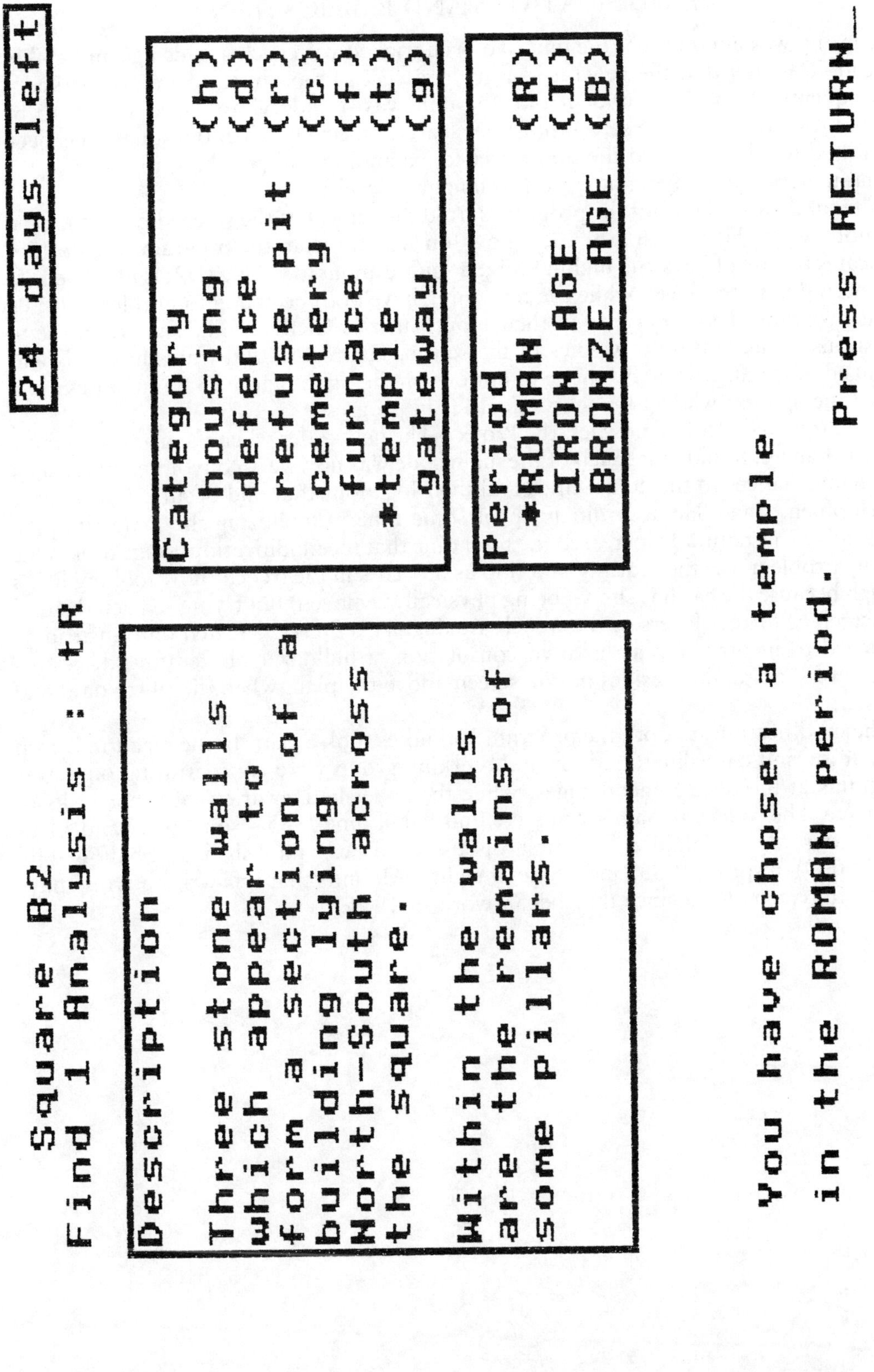

```
┌─────────────────┐
│ 24 days left    │
└─────────────────┘
```

Square B2
Find 1 Analysis : tR

```
┌──────────────────────────────┐
│ Category                     │
│ housing           (h)        │
│ defence           (d)        │
│ refuse pit        (r)        │
│ cemetery          (c)        │
│ furnace           (f)        │
│ *temple           (t)        │
│ gateway           (g)        │
└──────────────────────────────┘
```

```
┌──────────────────────────────┐
│ Period                       │
│ *ROMAN            (R)        │
│ IRON AGE          (I)        │
│ BRONZE AGE        (B)        │
└──────────────────────────────┘
```

```
┌──────────────────────────────┐
│ Description                  │
│                              │
│ Three stone walls            │
│ which appear to              │
│ form a section of a          │
│ building lying               │
│ North-South across           │
│ the square.                  │
│                              │
│ Within the walls             │
│ are the remains of           │
│ some pillars.                │
└──────────────────────────────┘
```

You have chosen a temple
in the ROMAN period.   Press RETURN_

FIGURE 13.6   Analysing Find 1 in square B2, with 24 days left

MODIFICATIONS AND PUBLICATION

The group was amazed that the unit had been trialled with such a wide age and ability spread. They felt that the general idea with respect to their historical aims worked – consequently, they felt confident that the unit was sound. More work seemed to be needed in two areas – the screen must be clearer, especially when the square has been identified for digging; and the notes needed expanding and polishing to improve the visual material and paying attention to language levels.

The fundamental idea of the program stayed the same, but the screen layout changed in subtle ways. Figures 13.3 to 13.6 show four frames from the program. Figure 13.4 indicates the use of lines and highlighting; a square about to be dug (D2) is indicated, Al has been dug to test level, while the remaining have both been dug to grid level. In the trials program, the users typed in their input, such as GRID or TEST, in response to questions in the bottom four lines of the screen. Figure 13.4 illustrates how this was changed to spacing through a menu of options on the right. Figure 13.5 illustrates a test trench being dug; while 13.6 shows analysis in progress.

The original coder had now left the Project. The new coder when incorporating these screen changes, found that much of the main code was now very convoluted because of the many changes to the actual finds and their locations that had occurred during the development stage. He accordingly spent some time rationalizing the main site plan internally. This naturally increased the total time that the modifications stage took. One thorny problem was the plotting of a find as it occurs in the trench (now looking like a trough because the earth is shown being physically removed) but trying to keep the find on screen as further layers of the trench are dug. This finally defeated him. Instead he managed to incorporate, as his own consolation, a bulldozer obliterating the cross-section of the site, that resides on the screen above the plan, when the thirty days had elapsed.

The modifications to both the program and notes took a year. In the meantime both the author and co-ordinator/editor and working group were concentrating on newer programs at the development stages, while the coder had a variety of other tasks to complete. The code and manuscript were finished in June 1985 – some three and a half years after the initial idea was first discussed. It was published as Shallow Hill (ARCHEO) in spring 1986, and is one of eight CAL units that this writing group have successfully completed since they began work in 1981.

14
LANDSCAPE ANALYSIS – LAND

This unit has a somewhat different path through development compared with that of ARCHEO described in Chapter 13.

THE WRITING GROUP

The unit was developed by a Geography working party based in a large mixed urban and rural Local Education Authority. They were not associated with any particular curriculum development project, although most of the teachers taught or had experience of the Geography for the Young School Leaver Project (GYSL). When they first met in the summer 1981, they were shown some of the existing Geography CAL materials and they agreed that they wanted to concentrate on the 13–16 age group to provide them with some sort of focus. The group was co-ordinated by a CAL developer who had been involved for many years in two earlier CIC writing groups. Again, programming support was provided locally by the CIC project, although as emerged with the history group, the coding was eventually taken over at Chelsea. One feature that is relevant to the work of the group is that the Co-ordinator himself does do some programming. He is an author/developer of many years experience and finds it a useful way to try out ideas and explore models for use in the CAL environment.

CONTOURS

THE IDEA AND SPECIFICATION

After the initial meeting of the group for a CAL awareness briefing, there followed a brainstorming weekend in the winter of 1981 for ideas for CAL units. Aware of the existing Geography CAL, they were keen to tackle new areas, and in particular to push the advantage of using the computer to do operations not hitherto possible. From a group consisting of twelve teachers, the group co-ordinator, the humanities CAL developer and two programmers, eight ideas emerged, one of which was for Contour Analysis. The following OPU was produced – note the emphasis placed on educational aims.

CIC – *outline of proposed unit: contour*

A   THE TOPIC
1. *Curriculum area and year*   Geography 11+
2. *Specific topic*   Mapping skills. Contour appreciation.
3. *How is the topic currently taught?*   Text book and local maps of various scales. Contour patterns are difficult to follow in built up areas and the construction of cross sections is not a very accurate method to show important physical details of site etc.
4. *List two or three questions which students should be able to answer after studying the topic.*   How important are physical features in determining possible sites for settlements? Why is the land above 1,500 feet or 500 meters not cultivated?
5. *What aspect of the topic will the computer cover?* The interpolation of contour lines from given spot heights and also visual cross-sections across selected contour profiles.

B   COMPARISON WITH TRADITIONAL TEACHING
6. *What are the difficulties faced by students in their study of the topic?*
Appreciation of the height/depth dimension on the map has always been a difficult idea to grasp even at advanced level map analysis. The slope angle as represented by contour interval/spacing and/or rock drawing is not readily appreciated. Drawing endless cross-sections is a time consuming exercise of dubious validity and tends to be inaccurate with less able pupils.
7. *How is it envisaged that the new unit will help with these difficulties or improve students understanding?*   To appreciate the lie of the land is not easily accomplished, even when using corresponding map and aerial photograph or even a stereo pair of photos. The purpose of the package is to help pupils appreciate the multi levels of contouring whether studying river profiles, valley cross-sections or flood plain morphology for settlement locations.

C   PROGRAM DESCRIPTION
8. *Outline sample dialogue showing parameters which the student will control and the form of the output.*   (All output forms in High Resolution Graphics). Which contour value do you want to plot 15, 30, 46m? Do you want to plot more than one value? The diagram shows the 30m contour pattern, where do you think the steepest slope is? a,b,c or d? The contour lines show a river valley. Each of the section lines A to D cross the valley from side to side. Which one would show that the valley has a typical U shape? Can you identify any other of the features shown in the contour pattern? a terrace? a bench? a. . .
9. *What model is to be used? What parameters are unseen by the student?*
The limits to this area depend on the complexity of the map extract and the level at which the exercise idea is to be pitched. Ideally it should have three versions to cope with the wide age/ability range. It is also possible to link the unit in with an aerial photograph to

aid aquisition of interpretation, using a transparent grid to help select features using co-ordinates to plot the Q/A dialogue.

10. *What limits to student input should be (a) mandatory and (b) educationally recommended?*

The limits will be set by the size of the program so that the basic interpretation can be followed and then subsequent work should come from the map extract itself. Hopefully if should be possible for pupils to request a line of section between given co-ordinates so that comparisons of a sketch section done by them can be compared with the screen version.

DEVELOPMENT

There then followed over a few months intense discussions about how to begin to fulfil the aims. These discussions were principally between a programmer and the co-ordinator. The author was asked to provide a map, with contour lines on it, representing a known geographical feature. This was then translated into a regular grid of spot height data covering a whole square. The initial code allowed this data to be read and a three dimensional view was drawn, by the simple method of drawing cross sections in sequence to build up the view. The draft code allowed you to 'look at' the map from four quarters – N, S, E, or W. Twenty cross sections would be drawn in sequence to build up a view of the landscape. To give a sense of distance and depth, the cross-sections further from the viewpoint would be drawn in fewer pixels, resulting in a fainter impression on the screen. This was all done initially to then identify the cross-sections for the slope analysis. New ideas however immediately emerged, stimulated by watching the build up of these sections across the screen. The key educational problem behind the Outline (OPU) and hinted at in Part 7 is the fact that it is very hard to teach pupils that a map with contour lines is a representation of a *real* three dimensional landscape. The classic method used in the classroom is the drawing of a cross-section to give a sense of shape to one 'slice' across the map. Here we had code that by putting all these cross-sections together, brought out the real shape of the whole.

Rather than pursue the style of exercises based on recognizing the contour features and degree of slope described in the OPU, it was agreed to explore this fundamental relationship between contour and landscape further. The map needed to be on the screen at the same time as the view in order to show the direct relationship between the two representations. Pupils needed to view the block not just from 4 compass points, but from a different variety of compass angles and also heights above sea level, as these both influence what the landscape acutally 'looks like' to the human eye. Somehow the operation of reading the data and drawing up the graphics had to be drastically speeded up otherwise the pupils would have fallen asleep at the keyboard.

This period coincided with the central team struggling to accommodate picture drawing on micros within the overall strategy of using the MINLIB structure for coding. A new programmer was available to the group, based in the LEA, who spent a significant part of a year struggling and exploring means of drawing these contours fast on both the RML and BBC machines. There were other related issues of file handling, speed, and a lack of memory. Essentially, the micro stored a data map of spot heights across the map. These were translated into cross-sections according to the angle, height and view chosen.

In the meantime a second main author emerged from the group, who took the unit over from the original author who now had a new post in a school and less time to devote

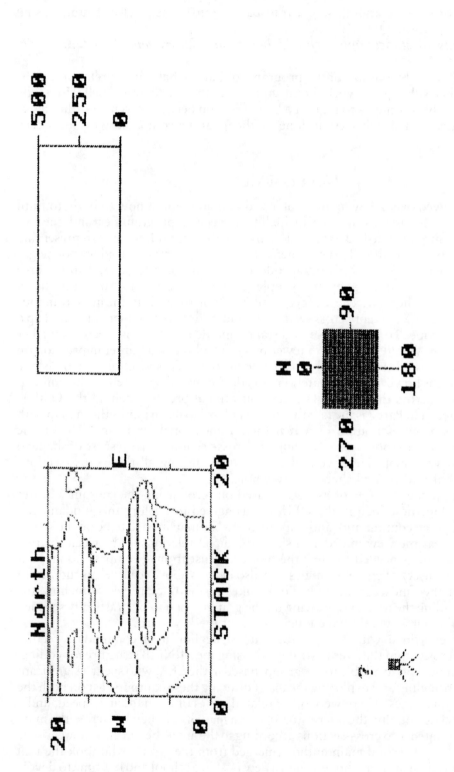

FIGURE 14.1 CONTOUR – Choosing a location

to the development. This author produced a series of eight different contour grid maps, as eight different examples of landscape features. The emphasis on a variety of landscape examples indicated how the aim had shifted from a contour exercise to a facility to explore a variety of landscapes from different perspectives. The program emerged which offered eight landscapes, each of which could be viewed from a range of angles of elevation and compass points. A cross-section could be drawn along any Northing or Easting and viewed simultaneously. Figures 14.1, 14.2 and 14.3 illustrate the sequence of choosing the angle and height and the resulting view.

TRIALS AND MODIFICATION

The unit was sent to trial in schools in the LEA but not involved with the development. While development had been progressing with this unit with the programmer over an eighteen month period, seven other units were also being explored, two of which were later abandoned. Some team members had left, but three key authors had emerged. Group meetings were taken up principally with reviewing and discussing the various development stages of the unit; the detailed work took place between the individual and the programmer.

There was a positive trials response. Discussions for modification centred on two areas.

1. The dictates of screen design meant that there was no room to put any contour height markings on the map itself. The trials teachers felt very wary about the pupils interpreting shapes without a related sense of scale. This point was accepted, although part of the purpose was to give the pupils that sense of shape that they themselves often do not have of landscapes. Many urban children have little experience or 'feel' for the shape of the land in an environment that is obscured by buildings. They certainly find it difficult to perceive the way the landscape appears to change according to the position from which it can be viewed. To satisfy these concerns, a spot height facility was added. Once the view was drawn, the user could opt for a spot on the map and located it by means of a marker. A marker could be moved simultaneously on the 3D view itself. This, in fact, helped the question of perception of location between map and view but not of the actual height. The authors still felt very uneasy about identifying an exact height due to the way the data was called up.

2. Could we add a facility for teachers to put in their own data maps? Exploring this second modification took nearly a year, while the main program remained static. The main achievement was to expose inaccuracies in the way the code was translating the data into the view. A whole new set of data and code was input. The authors took the opportunity to change two of the maps to represent data for different landscapes. Eventually the small group involved with the unit, that is, the two CAL developers, one author and the programmer, had a meeting to resolve an issue.

Here the management skills of the CAL developer were called into play to persuade the group to drop the data entry idea and to concentrate on the main program and begin to polish the screen design and user interface. The programmer and author were reluctant to drop the data entry – they had had to develop the appropriate code to check the existing data and edit it. Nevertheless, a piece of in-house code is not the same as a properly developed piece of user-friendly file-handling software. To do the job properly, more time and therefore funding would have been needed. The decision coincided with a cutback in general funding that had direct impact on the total number of units that CIC

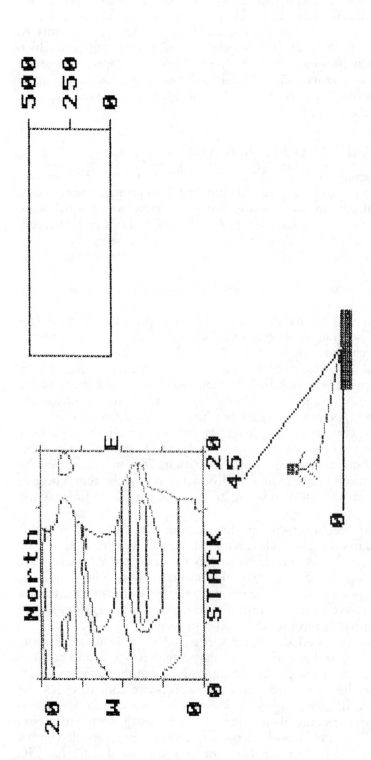

Type ANY NUMBER from 0 to 90 to show at
what angle you will look down? 15
Is that OK (Y/N)?

FIGURE 14.2 CONTOUR – Choosing a height

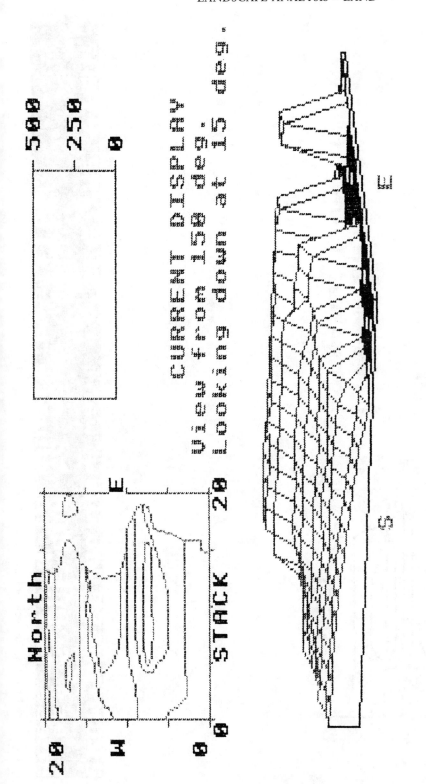

FIGURE 14.3   View in the draft program

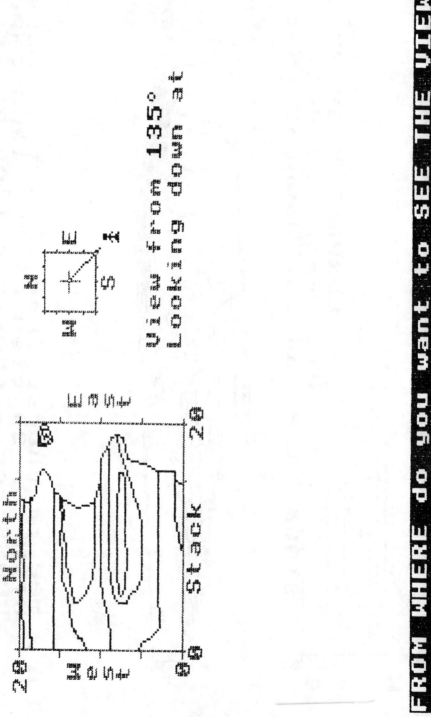

FIGURE 14.4   Choosing the angle of location – LAND

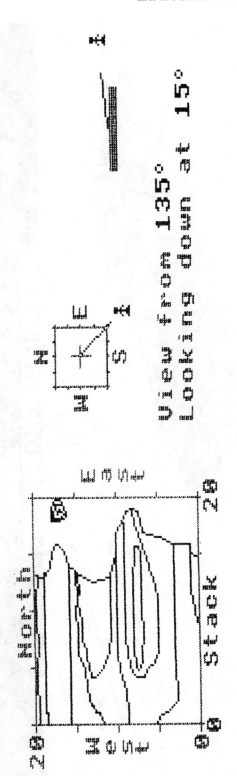

FIGURE 14.5   Choosing the angle of heights – LAND

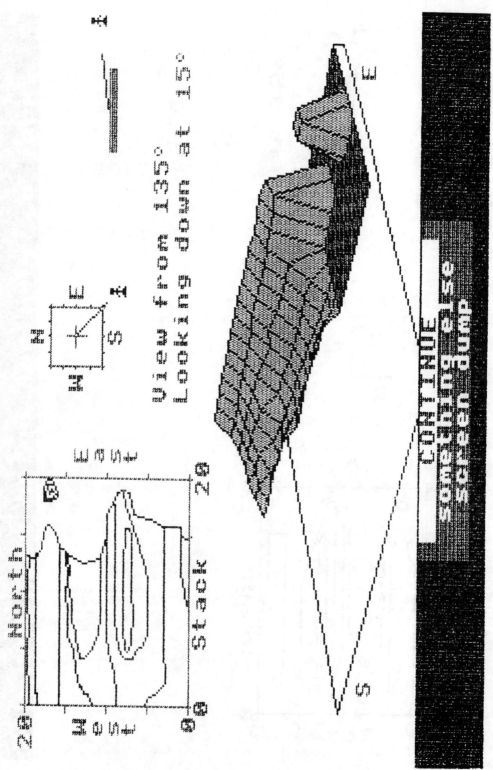

FIGURE 14.6   A view paused – LAND

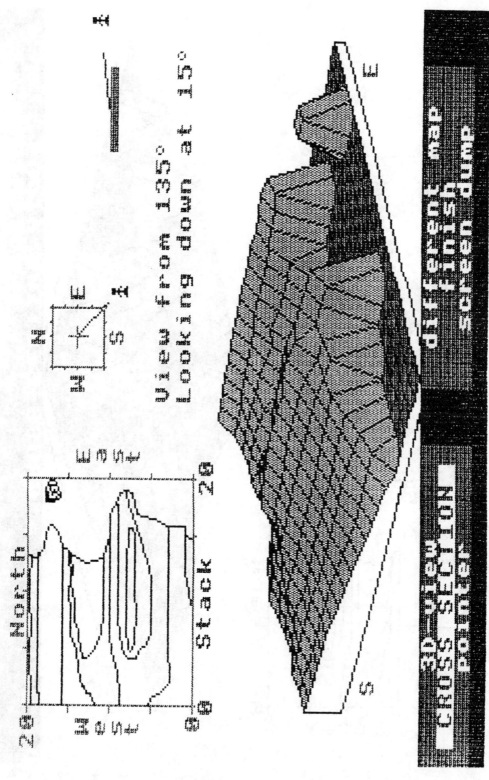

FIGURE 14.7   A view completed – LAND

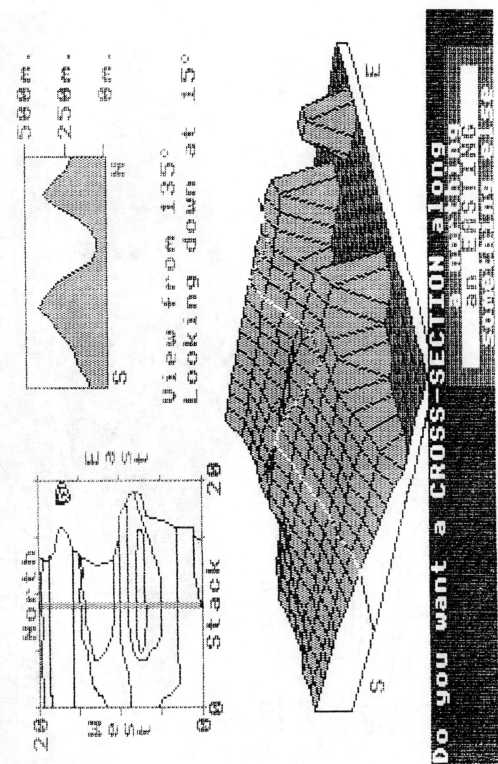

FIGURE 14.8   A cross section – LAND

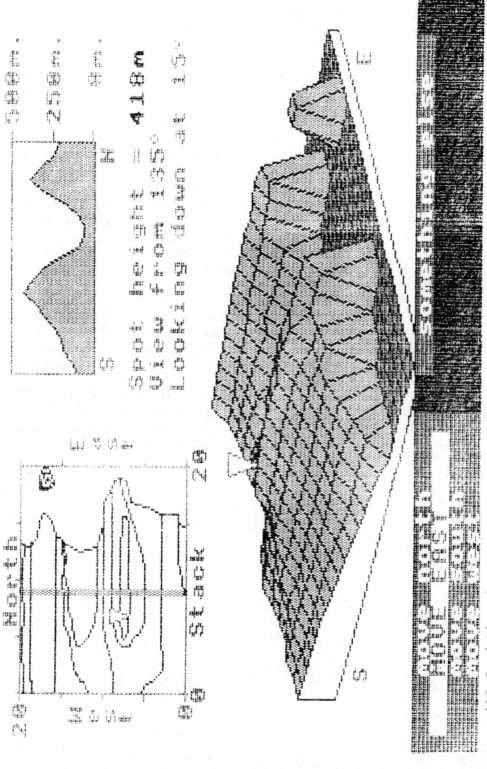

FIGURE 14.9   Spot height marker – LAND

could complete. The CAL developer felt it was essential to get the main program finished. If funds became available later, we could add on a data input unit.

There was in the meantime a significant amount of work still to be done on the screen design and user interface. During the two years of development, the CIC ideas and standards had changed, so selection by number and checking entry were eliminated; icons were used for choice of compass direction and angle of elevation; single letters where essential were replaced by full words; extraneous clutter of scales were removed; a four colour coding was incorporated. These changes indicate the style followed to minimize clutter on a dynamic screen. During these stages other aspects were incorporated. A print dump routine was added, and a facility for the user to use the space bar to pause during the drawing of a view. This latter facility adds considerably to the richness of the unit. Figures 14.4 to 14.9 illustrate the final version of the main screen which took some eight months to produce. Notice the new method of input, by spacing through the angles, for direction and height. Figure 14.6 shows the view with the pause facility, to be compared with the complete view at 14.7. 14.8 shows a cross-section located and drawn, while 14.9 has a spot height marker being located. In fact, the programmer decided that the code was now such a mess that it was better to start from scratch, using a comic strip to represent the dynamics required. Eventually, five years later, the specification for Contour Analysis became a unit called Landscape Appreciation (LAND) (Willson 1984).

LAND rapidly became the province of four people, one of whom was part of the central team and not the writing group. The initial idea in LAND was relatively narrow compared with the final scheme. There was significant polishing of the user interface to the program especially after trials. LAND changed as the capabilities of the machines and our perception of design changed.

The change in the name from Contour Analysis – CONTOUR – to Landscape Analysis – LAND – indicates the shift in educational perspective that progressed with the development of the unit. It was published in 1986, together with two other programs from this group. Two more are still under development.

15
FURTHER DEVELOPMENT EXAMPLES

The drawing up and following of guidelines has only been possible because CAL development in CIC has been ongoing. The experience of the development process has enabled us to chart patterns that have emerged, until it is only relatively recently that the combination and sequencing of the stages and issues to consider have become clearer. Over this time, as problems arose particularly in the design, whether in program structure, screen or interface, solutions were being sought and put into practice on units that were themselves at various stages of development. It is ironic that just as we begin to feel we have an understanding of the combination of issues involved and how to solve them in relation to the 8 bit environment, the actual environment in schools is moving rapidly into that of 16 bit with all the languages, software tools and new methods of interface that this implies.

It is unlikely that the actual development of any one unit will not have some major problem associated with it during its development stage: the model just does not seem to work; the screen is too cluttered; the idea does not seem to stand up to such sophisticated treatment after all. This chapter traces a few decision points in some units to compliment the examples already offered by ARCHEO and LAND.

LAYOUT OF TEXT AND GRAPHICS – AGCOM

AGCOM is the program that forms part of an economics CAL unit on Agricultural Commodity Price Stabilization. It provides two simulations for the study and comparison of two price support and stabilization schemes for farm products and other primary commodities. The first is about the EEC (European Economic Community) Common Agricultural Policy and its market intervention. The second is the former UK system of guaranteed prices and deficiency payments. It is designed for use by students of between sixteen and eighteen years who can explore the dynamics of fluctuating prices and of stabilizing policies using the supply and demand model. Before starting the work, students should be able to interpret simple supply and demand graphs and understand the determination of market price in a perfect market. They should also know about price and income elasticities of demand, elasticity of supply, and about what kind of factors affect these elasticities for particular products.

This unit was designed and developed during Phase I of the Project after the first major brainstorming weekend held by CIC, at Keele in 1974. A group of economists began to explore how the computer may help in their teaching. The individuals of the group came from different parts of the country and were not associated with any location. The programming was done by the author and project director, and was written to run on a mainframe. The program therefore ran line by line at a terminal. With the advent of microcomputers this was directly transferred across to run on an RML 380Z, Apple II and Commodore Pet. The user interface was of a dialogue style and there were no graphics. Figure 15.1 gives a sample printout, with the user choosing to look at the EEC option – beef as the commodity and run it for three years.

The unit was published as part of a pack in 1979. By this stage a new phase of development had started and the project was now designing specifically with the micro and graphics in mind. During the work on these new, Phase II, units, the original author, who was still involved, began to explore the possibility of a new graphics version of the program. Funding was found for the science re-writes of the Phase I packs in 1980, and by 1983, further funding was found to re-write the original economics and geography units.

The initial work on this re-write is illustrated in Figures 15.2–15.6. These figures are taken from the first draft working version. The graphs drawn illustrate the style of work that was underway in graphics in 1982 and 1983. The code was all there, written in the library. The model had transferred across from the original program. Therefore the subsequent work concentrated on the screen design.

Figures 15.7 – 15.12 provide a new sequence to be compared with the first draft. Figure 15.7 illustrates the new front end compared with the original credits page, which now appears second. Notice in the next three sequences the text was only changed slightly. The word 'attempt' has been replaced by 'do'; 'Your task' has been added, and 'is' has replaced the equals sign. It is the *layout* of the screen that makes these two frames different. A box has been used to break up the screen, and also to separate the two styles of information. A star has been used to identify each separate important piece of information. 'Press space' is now used to continue, as information is being paged. The remaining screens for comparison show a variety of methods of 'polishing' of the screen: by boxing, right justifying the quantities, adding labels to the graph, and clarifying the graph by use of extra lines for MP (Market Price) and GP (Guaranteed Price). 'Def'cy Pts' has been replaced by the word Deficiency. The last two screens, for Market Price, show the impact that re-locating relatively peripheral items such as the pound sign, the key, and overall boxing, has made. This last series of screens is taken from the finished published version.

FROM DIALOGUE TO OPTIONS – POND

POND, the program that belongs to the unit Pond Ecology, was re-written from its original text based version. This illustrates the dramatic impact graphics and use of the dynamic screen to illustrate the same basic material, can have. This is a classic option-driven program that provides total flexibility to the user over the earlier dialogue style. Figures 15.13 gives a run through showing the dialogue style, and the way the information was presented, inevitably line by line to the user. Figures 15.14–15.16 show the new dynamic graphic page in operation after the use of the option, and also the list of options and their explanation. This unit was published in this form in 1983. Although, with hindsight, CIC may want to polish the design, the options still provide a most useful method of operating a totally open-ended framework. Option keywords are still used in a large number of units, although their method selection may have changed.

ORDERING THE LIST OF OPTIONS – DEMOG2

DEMOG2 is one of three programs that make up the CAL unit Human Population Growth. DEMOG2 was also translated from a dialogue to our option program, as part of the geography re-writes between 1983 and 1986. Transfer to options was not totally straightforward, however. It was not always appropriate to allow the user total freedom to choose any option. For instance, they could not project to a future date until they had chosen which country they were viewing. So it was important to 'hide' some of the options, or make it obvious that they were not available for choice at some stages. Figure 15.17 illustrates one method chosen, to use of fuzzy letters for the inappropriate options in the list for choice at the time.

When drawing up the list of options, they first appeared in the following list:

COUNTRY
BASE YEAR
PROJECT
COMPARE
TABLES
MARKERS
COLOUR
FINISH

Country was a logical first word for the user to see, but after calling up country the next logical step is to project forwards to look at future years. Therefore *Project* should come before *Base Year* which is simply a method of returning to the Base Year on which the data starts. But *Markers* indicate an opportunity to mark a specific cohort and watch it move through five year projections, so logically *Markers* should come before *Project*. Also, the words used in the list were sometimes in an inappropriate part of speech. *Print All* is clear, it is an option that enables you to print all your output. What does the *Compare* option enable you to do? What are the *Tables* of? Different words were chosen that aimed to be more specific about each option, and are illustrated in the box on the left in Figure 15.18. *Pop/Rates* (*ex* Tables) represent the option for inputting new populations and rates. *Outline* (*ex* Compare) is the option that enables you to compare the new projection with the previous period by placing an outline over the top. The fuzzy images show that none of these options are yet relevant to the user as *Country* has not yet been selected. Inevitably you will not totally solve these problems, especially when in this case with a space that will carry a maximum of twelve characters. *Mark Cohort* has been criticised, because some users' response is 'Who is he?'!

Figures 15.18 and 15.19 illustrate the way these options are selected, by locating a box over each word through space bar selection, and then pressing the return key to confirm. In this case the confirmed selection remains boxed while the marker is being placed, in this case on the 10–14 cohort. The option *Print All* is still fuzzy because the user opted not to use the printer at the beginning of the run, so selecting to print would be inappropriate.

TO ROLL OR BOUNCE?

Selection by moving through a menu, either vertically or horizontally was first introduced by use of the cursor keys. Figure 15.20 illustrates our initial designs using this method, on AMWEST. Note the message to the user at the bottom of the key is quite explicit about the use of arrow keys, or U and D for those who do not have them. The arrow would move up and down the list accordingly. This method of user selection is reinforced by a subsequent screen; in Figure 15.21, where the user is by now assumed to understand the significance of the arrow, the message at the bottom has changed. Press Return is used in the same program to both confirm a choice or see the results of a choice.

Consistency of use of words and routines, such as Press Return, may be the ideal but it does become quite hard to implement in practice. Use of the arrow keys meant that when the user had reached the bottom of the menu lists they could then move back up it in reverse order, so that the cursor was bouncing up and down the list.

When developing the menu selection in DEMOG2, the first version also showed the cursor bouncing back up the list. However, after carefully working out a logical sequence for the users to work through the list, such bouncing was illogical. So in this program the cursor rolls back up to the beginning of the list and moves down again from the top with each key stroke entry.

With the space bar used to select a choice, the close relationship between the arrow and the cursor changed, and it is thought that boxing the whole option is actually clearer. This also allows for indicating that the box has been selected through inversion of colour or stippling the outline. One of the clearest examples of boxing the selection is given in Figure 15.22 taken from the Home Heater unit. Notice that the arrow and cursor keys are being used to make a selection, and not the space bar.

These three examples illustrate the individual differences between programs which use the cursor selection of a menu.

OVERLAYING WINDOWS – BURREG

A combination of both screen design and user interface decisions were taken during the design of a program on Burial Registers. This program began because the historians were concerned at their pupils misunderstanding of the term 'the average age of death'. They find it difficult to relate to a period that can have many grandmothers, when they learn that the average age of death at the time was twenty-six years old. 'Doesn't everyone die at 26 then?' This was linked to an involvement with local history and the role of Parish Records. The initial specification of the unit was for there to be a simple data handling and interrogation program. Pupils could enter up to forty records of deaths for any one year. The details would be simply those you would expect to cull from the parish records, thus they were: names, sex, age, and month of entry of death in the record. The first design was, therefore, a reflection of other data entry programs, with the appropriate checks such as to see if the year was within the given range. The records were not to be large, as the aim was for the pupils to be able to enter the data relatively easily and quickly and then see an analysis by either Age or Month against Males, Females or both. It was hoped that such an analysis would illustrate the combination of variety of entries over any twelve month period that could result in an average age of death.

The first draft program looked like any other data entry packages, so failed to highlight the teaching aspect about the average age of death. Accordingly after a further detailed workshop session it was agreed that the process needed to be entered graphic-ally, and with each entry point the average would be calculated. Within a few months CIC happened to be going through an intense discussion phase on the interlinking of screen design with the appropriate user interface. The programmer decided to move from dialogue entry to menu selection. The program then became particularly interest-ing, as by careful use of the logical menu and overlays, the unit began to be a useful illustration of the logical steps necessary to enter, or recall, and analyse data.

Figures 15.23–15.26 show a sequence of the user selecting to *Recall* data already on the file, choosing *which* of the four data files to select, deciding to *analyse* this data, to analyse it by Age against both Males and Females. This last frame shows that fifteen deaths, some of individuals in their seventies and eighties, others of infants, results in the Average age of death at 47.9. Figures 15.27 – 15.31 show the step by step sequence of the data entry section where the marker moves as each new entry is give. The basic education idea behind the unit has not changed, but the facility to use graphics and window overlaying has made its execution much richer.

SCREEN CLUTTER

The graphics area is neither as large nor as flexible as one would like. It is extremely easy to fill up the screen with extraneous clutter. Better chararcter definition now enables us to draw finer pictures, but these often become too complex. It is better to use a simple key than to always put all words on the screen. Users can refer to the paper-material for explanation (see Figure 15.32). It is very hard to see how to remove some clutter. One solution is to allow the user to select to turn some of the features off for clarity. Thus in MILL the contours can be toggled on or off. (See Figures 15.33 and 15.34.)

The key does not necessarily always have to appear, nor North, on maps, even though as a Geographer this all goes against my basic training! They can also be toggled. Alternatively a diagram need not always be labelled as long as it is clear to the user what the graphics or icons represent.

Some units need a significant amount of thought on how to increase clarity without reducing the richness. Figure 15.35 is taken from a trials version of the program Indian Farmer (INDFARM). It represents an Indian family, one member of which has died in the pevious year. The family works ten fields with their own labour and with the help of two bullocks. In year two, the rainfall was 1250mm. resulting in the yields of rice and maize as shown. This brought them enough grain to live on, but they have to use some to repay their debts. We are still re-jigging this design, which will be published in 1986. Readers may care to plan how they would re-design this screen.

DROPPING A UNIT

It is very hard to drop a unit, especially once it has been the subject of some considerable development time. The geography program Motorway (MWAY) allowed transport networks to be designed and modified. It was aimed at the lower half of the secondary school. Basically the users could locate a number of cities and give them a certain population. A motorway network and traffic flow would be calculated between them, using the simplest form of gravity model. This is that movement between two towns is directly proportional to the product of their populations; and inversely proportional to the square of this distance between them. Thus:

$$\text{Movement} = K \; \frac{(\text{population of town I}) \times (\text{population of town J})}{(\text{distance between town I and town J})^2}$$

Where K is constant.

In the BASIC program this is represented by:

$$IV = IE6 * P(I) * P(J)/D(I,J)/D(I,J)$$

This simplification means that pupils needed to be aware that:
● it does not allow for constraints on the construction, through physical factors, environmental factors, or ownership problems;
● it assumes the area already has an existing infra-structure and that the monetary network is to be added; and
● although the population figures are given for a city, the users must consider it an 'urban' field – that is the total area to be served by the motorway.

When using it, the pupils first enter the location of their cities on a grid, followed by the population size. This will be indicated by a square proportional to the size of the population. A relative traffic flow table is then given. The pupils then construct a network that they think may be appropriate. They can make direct links between cities, or link three together either by a triangle, or by a Y shape. The pupils are encouraged to build on the basis of the relative traffic flow table. The traffic, cost and efficiency of each network is then given. The sequence of Figures 15.36 shows the traffic flow after city location; Figure 15.37 the network once built up.

This was trialled by the writing group and others. The trials feedback varied from 'too difficult for our pupils' to 'the best graphics in Geography CAL I have seen' (!). This caused much amusement to the author and group co-ordinator. There are two areas of concern. The group wanted to be able to compare networks once drawn. This was just not possible with the current amount of space and the layout of the code. A 'Y' link could not be drawn if the angle was very obtuse. This would prevent the 'Y' link being executed where it would in fact be a better solution than 2 separate links, e.g. between A and B, and B and C. This would cause problems because of the sharp angle, so in this case the computer graphics will actually limit you from choosing what the model would compute as a best solution.

The graphics could not adequately represent the differences in scale of population in a meaningful way. 'Y' links could not be undone, and the author was increasingly concerned that the use of 'Y' links did not stand up in the model, which used cost on the basis of line length and could not take into account the efficiency of flow. The aim of the unit was to introduce in a simple way the difficult concept of networks. It was agreed that dynamic graphics and user interface problems could have been tackled again, but not while there was distinct uncertainty about the validity of the use of the model in this way. Also CIC already had developed a gravity model unit (GRAVITY) to cover the more complex aspects. It was agreed to drop the program.

Programs can be dropped for a variety of reasons – either the idea is simply not worthy of such detailed attention, or the model is suspect, or there are no resources left to finish properly what is still a good idea and good initial design. When some ideas become richer during their development, it is hardly surprising that others become poorer. Even with hindsight, it really is not easy to anticipate those ideas that will later prove to be weak. It can be an appalling blow however to the morale of a group, and particularly to the author who has worked away, often for a year or two, on an idea before it is scrapped. This makes the decision all the harder, but should not prevent it having to be taken.

```
SCHOOLS COUNCIL PROJECT
COMPUTERS IN THE CURRICULUM

AGRICULTURAL COMMODITIES 1 - VER 10
-------------------------

TEXT DISTRIBUTED BY
EDWARD ARNOLD (PUBLISHERS) LTD


SELECT MARKET :
POTATOES(1), BEEF(2), ANOTHER(3) ? 2

TIME LAG BETWEEN DECISION TO SUPPLY
AND SUPPLY REACHING MARKET = 1 YEAR

NO.OF FARMERS = 200

FREE MARKET PRICE YEAR 0 =   231
FARMERS' PRESENT INCOMES=  2552
PER FARM

FARMERS PROTEST ABOUT THEIR LOW AND
FLUCTUATING INCOMES. AS EEC COMMISIONER
FOR AGRICULTURE YOU MUST RAISE AND
STABILISE INCOMES AT A MINIMUM LEVEL OF
AT LEAST 3403 PER YEAR

YEAR   1

   TARGET P ? 245
  PLANNED S =  2350
   ACTUAL S =  2820
FREE MKT P =   181

I.B. ACTION ? BUY

  QUANTITY =   760
STOCKS NOW =   760
 MKT PRICE =   245
FARM INCOME=  3454

YEAR   2

   TARGET P ? 295
  PLANNED S =  2850
   ACTUAL S =  4275
FREE MKT P =    60

I.B. ACTION ? BUY

  QUANTITY =  2815
STOCKS NOW =  3575
 MKT PRICE =   295
FARM INCOME=  6305

YEAR   3

   TARGET P ? 345
  PLANNED S =  3350
   ACTUAL S =  3015
FREE MKT P =   165

I.B. ACTION ? SELL
++INAPPROPRIATE ACTION
I.B. ACTION ? BUY

  QUANTITY =  2155
STOCKS NOW =  5730
 MKT PRICE =   345
FARM INCOME=  5200

YEAR   4

   TARGET P ?
```

FIGURE 15.1   Teletype output of AGCOM

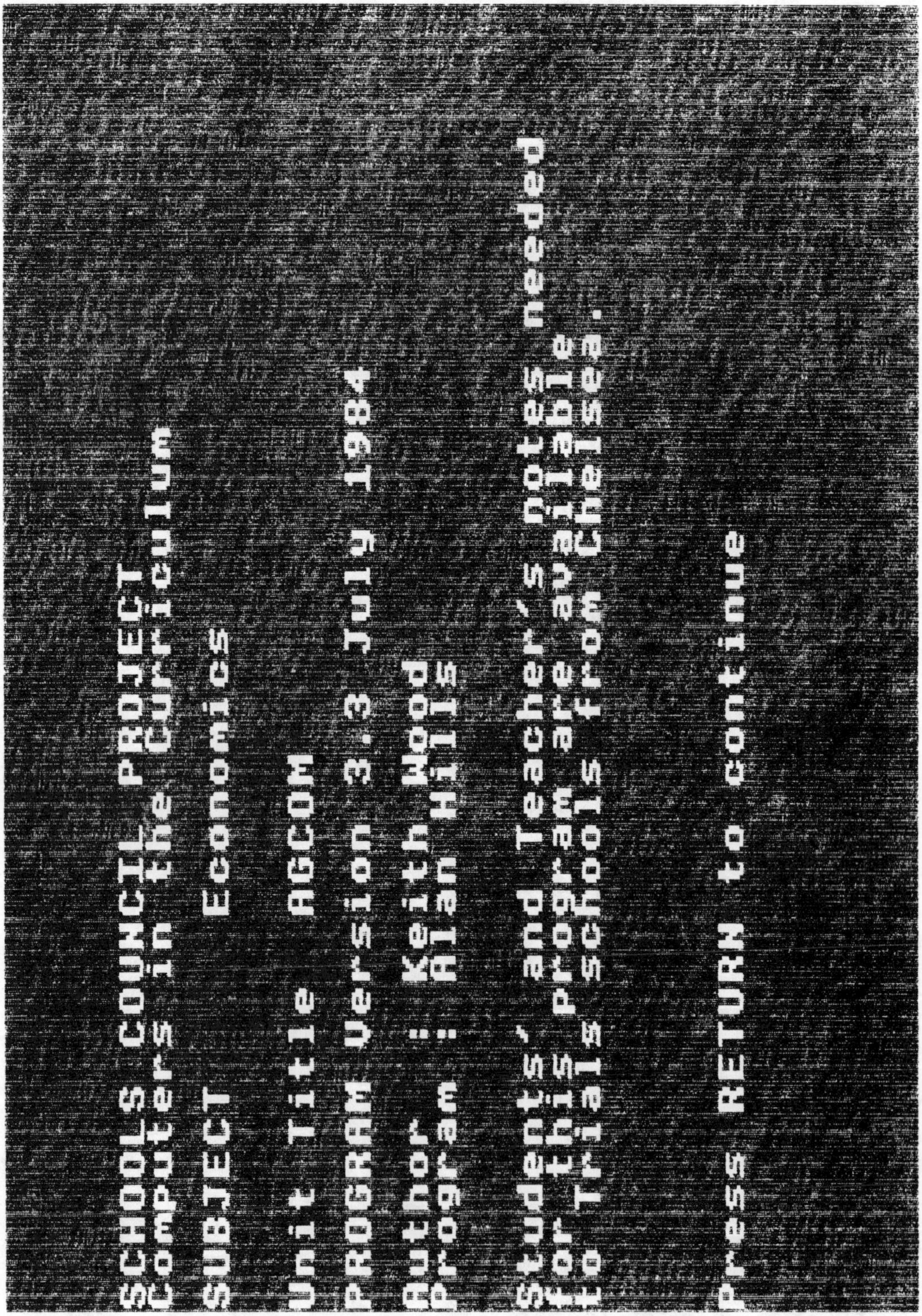

```
SCHOOLS COUNCIL PROJECT
Computers in the Curriculum

SUBJECT   Economics

Unit Title AGCOM

PROGRAM version 3.3 July 1984

Author: Keith Wood
Program: Alan Hills

Students' and Teacher's notes needed
for this program are available
to Trials schools from Chelsea.

Press RETURN to continue
```

FIGURE 15.2   Draft micro version – AGCOM

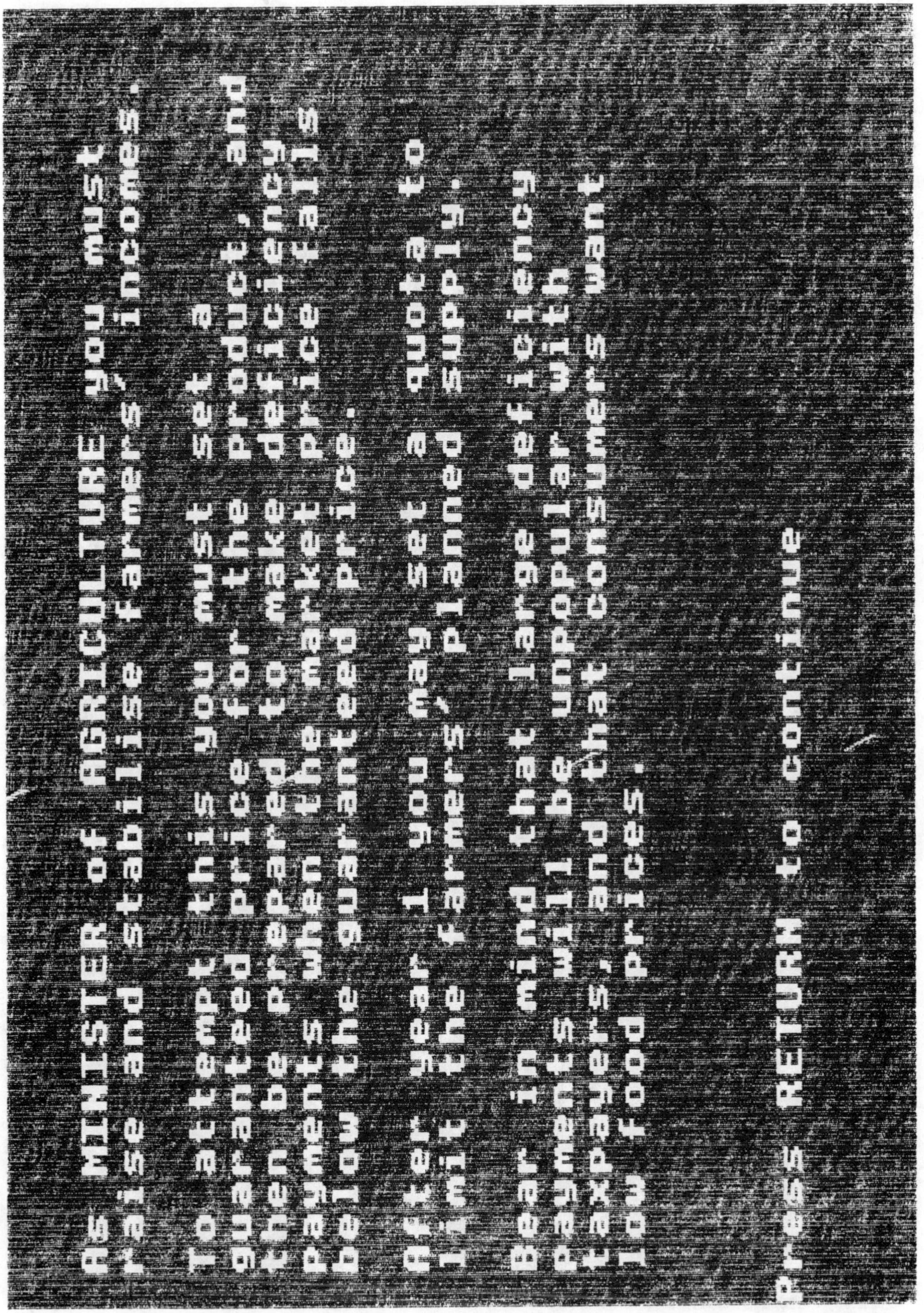

As MINISTER of AGRICULTURE you must raise and stabilise farmers' incomes.

To attempt this you must set a guaranteed price for the product, and then be prepared to make deficiency payments when the market price falls below the guaranteed price.

After year 1 you may set a quota to limit the farmers' planned supply.

Bear in mind that large deficiency payments will be unpopular with taxpayers, and that consumers want low food prices.

Press RETURN to continue.

FIGURE 15.3 Draft micro version – AGCOM

Time lag between decision to supply
and supply reaching market = 1 year

Number of farmers = 200

Free market price at present=£236

Income per farm = £2548

Farmers protest about low and fluctuating incomes. As Minister of Agriculture
your task is to raise and stabilise
incomes at £3397 a year at least.

Press RETURN to continue

FIGURE 15.4   Draft micro version – AGCOM

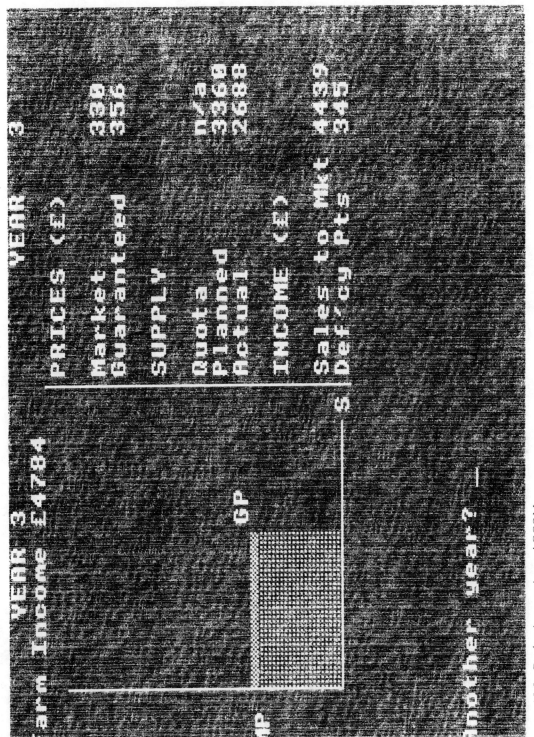

FIGURE 15.5   Draft micro version – AGCOM

FIGURE 15.6 Draft micro version – AGCOM

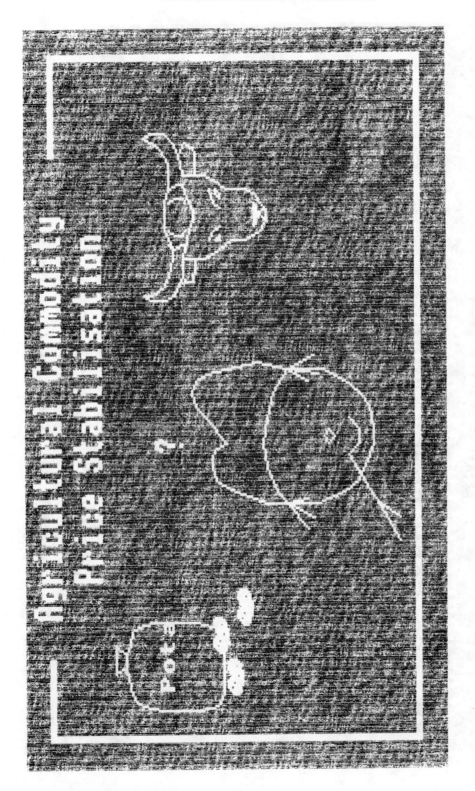

FIGURE 15.7 Final micro version – AGCOM

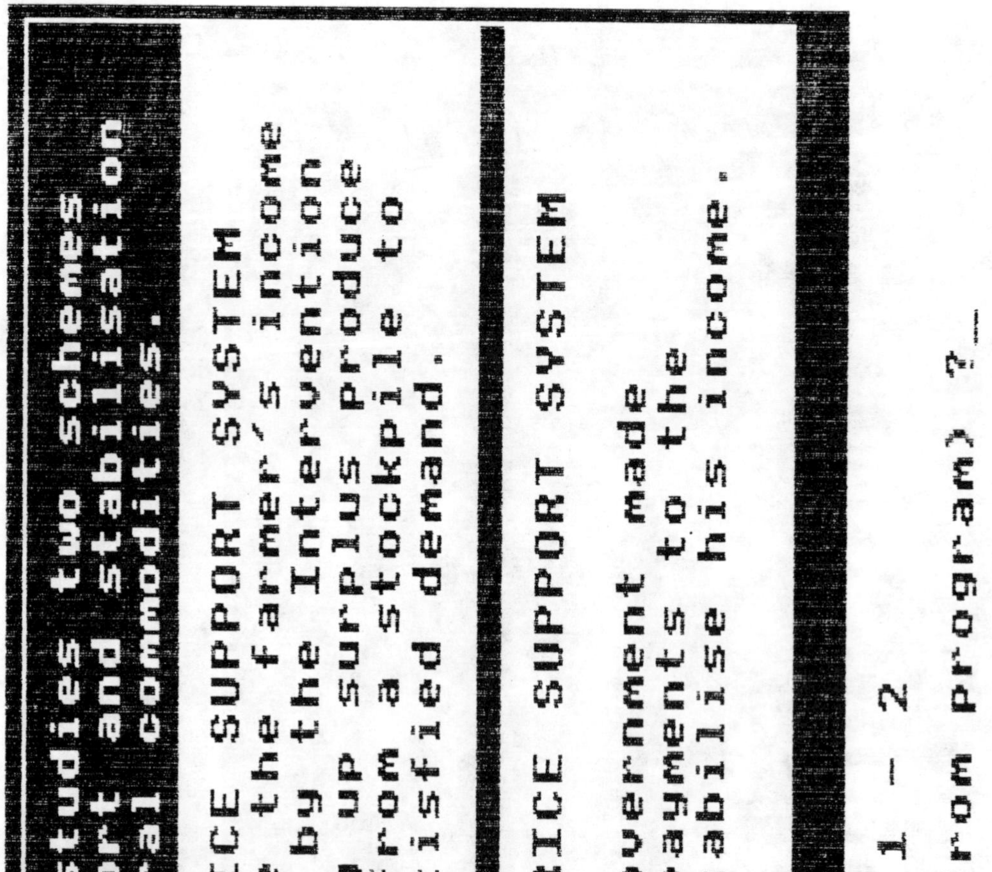

DEVELOPING CAL

This program studies two schemes
of price support and stabilisation
for agricultural commodities.

1 EEC FARM PRICE SUPPORT SYSTEM
In this case the farmer's income
is adjusted by the Intervention
Board buying up surplus produce
or selling from a stockpile to
fulfil unsatisfied demand.

2 FORMER UK PRICE SUPPORT SYSTEM

Where the government made
deficiency payments to the
farmer to stabilise his income.

WHICH SYSTEM 1 - 2
(or 3 to exit from program) ?_

FIGURE 15.8   Final micro version – AGCOM

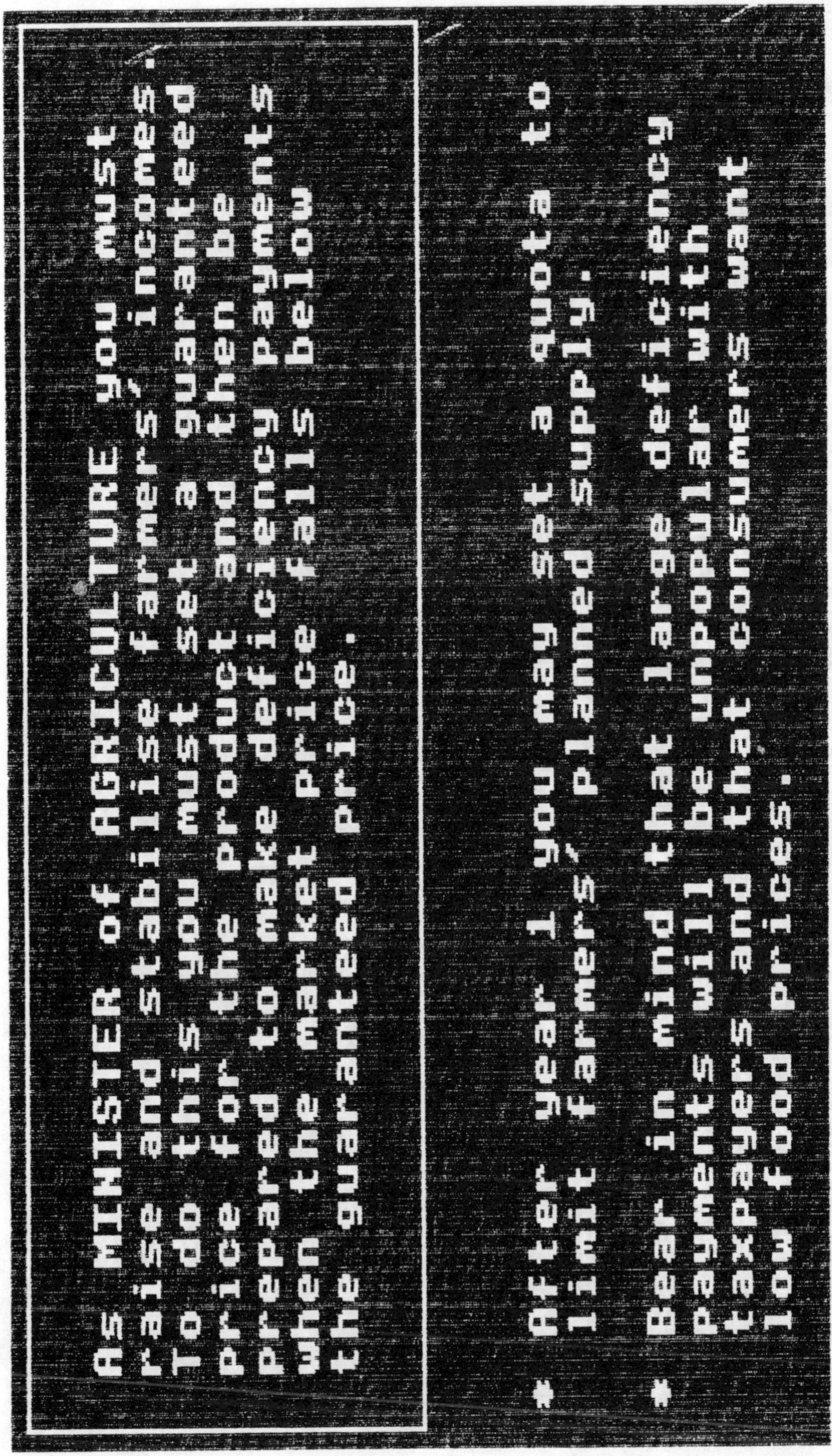

As MINISTER of AGRICULTURE you must raise and stabilise farmers' incomes. To do this you must set a guaranteed price for the product and then be prepared to make deficiency payments when the market price falls below the guaranteed price.

* After year 1 you may set a quota to limit farmers' planned supply.

* Bear in mind that large deficiency payments will be unpopular with taxpayers and that consumers want low food prices.

Press SPACE BAR to continue

FIGURE 15.9   Final micro version – AGCOM

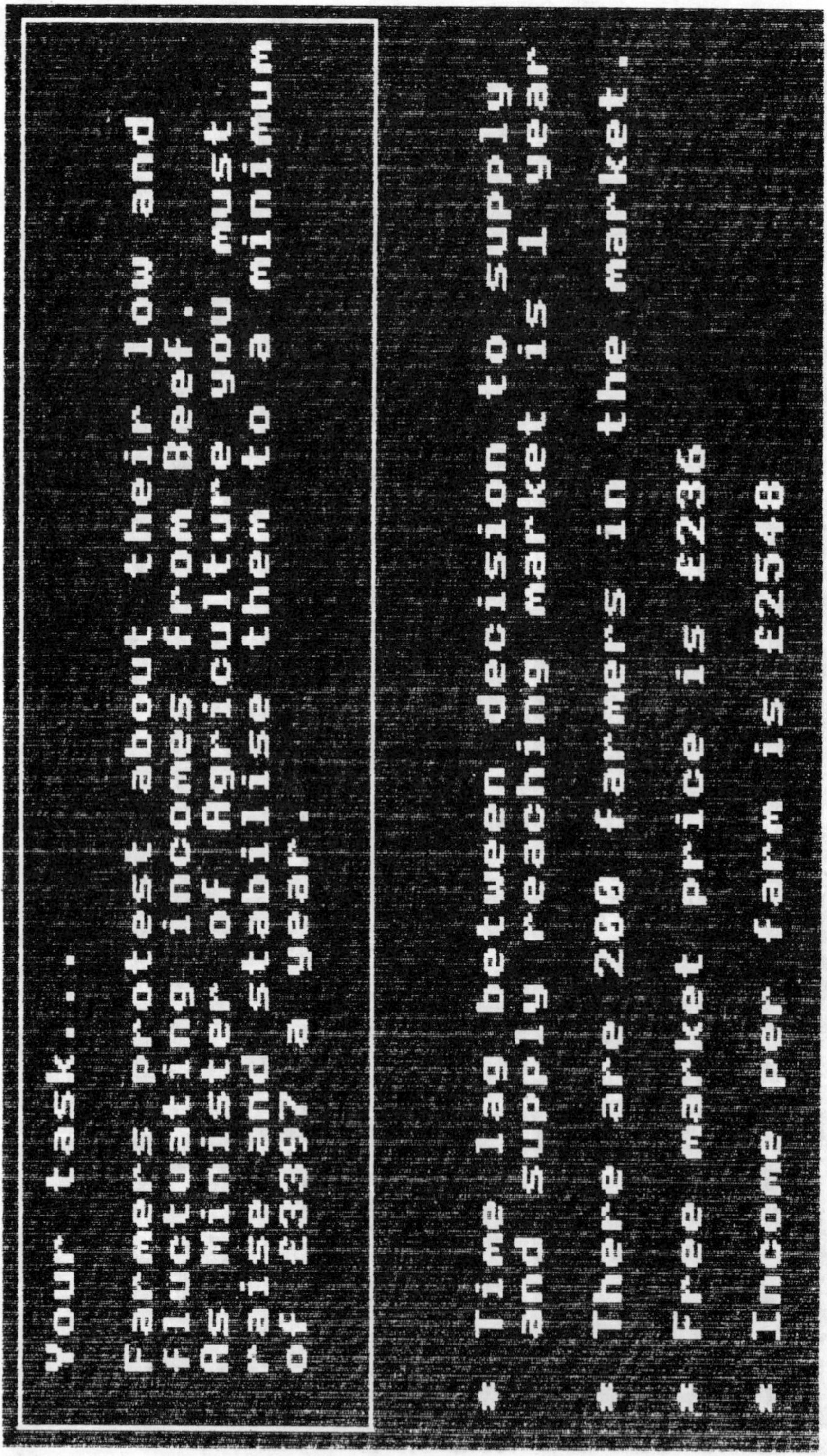

Your task....

Farmers protest about their low and
fluctuating incomes from Beef.
As Minister of Agriculture you must
raise and stabilise them to a minimum
of £3397 a year.

* Time lag between decision to supply
  and supply reaching market is 1 year.

* There are 200 farmers in the market.

* Free market price is £236

* Income per farm is £2548

Press SPACE BAR to continue

FIGURE 15.10   Final micro version – AGCOM

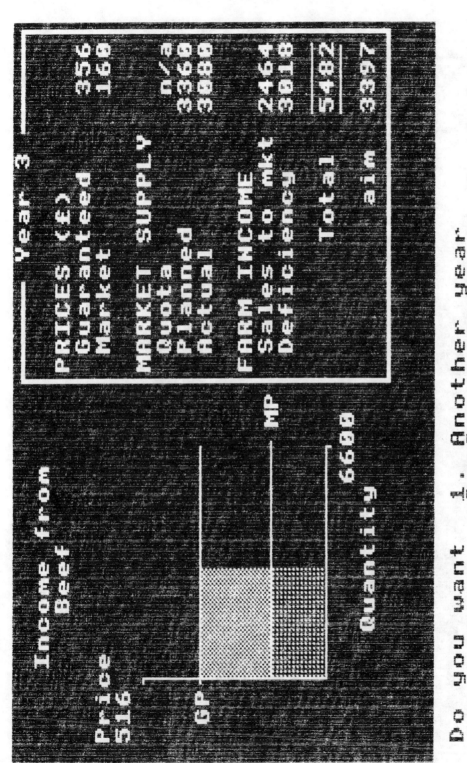

FIGURE 15.11   Final micro version – AGCOM

FIGURE 15.12   Final micro version – AGCOM

```
SCHOOLS COUNCIL PROJECT
COMPUTERS IN THE CURRICULUM


POND ECOLOGY - POND1 (VERSION 5)
---------------------

TEXT DISTRIBUTED BY
EDWARD ARNOLD (PUBLISHERS) LTD



WHICH STAGE DO YOU WANT
(TYPE 0 FOR A LIST)? 0
     YOU CAN
  1  CATCH FISH
  2  SET INITIAL NUMBERS OF
     PHYTOPLANKTON, HERBIVORES & FISH
  3  POLLUTE THE POND
++TYPE 1 2 OR 3 ? 2

WHAT ARE THE INITIAL NUMBERS OF
  PHYTOPLANKTON (0-250) ? 200
  HERBIVORES (0-50) ? 45
  FISH (0-1000) ? 800

YEAR PHYTOPLANK HERBIVORES   FISH
  1  (BILLIONS) (MILLIONS) (THOUSANDS)
     0   .2    0    40    0    2
     +.....+.....+.....+.....+.....+.....
JA .     P      .      H   .  F
FE .  .   P     .       H   . F
MA .     P      .       H   . F
AP .          P    81 MILL  .    F
MY  .4 BILL    .       H   .         F
JN .       P   .   H       .      F
JL .       P   .       H   .      F
AU .      P    .       H   .    F
SE .      P    .       H    .  F
OC .;     P    .       H    .  F
NO .   P       .       H    .  F
DE .  P        .       H    .  F
ANOTHER YEAR ? YESNO
DO YOU WANT
DIFFERENT INITIAL NUMBERS ? NO
DO YOU WANT STAGE 1 OR STAGE 3 ? 1
++TYPE EITHER YES OR NO ? YES

WHICH STAGE ? 1

HOW MANY GO FISHING AT ONCE (0-20) ? 8

HOW OFTEN DO THESE  8  FISHERMEN
  GO FISHING (1 2 OR 4) ? 2

ARE YOU GOING TO KEEP THE FISH ? NO


YEAR  1  FISH LEFT    FISH CAUGHT BY
MONTH    IN POND    YOU   EVERYBODY
  JA      881        5       42
  FE      768       15      123
  MA      680      CLOSE SEASON
  AP     1602      CLOSE SEASON
  MY     3734      CLOSE SEASON
  JN     3034       60      481
  JL     2482       27      213
  AU     2023       32      254
  SE     1651       23      185
  OC     1352       13      107
  NO     1181       21      168
  DE     1034       14      114
   8  PEOPLE CAUGHT  1687  FISH.
    YOU CAUGHT  210  FISH
DO YOU WANT TO CONTINUE FOR
ANOTHER YEAR ? NO
DO YOU WANT A NEW FISHING RATE ? NO
```

```
DO YOU WANT TO START FISHING AGAIN ? NO
DO YOU WANT STAGE 2 OR STAGE 3 ? 3
++TYPE EITHER YES OR NO ? YES

WHICH STAGE ? 3

WHAT LEVEL OF POLLUTION
   LOW (1), MODERATE (2) OR HIGH (3) ? 1


YEAR PHYTOPLANK HERBIVORES   FISH
  1  (BILLIONS) (MILLIONS) (THOUSANDS)
     0   .2    0    40    0    2
     +.....+.....+.....+.....+.....
JA .     P      .    H      .  F
FE .      P     .    H      . F
MA .        P   .    H      . F
AP .       P    .    H      .    F
MY  6.8 BILL    .          H.      F
JN  55.3 BILL      161 MILL  .F
JL  1.7 BILL       315 MILL  .F
AU .      P        190 MILL  .F
SE .      P        140 MILL  .F
OC .      P      .          H.F
NO .      P      .    H      .F
DE .  P          .    H      .F
ANOTHER YEAR ? YES

YEAR PHYTOPLANK HERBIVORES   FISH
  2  (BILLIONS) (MILLIONS) (THOUSANDS)
     0   .2    0    40    0    2
     +.....+.....+.....+.....
JA .     P      .    H      . F
FE .      P     .    H      . F
MA .        P   .        H F
AP .          P.         H .F
MY .        P   .        H .F
JN .          P   93 MILL   F
JL .        P     93 MILL   F
AU .        P     86 MILL   F
SE .      P      .         HF
OC .      P      .       H F
NO .   P         .    H      F
DE .   P         .    H      F
ANOTHER YEAR ? NO
DO YOU WANT A
DIFFERENT LEVEL OF POLLUTION ? NO
DO YOU WANT STAGE 1 OR STAGE 2 ? NO


END OF PROGRAM
```

FIGURE 15.13 Teletype output for POND

```
Type one of these keywords when
Option ? appears on the screen

GO          to start with new pond
CONTINUE    to continue for another year
RESET       to restore starting conditions
NUMBERS     to set the initial numbers
FISH        to set the number of anglers
KEEP        to keep the fish caught
REPLACE     to return fish caught to pond
CLOSE       to set a close season
OPEN        to remove the close season
POLLUTE     to pollute the pond
FINISH      to end the program
EXPLAIN     for an introductory text

Option ?
```

FIGURE 15.14   Option list for POND

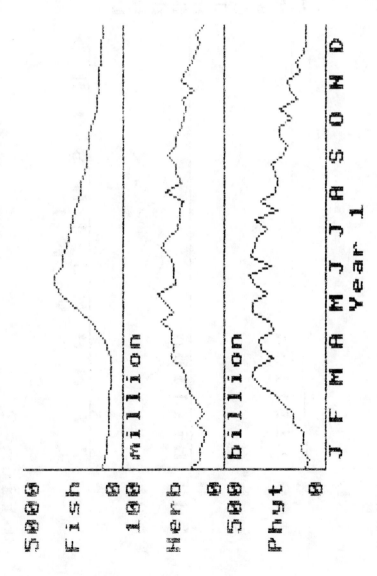

FIGURE 15.15 POND graphs

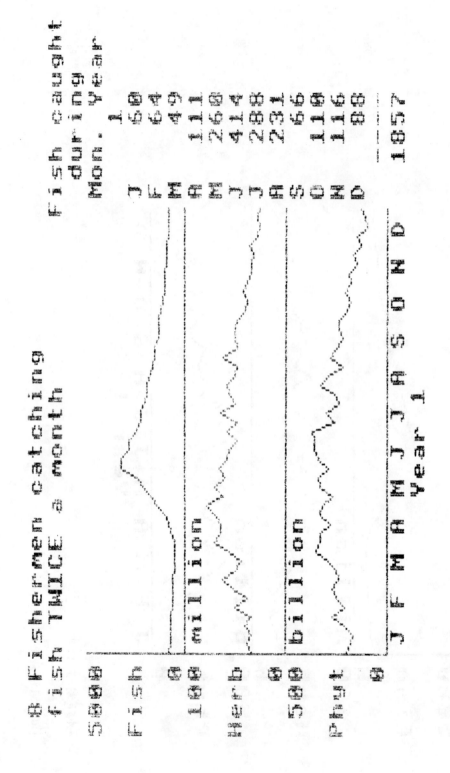

FIGURE 15.16   POND graphs

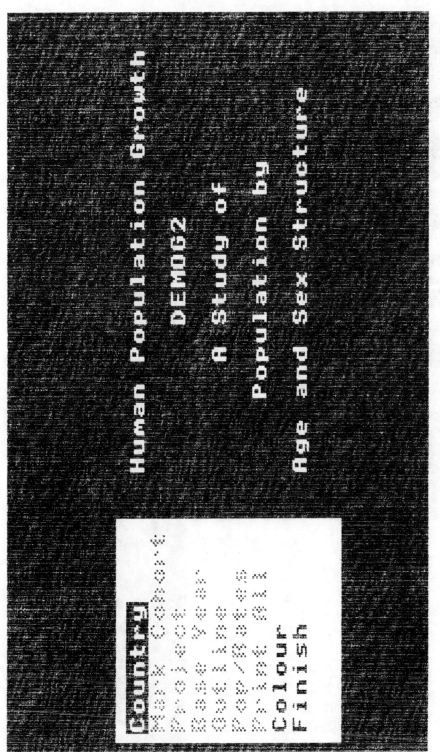

FIGURE 15.17   DEMOG menu lists

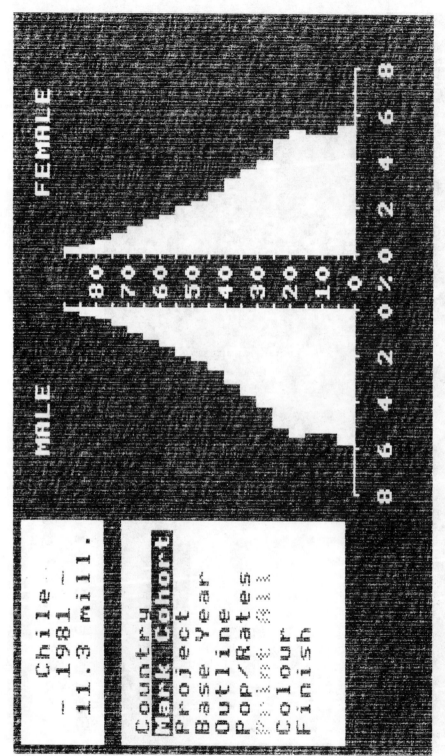

FIGURE 15.18   DEMOG menu lists

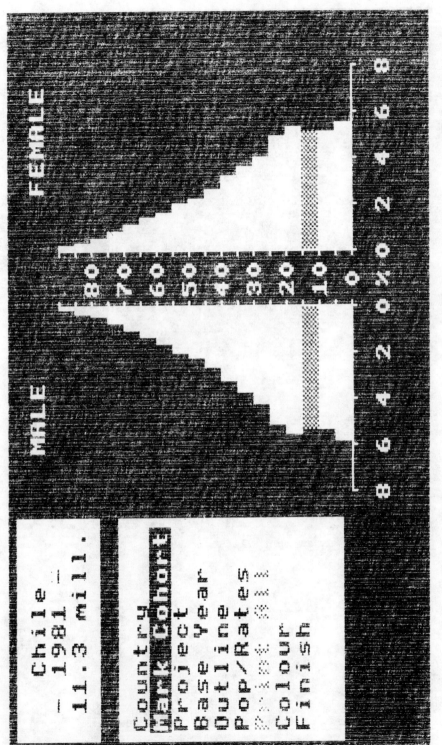

FIGURE 15.19 DEMOG menu lists

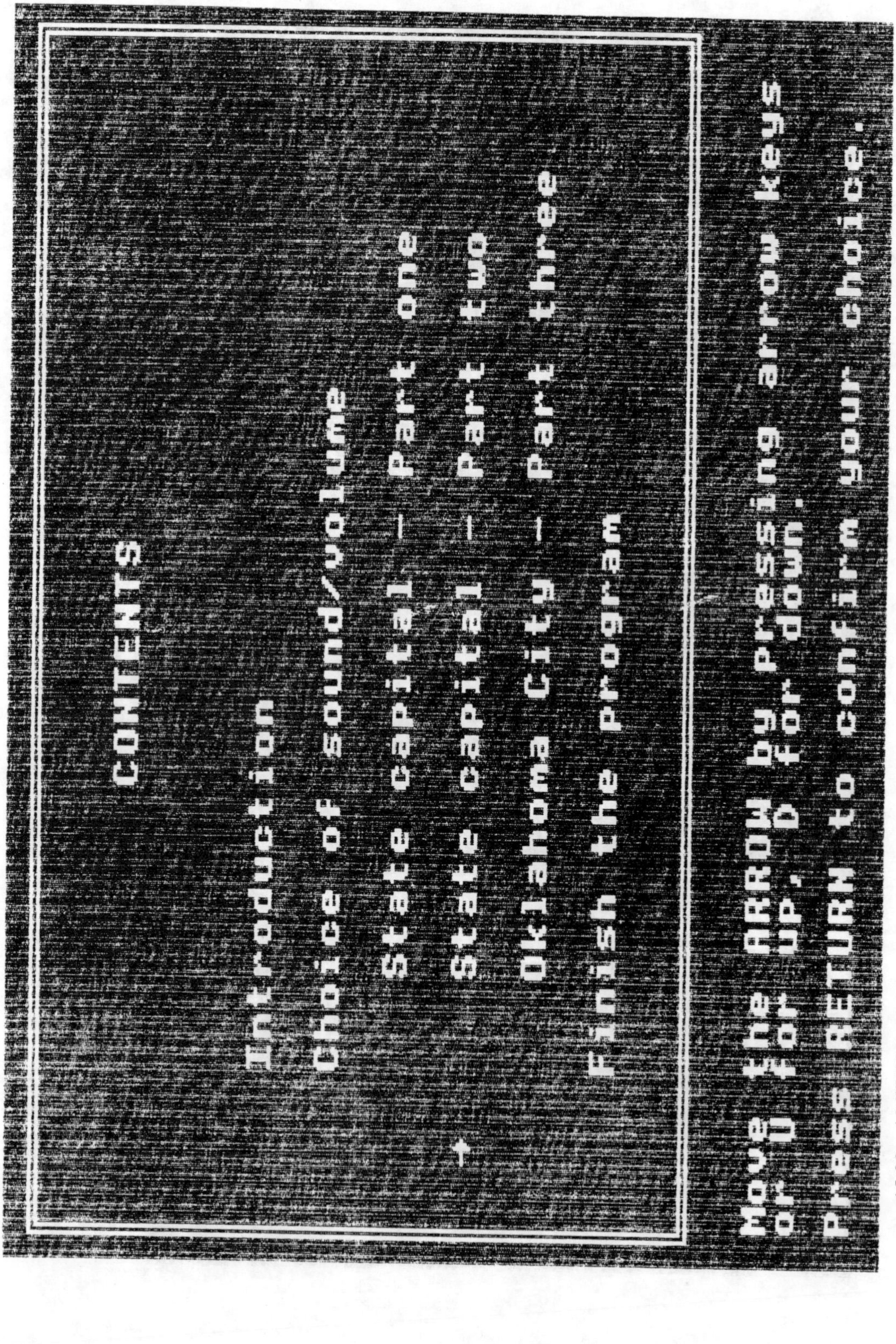

CONTENTS

Introduction

Choice of sound/volume

State capital - Part one

State capital - Part two

Oklahoma City - Part three

Finish the program

Move the ARROW by pressing arrow keys
or U for up, D for down.

Press RETURN to confirm your choice.

FIGURE 15.20 AMWEST selections

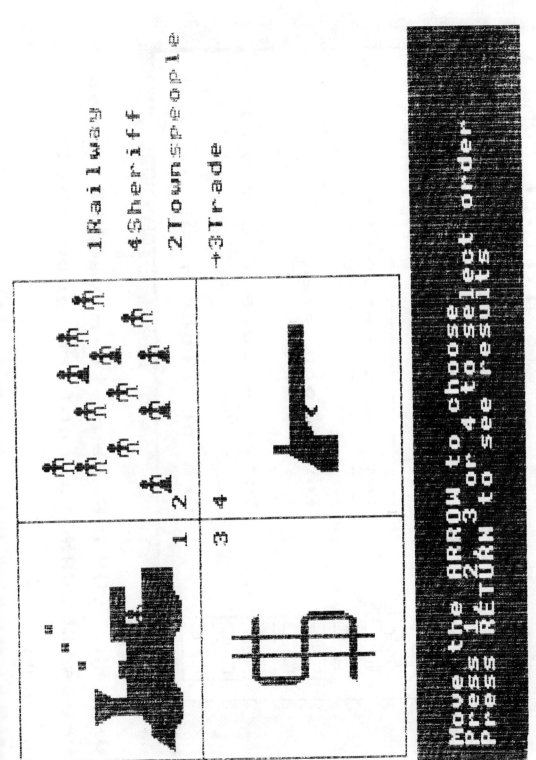

FIGURE 15.21   AMWEST selections

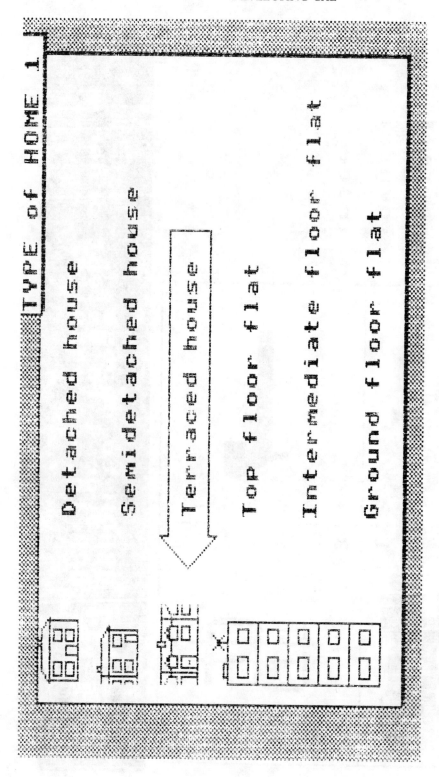

FIGURE 15.22   HEATER selection

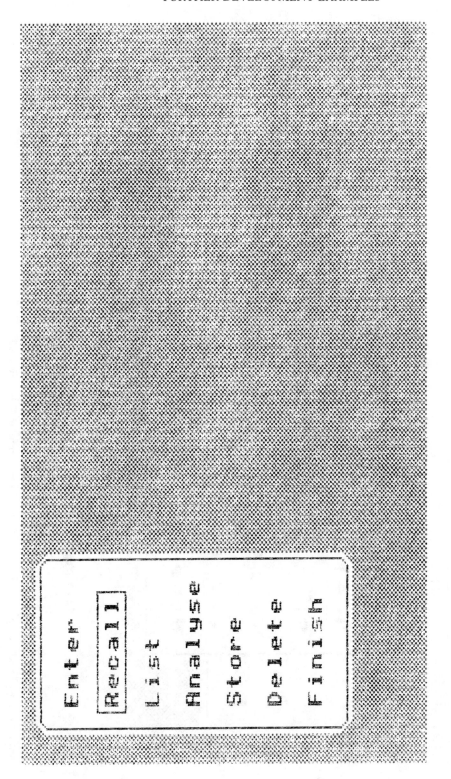

FIGURE 15.23 BURREG menus, overlaying windows and graphical display

```
Ent    Recall which data ?

Rec    Adel church 1788

Lis    Adel church May 1809-Apr 1810

Ane    Adel church 1812

Stc    St. James' Church

Del    ... empty ...

Fir    ... empty ...

       None of these


Recall complete.            Press RETURN....
```

FIGURE 15.24   BURREG menus, overlaying windows and graphical display

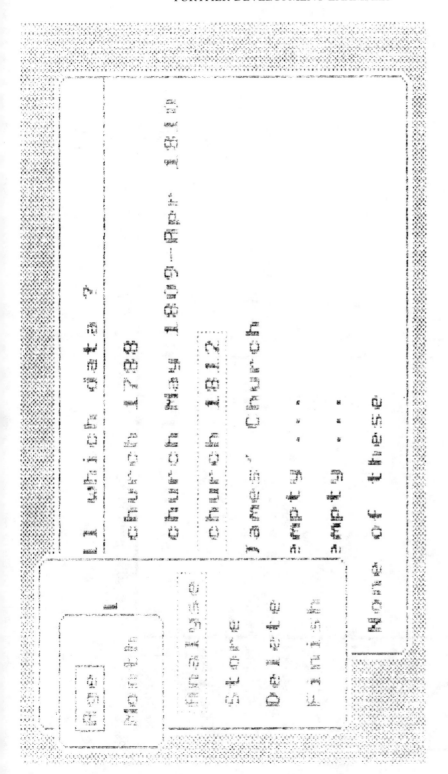

FIGURE 15.25   BURREG menus, overlaying windows and graphical display

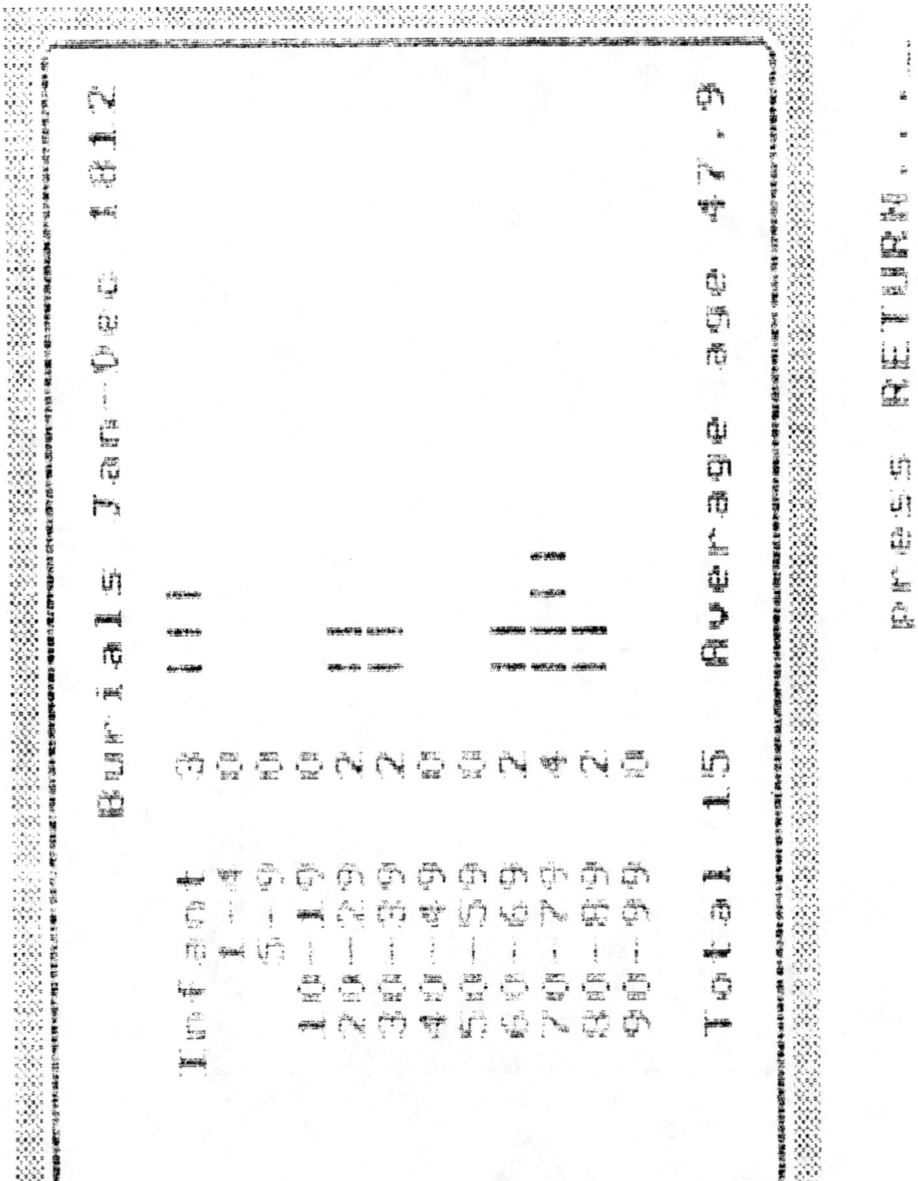

FIGURE 15.26 BURREG menus, overlaying windows and graphical display

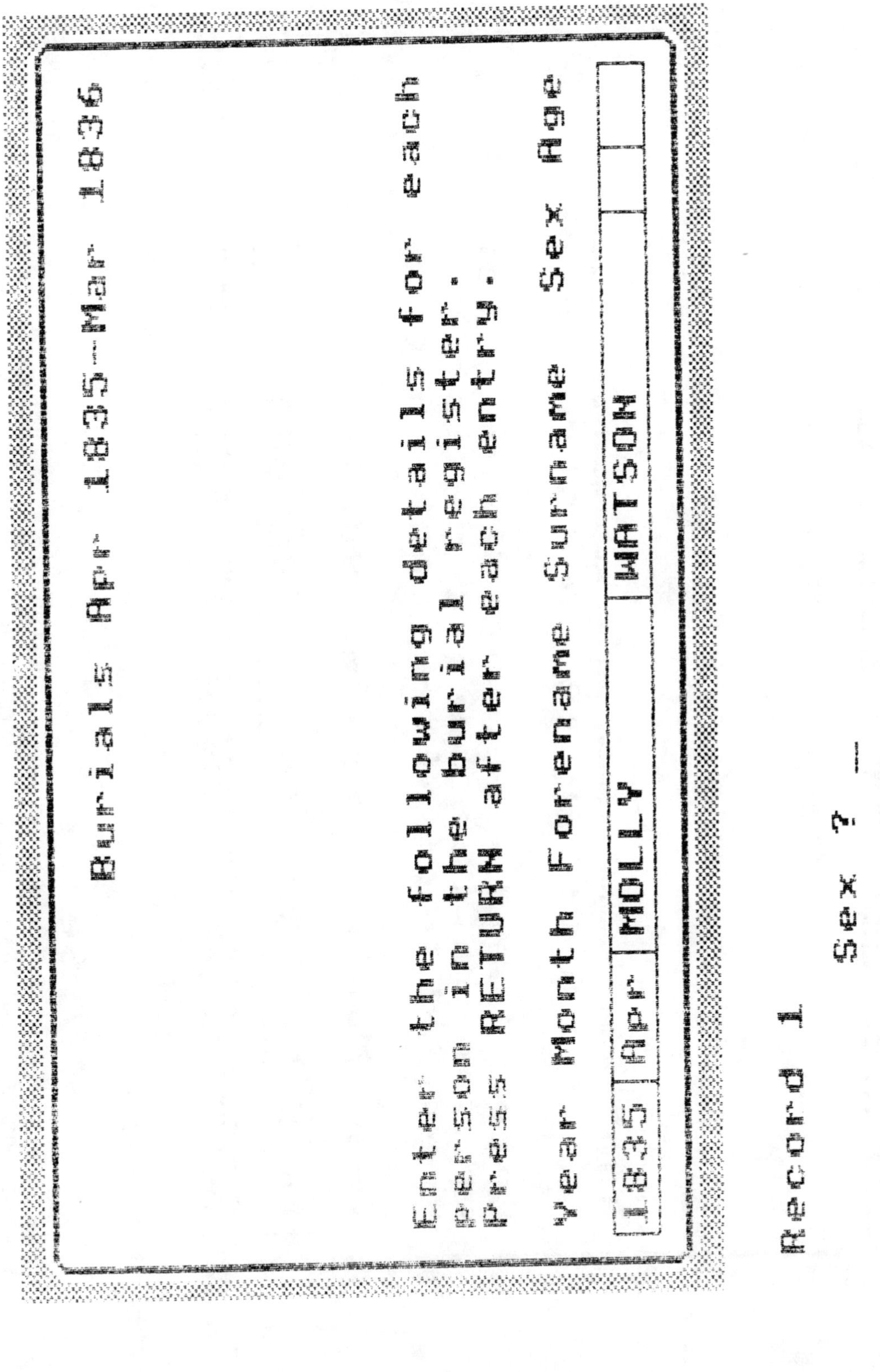

```
            Burials Apr 1835-Mar 1836

    Enter the following details for each
    person in the burial register.
    Press RETURN after each entry.

    Year Month Forename Surname Sex Age

    1835 Apr MOLLY     WATSON


Record 1

    Sex ? —
```

FIGURE 15.27 BURREG menus, overlaying windows and graphical display

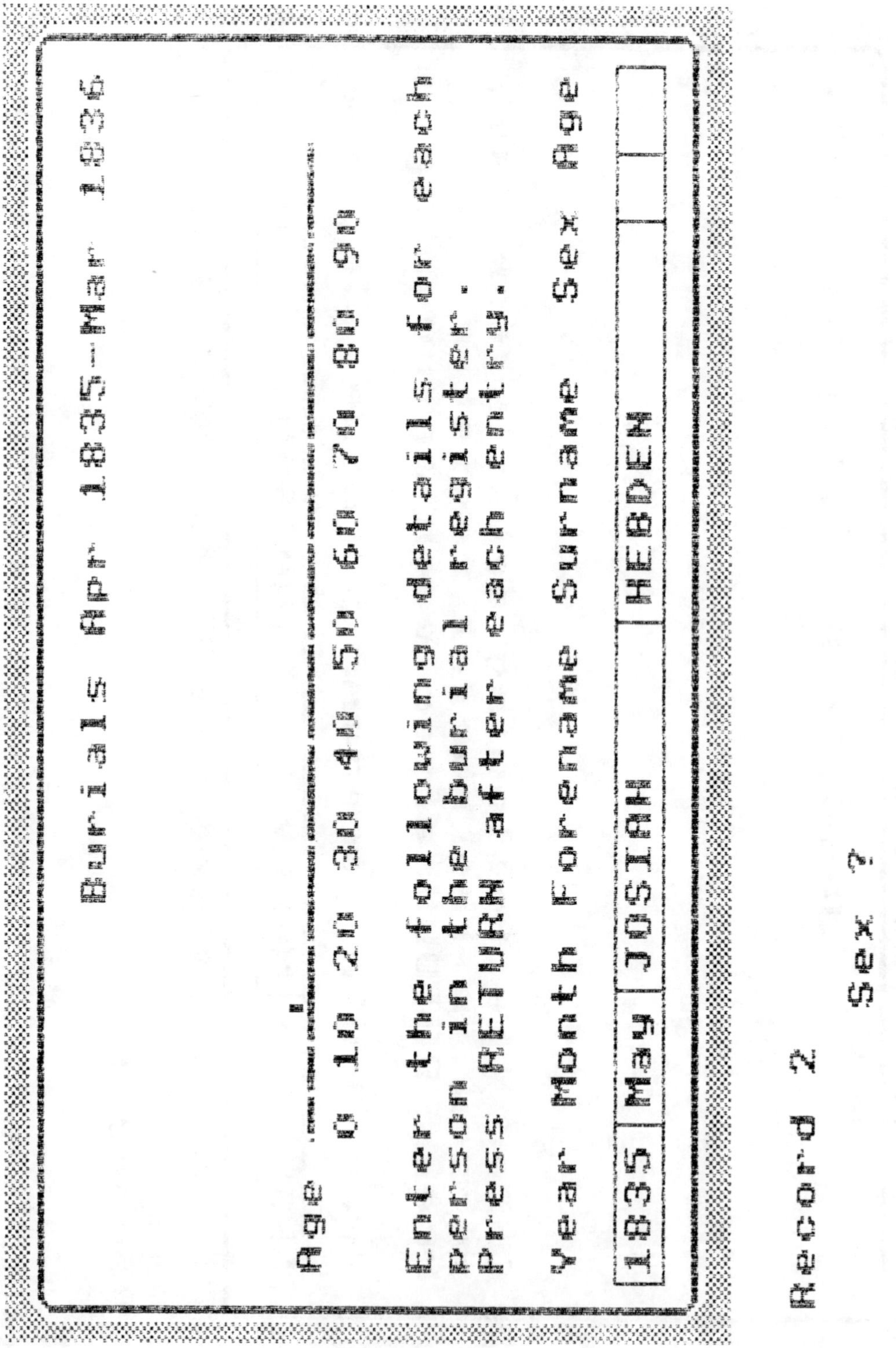

Burials Apr 1835-Mar 1936

Age |_____
    0 10 20 30 40 50 60 70 80 90

Enter the following details for each
person in the burial register.
Press RETURN after each entry.

Year Month Forename Surname Sex Age

| 1835 | May | JOSIAH | HEBDEN |
| | | | |

Record 2

Sex ?

FIGURE 15.28   BURREG menus, overlaying windows and graphical display

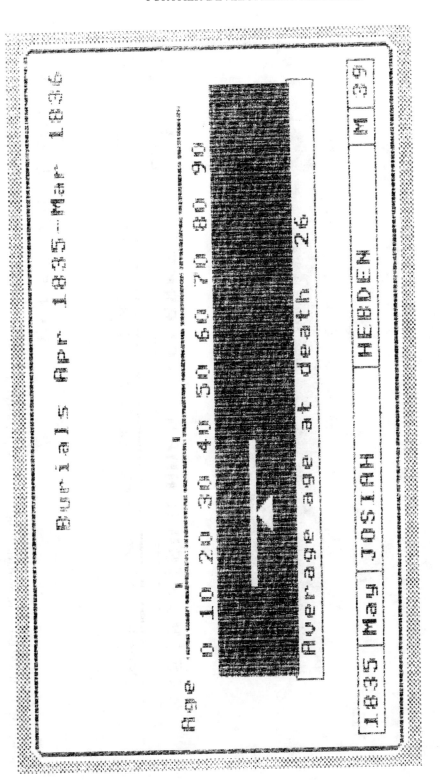

FIGURE 15.29 BURREG menus, overlaying windows and graphical display

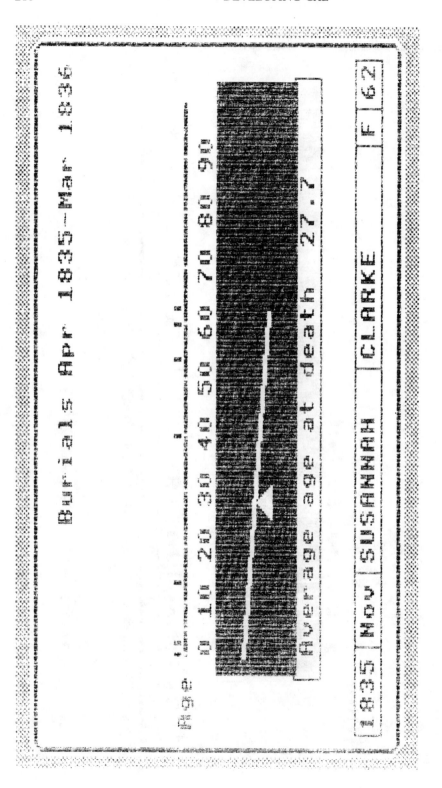

FIGURE 15.30   BURREG menus, overlaying windows and graphical display

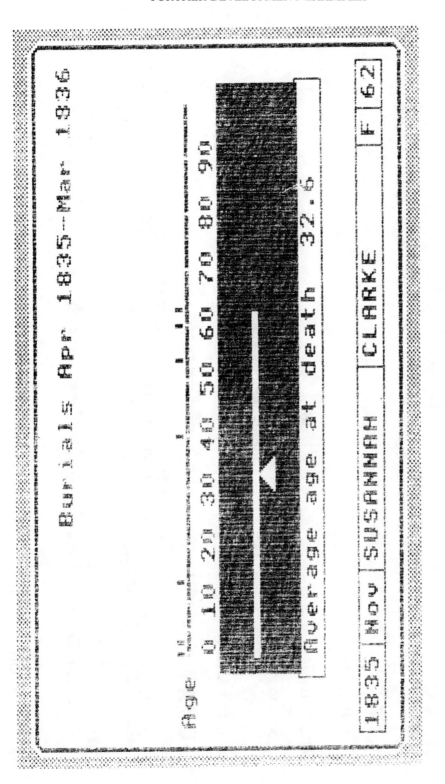

FIGURE 15.31 BURREG menus, overlaying windows and graphical display

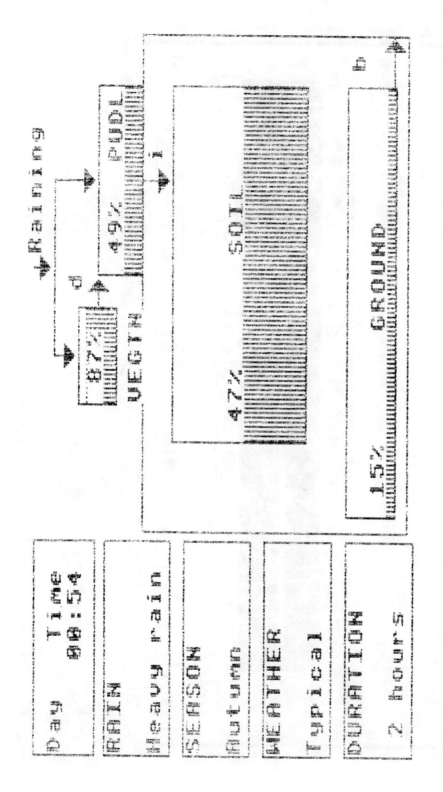

FIGURE 15.32   PUDDLE

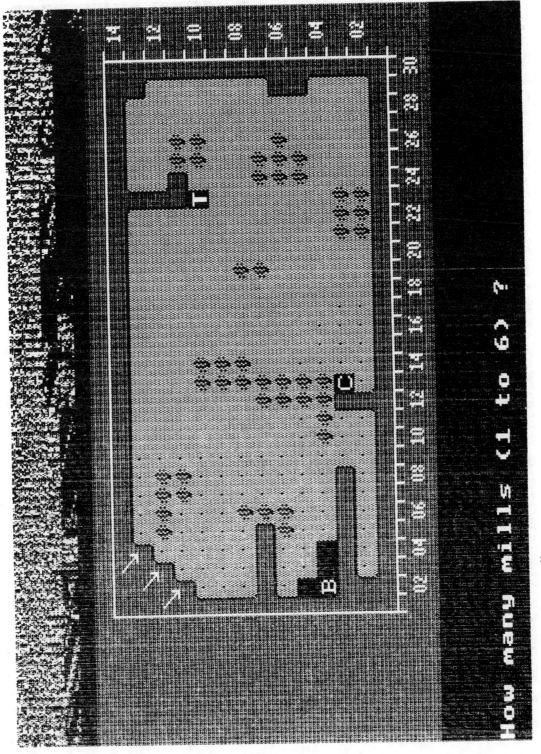

FIGURE 15.33   MILL contours off

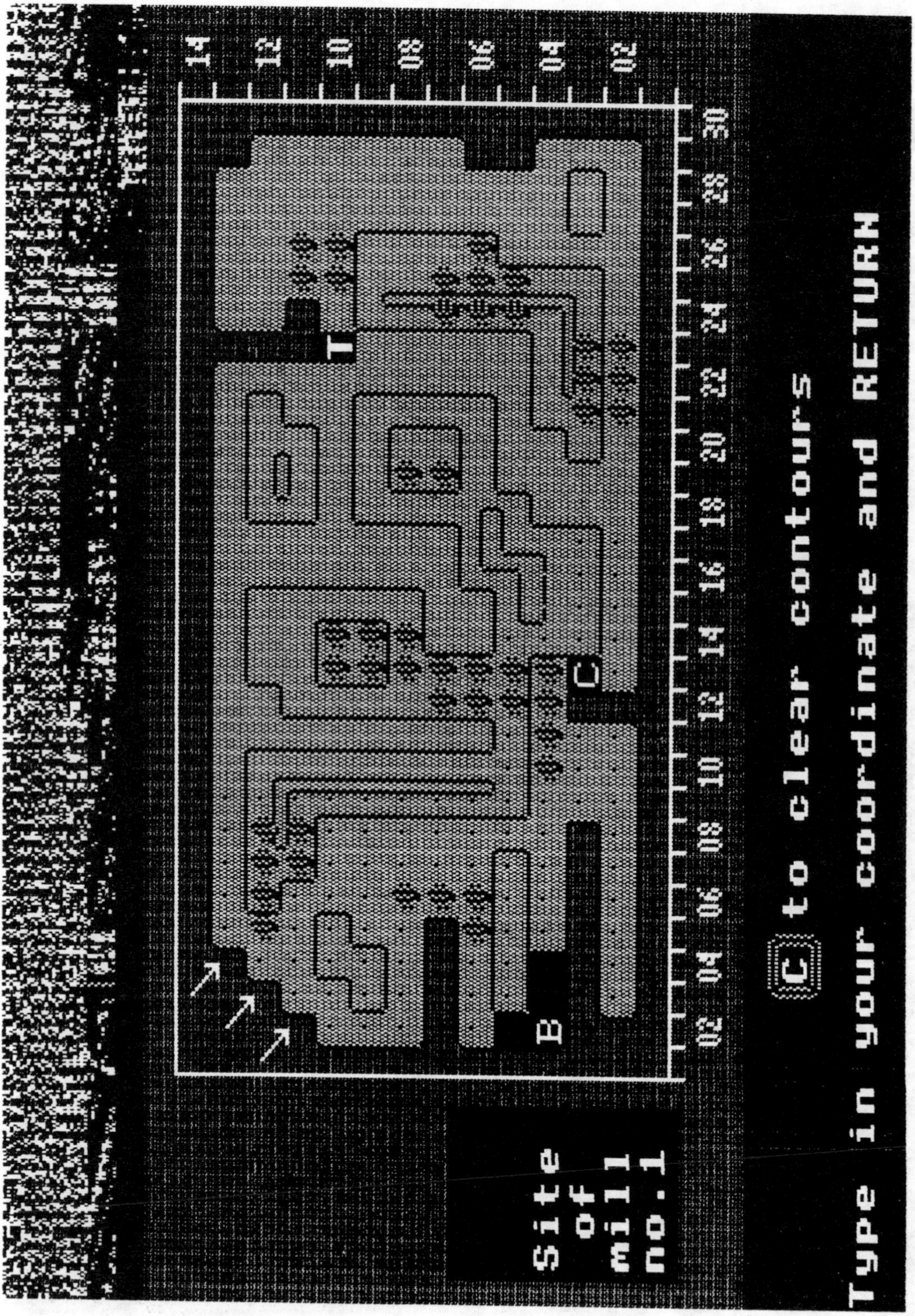

FIGURE 15.34 MILL contours on

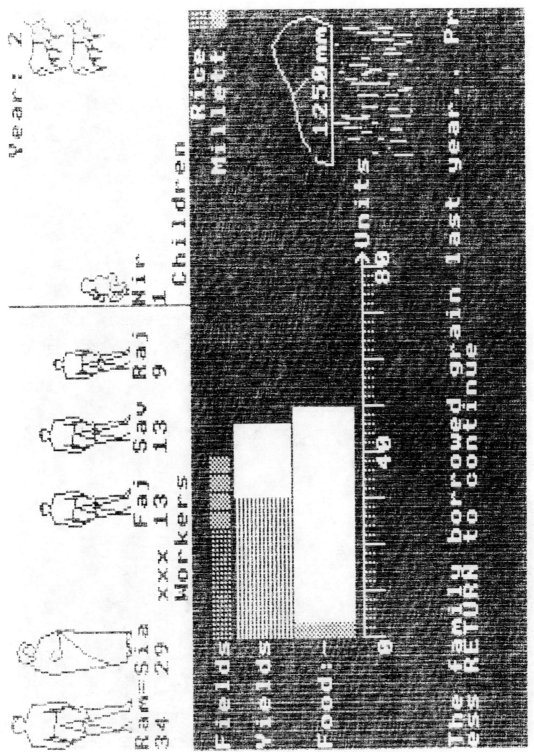

FIGURE 15.35. Indfarm – the design problem

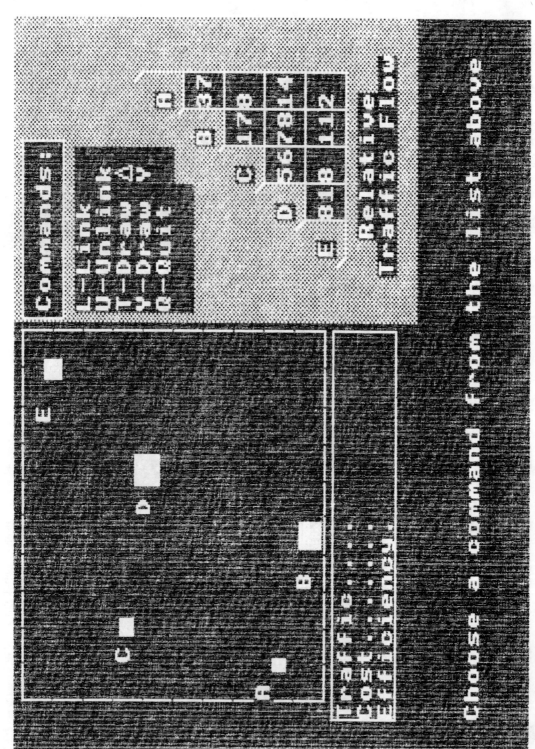

FIGURE 15.36   Motorway planning

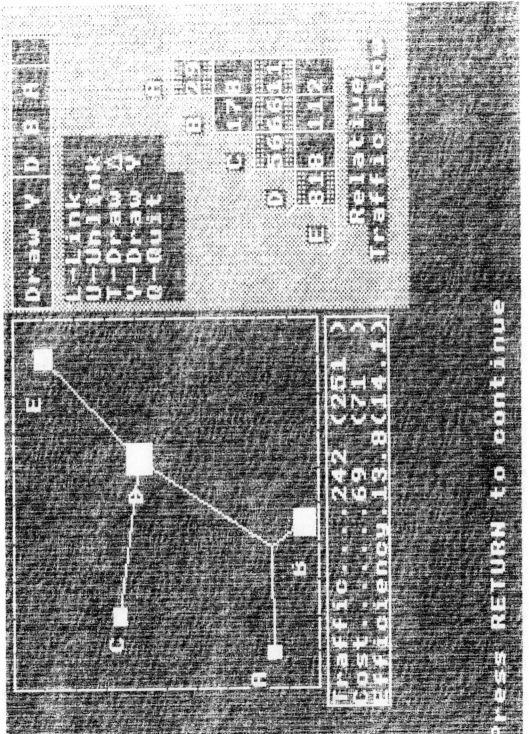

FIGURE 15.37   Motorway planning

16
A VARIETY OF CAL DEVELOPMENT MODELS

Placing the way the Computers in the Curriculum Project has devised a working schema, or model, for the development of CAL, in perspective is difficult. The following brief descriptions of some other CAL development groups are derived from the literature and in some cases personal conversations. It really is not appropriate to attempt to provide a framework for comparison. Nevertheless certain similarities or differences will emerge between these systems and that of the Project.

The essential character of each will derive from answers to the following:
- for what purpose is the software being developed?
- what expertise is embedded in the team?
- who devises the specification?
- who does the programming?
- what design tools and documentation are used?
- is the product tested?

FIVE WAYS SOFTWARE

This development group, now a company, has evolved from a school-based team in Birmingham, UK. The approach relies on the bright idea of a particular teacher or programmer which is then drawn up into a specification, and programmed by a team of pupils at the school-based site. These programmers are sometimes ex-pupils employed for a year before moving on to further education or into employment. The emphasis is on a central team of young programmers who are responsible for nearly all of the development. It has been reported that the director finds this is a faster, and therefore a very welcome method of production (Cross, 1982). In 1982, all the programs had been developed in response to requests from outside the unit, mostly from individual subject teachers. After receiving a rough idea about what is wanted, the whole process – from discussion between teacher and programmer, programmer and unit's designer, through the production of trials programs, modifications to meet the teacher/originator's aims, the production of technical documentation and acceptance as a published program – is supposed to take 4–12 weeks.

This process has been modified by 1985 to include field trialling. Due to cost and to commercial pressures, 5 Ways operates a model whereby trialling must take place at an early stage before production costs have started to mount. The original idea is developed and a storyboard mock-up produced. This is done by graphic designers working with the company. The flow of the program – showing what appears on the screen, and what users have to do – is presented in a non-technical fashion. This storyboard is then the subject of a critical review both by 5 Ways and by external consultants. Experienced teachers are asked to form a full impression of the planned software and comment on how they feel the program would be used in class – from the evidence of the storyboard.

A full technical specification and draft documentation is drawn from those of the teachers above who reacted positively to the storyboard. This specification is then reviewed again, and a decision is taken as to whether or not to proceed to the major coding stage. If the unit is abandoned at this stage, it is at no great cost. The director stresses that once coding has begun, major reprogramming tasks must be avoided. Feedback is still welcome particularly during the classroom use of the material. It is too late, however, for teachers suggestions to be incorporated into the current package (Alexander and Blanchard, 1985).

This process is partly driven by commercial considerations so that substantial changes to software are simply not possible; if a major deficiency arises in the product at such a late stage it is reported to have severe consequences for the company. Nearing the time for publication, 5 Ways demonstrates the new material to audiences of teachers and send the packs to selected schools for trial. The feedback from these meetings and trials however cannot be incorporated into the unit, but are useful for providing new ideas for further packages.

THE SINGLE DEVELOPER

A different alternative, and one that removes itself from larger projects with their structure, is when an individual teacher with an idea develops a program either himself or working closely with a programmer colleague. The Microelectronics Education Program funded a number of individuals under their 'Buckshot' scheme in 1981–2 to produce software. The teacher has not necessarily been involved with developing CAL before; it encourages teachers themselves to become active programmers. This method of operation is neither costly in resources or in time, although there may be ancillary costs later on in preparing the software for a wider audience. It is not known how much of the buckshot fell on stony rather than fertile ground.

King (in Alexander and Blanchard, 1985) has reported on the development of his idea for the program SLY FOX. While attending a diploma course he explored the idea for a simulation based around the life of a suburban fox moving around his territory. He devised a game approach to the simulation and drew up the information that pupils would need on a series on cards. In the early stages his specification for the program was little more than an outline including pencil sketches of the scenes. However, it was sufficiently detailed for the programmers to make a start. A college programmer began to code and the two worked together, the teacher concentrating on the design of the simulation, leaving the programmer to choose such issues as character design, choice of colours, and screen display. The teacher acknowledged that the coder knew more about the machine, while he still retained overall control of the design and development.

During the development the teacher discussed the program and the general idea with other colleagues on the course and teachers in schools, which led to modifications and new ideas being incorporated. The teacher reports that the approach was flexible and he allowed other teachers' comments to influence the developments of the package. They only trialled the whole unit late in the development, and concentrated on finding scope for improvement (e.g. the messages appeared for too brief a time) in the execution of the idea, rather than judging the package's overall appeal.

This successful development obviously depended upon the teacher having both time available and access to a skilled programmer in the college. It does highlight the importance of the relationship between the two individuals.

There are undoubtedly a lot of teachers who develop material for their own classroom. What is not easy to find in the documentation is evidence of individuals who have produced CAL in a way that has travelled beyond their own environment to the extent of becoming available nationally. Nor is it easy to elicit information on whether those individuals, or pairs, who produce a single unit go on to produce another. If it is successful, they may be commissioned to produce more, and become an established CAL authoring point.

Landa (1984) reports developing her own software to use in her school and how this method has been expanded to form Brainbank Inc. She outlines a scheme for teachers to harness their imagination, design lessons on the computer (referred to as courseware) and know enough about the computer to prepare these detailed lessons on paper, to be implemented by a programmer.

NEWMAN COLLEGE

Newman College is a College of Education in Birmingham, UK, that has a software unit. This unit is a separate financial entity, but is based in the Computer Centre. It depends upon the fact that there are educational lecturers, who by working with the programmers employed in the unit, can together produce educational software.

The ideas come from two sources – staff and teachers at the college, and educational publishers who commission the unit. Following a specification workshop, where ideas are discussed, an idea emerges that one person feels able to identify with. A specification is then handed over to a programmer, who works for the section in the college. Keeling (1986) has reported that there then follows a period of close interaction between programmers and teachers who constantly monitor developments. Here the college is fortunate in that, in any one year, they always have at least fifteen primary school teachers working in the computer centre on a year's secondment leading to an Advanced Diploma in Educational Computing. This represents what Keeling has described as a large reserve of enthusiastic expertise all ready to contribute to the specification and to trial the programs in school. Following these trials, the units are adapted and modified, and finally the documentation and resource material is written. Where this process is unique is the use of a pool of resident teachers on an inservice course as developers and triallers. Keeling also values the frequent contact between the programmers and resident teachers.

This development process at Newman takes anything from four to twelve months, including writing the accompanying resources for the software. It is a self-funding operation relying on copyright income to proceed.

THE COVENTRY COMPUTER BASED LEARNING UNIT

This unit was established at Coventry in 1984 following a successful project funded by the Manpower Services Commission (MSC) using Control Data Plato Systems. The unit works in two areas, the provision of resources and support for the use of computer based learning, and the production of new CBL material. They consider that the latter includes both the software and the associated text-based materials. The aim of this courseware is to be integrated into the training programs.

Bell (1986) has recognised that it is necessary to draw together expertise from several areas, including:

- knowledge of the subject area;
- knowledge of education/training;
- Computer Based Learning techniques;
- programming; and
- using Computer Based Learning (i.e. the students).

The process for development depends upon a curriculum development group. They receive the request for CBL development, allocate resources, control and monitor the work, and maintain standards. Once the idea has been approved, the working party is established, which is made up of three or four subject and education/training specialists working with a member of the CBL support staff, who is called the Curriculum Development Officer. This individual directs the flow of work. A clear 'statement of requirement' is produced. There then follows well-designed structured stages of development: analysing of the design; detailed lesson design; production of program specification sheets; programming; lesson review and amendments; lesson testing; pilot run of courseware; validation; and the production of supplementary material.

In essence the Program Specification is handed over to professional programmers who code the program and create the design. The working group reads it and makes amendments which are coded. It is then carefully piloted.

Bell has reported that this curriculum development model ensures that the design is relevant to teachers and trainers and that they recognise and relate to the approach being taken. Because the designers are not computer experts, they are initially told to assume the computer can do everything, which reportedly results in very imaginative use of the computer and unexpected designs. The curriculum development officer's presence ensures continuity and control in the development process; expertise from group to group is passed by this member of staff; there is ready feedback to the central team.

Programs are robust and adhere to structured programming standards. The lessons learnt at the trials stage are documented in the manuals.

SOUTHAMPTON

Layman and Hall (1986) have reported on their development of a package for the Electricity Supply Industry. They follow the processes involved in the design development of computer based teaching material outlined by Burkhardt et al. (1982). They indicate that there is a new part of the equation because they are using a model for the production of material to match the needs of both industry and education. They state that the linear development model outlined in Burkhardt et al. is inappropriate for industry-linked projects because:

1. The generative principle of curriculum need can be too narrow for successful industrial involvement in the curriculum process.

2. The starting point of curriculum need can constrain the outcome within the confines of single subject areas. Industrial applications often cut across subject boundaries as well as drawing on separate contributions from different fields.

The development team at Southampton acted as co-ordinators; both individuals were lecturers in educational computing. They felt it was important that the following expertise was present:

● awareness of curriculum needs;
● a working knowledge of hardware and the programming language chosen for the project;
● an understanding of industrial concepts;
● experience of school environments; and
● the necessary expertise and resources to establish, monitor, and evaluate field trials in schools.

THE EDUCATIONAL TECHNOLOGY CENTER AT THE UNIVERSITY OF CALIFORNIA

This is one of the oldest established development centres for CAL materials in the USA. The development process works around what Bork (1980) describes as 'an authoring system'. He emphasizes that early on it was felt important that the authoring system was not to be allowed to restrict, in any way, the types of materials produced. The system works through seven stages – and for each step, different types of persons will play the dominant role.

Step 1   The development of the pedagogic specification for the material – using education faculty members.

Step 2   Using the experienced team to edit ideas.

Step 3   The use of competent graphics designers.

Step 4   Developing the logic design – which Bork relates to traditional computer programming activities.

Step 5   Allowing time on development for language environment considerations.

Step 6   Group reworkings of the program.

Step 7   Evaluation of class use, and subsequent modification.

Bork (1981) encourages calling the author the 'dialogue writer', as he considers the computer dialogue to be a representation of a conversation between the student and teacher, where the teacher is conducting the dialogue through the medium of the program. The dialogue writer is encouraged to consider how, when teaching a particular subject area, you could gain unusual leverage through using the computer. Bork (1981) reports that this approach has been modelled on the course design activities of the Open University. The dialogue writer is asked to express clear learning goals, and to consider the variety of types of unit appropriate to the subject matter. Dialogue writers often work in groups of three, one of whom should have had previous experience at dialogue writing.

The material is then prepared as an outline – either giving full details line by line, or the general idea in a frame by frame sequence. The group then frequently uses an authoring language, APL, for the execution of the author dialogue. If APL is not appropriate, the team at Irvine will develop routines as required. Bork repeatedly emphasizes that it is education rather than technology that should drive the process.

ITMA

A thoroughly well documented model for development is that of the ITMA Project. One of its principle factors is that the initial brainstorming takes place amongst the development team. The idea is then taken to teachers to be involved with the development and finishing process. Thus ITMA capitalizes on the CAL design skills of its team at inception stage; teachers then follow on as responders and developers. Much of the development takes place through closely observed classroom practice, for which the ITMA project has produced a particular methodology, SCAN. Field (in Alexander and Blanchard, 1985) has reported the detailed operation of these trials, and it is quite clear that suggestions for major 'spin offs' may arise during development. Phillips *et al.* (1984) have also reported that it is essential for these classroom observations to be undertaken by the Project team, because it has never been found to be very useful to ask teachers to report on their own lessons. He considers that even the most skilful and imaginative teachers seem unable to report effectively on their own performance. The observations result in a large amount of ergonomic information – that is facts that cast light on the efficiency of the man–machine interface. He believes teachers, as well as finding it difficult to be objective observers of their own lessons, cannot always make the time available to fill in detailed questionnaires. The main cost in this method is the time it takes.

The ITMA Project (Fraser, 1981, Burkhardt *et al.*, 1982) identified a sequence of nine events with two strands following through – writing and development. In essence these events are:

The ITMA design diagram

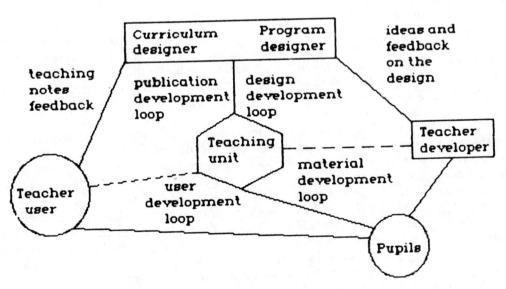

FIGURE 16.1   The ITMA design diagram (after Burkhardt *et al.*, 1982)

1. state aims;
2. accept ideas;
3. draft program;
4. revise program;
5. report on trials progress;
6. revise further;
7. rewrite in light of evidence;
8. polish; and
9. publish.

A clear indication is given of how the development progresses through these writing events. These events when incorporated into their design structure reflect the four development loops that they identify – that of design, materials, user, and of publication. This is illustrated in Figure 16.1.

OTHER STRANDS

The MEP Educational Software Creators' Handbook (Alexander and Blanchard, 1985) does not identify stages of development but rather list at least thirty-four activities that need to occur, and places them in a related time sequence, in order to illustrate issues of management. This list runs from:

- (2)   develop specification with advisory group;

through to:

- (8)   select software house;
- (11) generate relevant idea;
- (13) code program;
- (14) write documentation;

eventually to:

- (24) publisher assesses product;
- (26) generate artwork;
- (31) publication; and
- (34) versioning and other markets.

These activities are described as occurring within a linear progression, but do not necessarily relate to the roles of individuals within the whole scheme. This text suggests that different events are undertaken by different teams under the overall management of one individual. The development of a specification for the flow of a program is referred to (as in Five Ways software) as the Storyboard – a useful alternative phrase to that of 'comic strip' that I have used earlier.

Hinton (1985) working at the University of Surrey also refers to the importance of producing appropriate documentation to aid the design stage of developing CAL courseware. He advocates the use of block structured charts for CAL design, and in particular suggests that the absence of arrows enables one to appreciate the complex intermingling of the constituent parts rather than a linear flow.

Ramberg (1986) has reported that both programming and design structures built upon blocks have been used in Norway. Indeed the idealized design resembles a large market hall with a variety of smaller side halls running off, some of which interlink.

Mackay (1986) considers the distinction between software (to mean the program) and courseware (to mean the associated classroom aids) to be outdated.

Schoenmaker, van der Mast and Moonen (1986) have reported on the need to produce a structured approach to the problem of providing good quality software. They advocate three stages:

1. the development of experimental programs in order to explore new technologies and learning theories;
2. the development of prototypes, where the demands and expertise of the largest group is taken into account; and
3. the production of software according to an industrial approach for different machines.

He considers that by the time the third stage is reached a program design framework would be available into which the appropriate material for each individual program would be incorporated.

Tinson and Smith (1986) report on the ever-present need to consider software portability. They remind us that this involves not just technical portability, including the establishment of standards for languages, graphics and numerical routines, but also academic portability through a careful consideration of both the academic content and educational philosophy of the material. They speak from many years of experience gained through the Engineering Science Project and Engineering Science Program Exchange.

ENDPIECE

This chapter is by no means an exhaustive cross-section of the activities of CAL developers. There are many development groups such as the Minnesota Educational Computing Consortium, Netherhall Software, Homerton College, the Open University, Exeter University, ILECC, AUCBE, and so on, whose development systems I have not recounted. I would encourage those interested in the field to seek details directly from all these sources. This will enable them to place the work and guidelines of CIC in a more appropriate perspective.

Developing CAL is now an activity that does not just sit on the fringe of curricular or technical concerns, but is becoming an integral part of both. With the increasing interest in tools for structured design and programming, a team environment becomes essential. Teams work on a basis of mutual respect for both the technical and educational concerns; although the operation of such a team can regularly present dichotomies between different aspects, the resultant dynamism can be both creative and innovative.

Appendix I
LIST OF PROGRAMS

All the programs referred to in the text have been developed by the Computers in the Curriculum Project with the exception of one Chelsea Science Simulation Project unit. The following is a list of the program names, unit titles and publisher. Further details of these and other units may be obtained from the publishers catalogues or by writing to CIC.

PROGRAM NAME	UNIT TITLE	PUBLISHER
ACCDNT	Accident and Illness	M
AGCOM	Agricultural Commodity Price Stabilisation	L
AMWEST	The American West	L
ARABIS	Palestine 1947	L
ARCHEO	Shallow Hill	L
BURREG	The Analysis of Data from Burial Registers	L
CANAL	Canal Building	L
CBLUFF	Call My Bluff	M
CENSUS	Census Analysis	L
COSBEN	Cost Benefit Analysis	L
COURT	Elizabethan Court	L
DALCO	Siting an Aluminum Plant	L
DEFCIT	Balance of Payments	L
DEMOG	Human Population Growth	L
DMS	Dynamic Modelling System	L
HEATER	Domestic Heating	L
INDFARM	Indian Farmer	L
LAND	Landscape Analysis	L
MALTHUS	Malthus	L

MILL	Windmill Location Game	L
MWAY	Motorway Networks	L
NEWTON	Satellite Orbits	Chelsea Science Simulations Project
POND	Pond Ecology	L
PUDDLE	Water on the Land	L
RADACT	Radioactive Decay	L
RELATE	Relationships	BBC Publications
SCRIPTWRITER	under development	CIC
TFORM	Transformation matrices	L
WINDS	Sailing Ships Game	L
WORKER	Workers and Machines	L

BBC: BBC Publications, 35 Marylebone High Street, London, WIM 1AA.
CIC: Computers in the Curriculum, Educational Computing Unit, King's College KQC, 552 Kings Road, London SW10 0UA.
L: Longman Group Ltd., Longman House, Burnt Mill, Harlow, Essex CM20 2JE.
M: Macmillan Ltd., Houndmills, Basingstoke, Hants. RG21 2XS.

Appendix II
ABBREVIATIONS AND ACRONYMS

AI	Artificial Intelligence
AUCBE	Advisory Unit for Computer Based Education (Hatfield)
CAI	Computer Assisted Instruction
CAL	Computer Assisted Learning
CES	Centre for Educational Studies (King's College, Chelsea)
CIC	Computers in the Curriculum
CML	Computer Managed Learning
CSME	Centre for Science and Mathematics Education
CSSP	Chelsea Science Simulations Project
CUSC	Computers in the Undergraduate Science Curriculum
DES	Department of Education and Science
DTI	Department of Trade and Industry
ILECC	Inner London Educational Computing Centre
ITMA	Investigations into Teaching Using Microcomputers as an Aid
K	Kilobytes
KQC	King's College, Queen Elizabeth College, and Chelsea College
LEA	Local Education Authority
MEP	Microelectronics in Education Programme
MESU	Microelectronics in Education Support Unit
NDPCAL	National Development Programme in Computer Assisted Learning
OPU	Outline of a Proposed Unit
RML	Research Machines Limited

REFERENCES

Alderson, G. and DeWolf, M. (eds.) (1984) *Guide to Effective Screen Design*, Computers in the Curriculum, London.

Alderson, G. and Blakeley, B. (1986) TFORM: the design and development of a computer aided learning package in D.C. Johnson (ed.) *The Application of Microcomputers to Mathematics and Science Teaching*, UNESCO Pilot Project, UK Report No. 2.

Alexander, K. and Blanchard, D. (eds.) (1985) *Educational Software, A Creators Handbook*, Council for Educational Technology on behalf of the Microelectronics Education Programme, London.

Baker, C. (1984). A critical examination of the effect of the microcomputer on the curriculum, in C. Terry (ed.) *Using Microcomputers in Schools*, Croom Helm, Beckenham.

Becher, A. and Maclure, S. (1978) *The Politics of Curriculum Change*, Hutchinson, London.

Bell, M. (1986) The Coventry computer based learning project, *Computers and Education*, Vol. 10, No. 1.

Blenkin, G. (1980) The influence of initial styles of curriculum development, in A. V. Kelly (ed.) *Curriculum Context*, Harper & Row, London.

Bloom, B. (ed.) (1956) *Taxonomy of Educational Objectives*, Longman, London.

Blow, F. (1986a) Evaluation of CAL in the humanities, in T. Plomp (ed.) *Proceedings of EURIT 86*, Pergamon, Oxford (in press).

Blow, F. (1986b) Evaluation of computer-assisted learning in history, in A. Kent (ed.) (1986) *Computer-Assisted Learning in Social Sciences and Humanities*, Blackwell, Oxford.

Bork, A. (1980) The educational technology centre at the University of California, in R. Lewis and E. D. Tagg (eds.) *Computer Assisted Learning – Scope, Progress and Limits*, Heinemann, London.

Bork, A. (1981) *Learning with Computers*, Digital Press, Mass., USA.

Bullock Report (1975) *A Language for Life*, HMSO, London.

Burkhardt, H., Fraser, R., Clowes, M., Eggleston, J. and Wells, C. (1982), *Design and Development of Programs as Teaching Material*, Council for Educational Technology on behalf of the Microelectronics Education Programme, London.

Chandler, D. (1983) *Exploring English with Microcomputers*. Council for Educational Technology, London.

Chapman, R. E. (1977) *Computers in Undergraduate Science Curriculum (CUSC) Graphics Package (BASIC version)* Council for Educational Technology, London.

Chatterton, J. L. (1985) CAL in the classroom: a force for change, abstract in *CAL '85 Conference Handbook*, Pergamon, Oxford.

Cross, J. (1982) School-based programs, *Times Educational Supplement*, 9 June.

Cummings, R. (1985) Small group discussions and the microcomputer, *Journal of Computer Assisted Learning*, Vol. 1, No. 3.

Ennals, R. (1984) Possibilities and priorities for the future, in K. Randall (ed.) *The Use of the Computer in the Study and Teaching of History*, Historical Association, London.

Fothergill, R. (1981) *The Microelectronics Education Programme – a strategy*, Department of Education and Science, London.

Fraser, R. (1981) Design and evaluation of educational software for group presentation, in J.A.M. Howe and P.M. Ross (eds.) (1981) *Microcomputers in Secondary Education*, Kogan Page, London.

Fraser, R. (1983) *Drivecharts Investigations into Teaching Using Microcomputers as an Aid*, College of St Mark and St John, Plymouth.

Fraser, R. (1984) The ITMA collaboration – history, tasks – some questions answered, in C. Terry (ed.) *Using Microcomputers in Schools*, Croom Helm, Beckenham.

Freeman, D. (1983) CAL in geography: a case study of Hertfordshire schools, in A. Kent, (ed.) *Geography Teaching and the Micro*, Longman, Harlow.

Freeman, D. and Tagg, W. (1985) Databases in the classroom. *Journal of Computer Assisted Learning*, Vol. 1, No. 1.

Galton, M. and Moon, B. (eds.) *Changing Schools . . . Changing Curriculum*, Harper & Row, London.

Harris, J. (1980) Using a computer to assist in the teaching and learning of science, in J.L. Moore and F.H. Thomas Computers in schools: aspects of education, *Journal of the Institute of Education*, University of Hull, No. 23.

Hartley, J.R. (1978) An appraisal of computer assisted learning in the United Kingdom, in N. Rushby (ed.) *Selected Readings in Computer Based Learning*, Kogan Page, London.

Hartley, J.R. (1981) Learner initiatives in computer assisted learning, in J. A. M. Howe and P. M. Ross (eds.) *Microcomputers in Secondary Education*, Kogan Page, London.

Hassell, D. (1983) Teaching style of CAL in geography in A. Kent (ed.) *Geography Teaching and the Micro*, Longman, Harlow.

Havelock, R. (1969) *Planning for Innovation through Dissemination and Utilisation of Knowledge*, University of Michigan.

Heppell, S. (1986) The use of business software as a content-free teaching tool: evaluation or simulation, in T. Plomp (ed.) *Proceedings of EURIT 1986*, Pergamon, Oxford (in press).

Hinton, T. (1985) A methodology for design documentation for CAL, abstract in *CAL 85 Conference Handbook*, Pergamon, Oxford.

Holt, M. (1981) *Schools and Curriculum Change*, McGraw-Hill, London.

Hooper, R. (1975) Introduction and overview, in R. Hooper and I. Toye (eds.), *Computer Assisted Learning in the United Kingdom – Some Case Studies*, Council for Educational Technology on behalf of the National Development Programme in Computer Assisted Learning, London.

Hooper, R. (1977) *National Development Programme in Computer Assisted Learning – Final Report of the Director*, Council for Educational Technology, London.

Howe, J.A.M. (1978) Artificial intelligence and computer-assisted learning: ten years on. in N. Rushby (ed.) (1981). *Selected Readings in Computer Based Learning*, Kogan Page, London.

Howe, J.A.M. (1983) Towards a pupil-centred classroom, in J. Megarry, D.R.F. Walker, S. Nisbet and E. Hoyle (eds.) *Computers and Education*, Kogan Page, London.

Hoyle, E. (1983) Computers and education: a solution in search of a problem? in J. Megarry, D.R.F. Walker, S. Nisbet and E. Hoyle (eds.) *Computers and Education*, Kogan Page, London.

Jenson, T.A. (1980) Ten years on – in a Danish project, in R. Lewis and E.D. Tagg (eds.) *Computer Assisted Learning – Scope, Progress and Limits*, Heinemann, London.

Keeling, R. (1986) An educational software unit as part of a college of education, *Proceedings of EURIT 86*, Pergamon, Oxford (in press).

Kelly, P.J. (1973) *Nuffield A-Level Biological Science Project*, Schools Council, London.

Kelly, A.V. (1977) *The Curriculum – Theory and Practice*, Harper & Row, London.

Kelly, A.V. (1980) Ideological constraints on curriculum planning, in A.V. Kelly (ed.) *Curriculum Context*, Harper & Row, London.

Killbery, I. (1984) Not just geography, in D. Watson (ed.) *Exploring Geography with Microcomputers*, Council for Educational Technology on behalf of the Microelectronics Education Programme, London.

Killbery, I., Labbett, B.D.C. and Randall, K. (1979) Computers in history, in J. Hunt (ed.) *Computers in Secondary School History Teaching*, History Association, London. No. 40.

Labbett, B. (1980) Using the computer for the teaching of history, in J.L. Moore and F.H. Thomas (eds.). Computers in schools: aspects of education, *Journal of the Institute of Education*, University of Hull, No. 23.

Landa, R.K. (1984). *Creating Courseware*, Harper & Row, New York.

Luarillard, D. (1983) The student experience of computer-assisted learning, in J. Megarry, D.R.F. Walker, S. Nisbet and E. Hoyle (eds.) *Computers and Education*, Kogan Page, London.

Lawn, M., and Barton, L. (1981) (eds.) *Rethinking Curriculum Studies*, Croom Helm, London.

Layman, J., and Hall, W. (1986) Teaching about the electricity supply industry – the development and evaluation of a computer-based teaching package for schools, *Computers and Education*, Vol. 10, No. 11.

Leiblum, M.D. (1981) Factors sometimes overlooked and underestimated in the selection and success of CAL as an instructional medium, in R.E.J. Lewis and E.D. Tagg (eds.) *Computers and Education*, North Holland, Amsterdam.

Lewis, R. (1981a) Pedagogical issues in designing programs, in J.A.M. Howe and P.M. Ross (eds.) *Microcomputers in Secondary Education*, Kogan Page, London.

Lewis, R. (1981b) *Project Paper 16 – Trial Mechanism during Phase 2*, Computers in the Curriculum (internal document).

Lewis, R. (1983) The microcomputer and the teacher's needs, in J. Megarry, D.R.F. Walker, S. Nisbet and E. Hoyle (eds.) *Computers and Education*, Kogan Page, London.

Lewis R. and Smith, P. (1980) *Project Paper 15 – The New Software Standards*, Computers in the Curriculum (internal document).

Lewis, R. and Want, D.L. (1980a). Educational computing at Chelsea (1969–79), in R. Lewis and E.D. Tagg (eds.) *Computer Assisted Learning – Scope, Progress and Limits*, Heinemann, London.

Lewis, R. and Want, D.L. (1980b) *Project Paper 20 – Guidelines for Program Development*, Computers in the Curriculum (internal document). London.

McCormick, S. (1986) The design, development and evaluation of an educational science software package: domestic electrical fault finding (DEFT), in D.C. Johnson (ed.) *The Application of Microcomputers in Mathematics and Science Teaching*, UNESCO Pilot Project, UK Report No. 2.

McCormick, S. (1984) *Microcomputers and Teaching Biology*, Longman, Harlow.

Macdonald, B., Atkin, R., Jenkins, D. and Kemmis S. (1977a). Computer assisted learning: its educational potential, in R. Hooper (ed.) *NDPCAL: Final Report of the Director*, Council for Educational Technology, London.

Macdonald, B., Atkin, R., Jenkins, D. and Kemmis, S. (1977b). The educational evaluation of NDPCAL, *British Journal of Educational Technology*, Vol. 8, No. 3.

Macdonald, B. and Walker, R. (1976) *Changing the Curriculum*, Open Books, London.

Mackay, B. (1986) Effective educational courseware, in *Proceedings of EURIT 86*, Pergamon, Oxford (in press).

Maddison, A. (1982) *Microcomputers in the Classroom*, Hodder & Stoughton, Sevenoaks.

Maddison, J. (1983) *Education in the Microelectronics Era*, Open University Press, Milton Keynes.

Megarry, J. (1983) Thinking, learning and educating: the role of the computer, in J. Megarry, D.R.F. Walker, S. Nisbet and E. Hoyle (eds.) *Computers in Education*, Kogan Page, London.

Miller, L. and Burnett, J.D. (1986). Theoretical considerations in selecting language arts software, *Computers and Education*, Vol. 10, No. 1.

Millwood, R. (1983) *Subroutine Library Manual*, Computers in the Curriculum, London.

Millwood, R., Sellman, R. and Creasy, D. (1984) *Stages in the Development of a Unit (Programming)*, Computers in the Curriculum (internal document), London.

Nash, A. and Ball, D. (1982) *An Introduction to Microcomputers in Teaching*, Hutchinson, London.

Newman, W.M. and Sproull, R.F. (1979) *Principles of Interactive Computer Graphics*, McGraw-Hill Kogakusha, Tokyo.

Nicholas, E.J. (1980) A comparative view of curriculum development, in A.V. Kelly (ed.) (1980) *Curriculum Context*, Harper & Row, London.

Nicol, J., Briggs, J. and Dean, J. (1986) Authoring programming and curriculum development, in A. Kent (ed.) *Computer Assisted Learning in the Social Sciences and Humanities*, Blackwell, Oxford.

Nisbet, J. (1974) Innovation – bandwagon or hearse? in A. Harris *et al.* (eds.) (1974) *Curriculum Innovation*, Croom Helm, London.

O'Shea, T. and Self, J. (1983) *Learning and Teaching with Computers*. Harvester, Brighton.

Papert, S. (1980) *Mindstorms, Children, Computers and Powerful Ideas*, Harvester, Brighton.

Payne, A., Hutchings, B. and Ayre, P. (1980) *Computer Software for Schools*, Pitman, London.

Phillips, R., Burkhardt, H., Coupland, J., Fraser, R. and Ridgeway, J. (1984) The future of the microcomputer as a classroom teaching aid: an empirical approach to crystal gazing, *Computers and Education*, Vol. 8, No. 2.

Pring, R. (1973) Objectives and innovation: the irrelevance of theory, *London Educational Review*, Vol. 2, pp. 46–54.

Ramberg, M. (1986) A new model for designing, developing and testing educational software, *Proceedings of EURIT 86*, Pergamon, Oxford (in press).

Reid, W., (1975) The changing curriculum, in W.A. Reid and D.F. Walker (eds.) *Case Studies in Curriculum Change, Great Britain and the United States*, Routledge & Kegan Paul, London.

Riddle, D.P.R. (1986) Fifteen Years of CAL – the Chelsea experience, in T. Plomp (ed.) *Proceedings of EURIT 86, Development of Educational Software and Courseware*, Pergamon, Oxford (in press).

Ridgeway, J., Benzie, D., Burkhardt, H., Coupland, J., Field, G., Fraser, R. and Phillips, R. (1984). Conclusions from catastrophes, *Computers and Education*, Vol. 8, No. 1.

Riley, D. (1984) Making a splash with models, in D. Watson (ed.) *Exploring Geography with Microcomputers*, Council for Educational Technology on behalf of the Microelectronics in Education Programme, London.

Rushby, N. (1979) *An Introduction to Educational Computing*, Croom Helm, Beckenham.

Rushby, N. (1981) Educational innovation and computer based learning, in N. Rushby (ed.) *Selected Readings in Computer Based Learning*, Kogan Page, London.

Rushby, N. (1984) Styles of computer based learning, in C. Terry (ed.) *Using Microcomputers in Schools*, Croom Helm, Beckenham.

Rushby, N., Anderson, J., Howe, A., Marrow, F. and Piper, D.W. (1981). A recursive approach to teacher training in the use of CBL, in R.E.J. Lewis and E.D. Tagg (eds.) *Computers in Education*, North Holland, Amsterdam.

Schoenmaker, J., van der Mast, C., Moonen, J. (1986) A methodology for the development of educational software, in T. Plomp (ed.) *Proceedings of EURIT 86*, Pergamon, Oxford, (in press).

Schon, D.A. (1971) *Beyond the Stable State – Public and Private Learning in a Changing Society*, Temple Smith, London.

Self, J. (1985) *Microcomputers in Education: a critical appraisal of educational software*, Harvester, Brighton.

Shaw, K. (1979) Some educational uses of computers in UK schools, in N. Rushby, (ed.) *Selected Readings in Computer Based Learning*, Kogan Page, London.

Shepherd, I. (1983) The agony and the ecstacy – reflections on the microcomputer and geography teaching, in A. Kent (ed.) *Geography Teaching and the Micro*, Longman, Harlow.

Shepherd, I.D.H., Cooper, Z.A. and Walker, D.R.F. (1980) *Computer Assisted Learning in Geography*, Council for Educational Technology with the Geographical Association.

Shipman, M. (1974) *Inside a Curriculum Project*, Ward Lock Educational, London.

Skilbeck, M. (1975) School-based curriculum development and the task of in-service education, in E. Adam (ed.) *In-Service Education and Teachers Centres*, Pergamon, Oxford.

Smith, C. (1985) *Exploring Biology with Microcomputers*, Council for Educational Technology on behalf of the Microelectronics Education Programme, London.

Smith, D. (1983) *Evaluation Report on the School Trials of CAL Materials Developed Jointly in Staffordshire*, University of Manchester for Computers in the Curriculum/Economics Education 14–16 Project/Staffordshire County Council.

Sparrow, F.H. (1973) The role of the evaluator, in *Evaluation in Curriculum Development: Twelve Case Studies*, Schools Council Research Studies, Macmillan, London.

Squires, D.J. (1981) Environmental studies and computer assisted learning, in R. Lewis and E.D. Tagg (eds.) *Computers in Education*, North Holland, Amsterdam.

Stenhouse, L. (1975) *An Introduction to Curriculum Research and Development*, Heinemann, London.

Stenhouse, L. (ed.) (1980). *Curriculum Research and Development in Action*, Heinemann, London.

Taba, H. (1962) *Curriculum Development: Theory and Practice*, Harcourt, Brace & World, New York.

Tagg, W. (1980) *A Standard for CAL Dialogue*, Advisory Unit for Computer Based Education, Hertfordshire.

Tawney, D. (1973) Evaluation and curriculum development, in *Evaluation in Curriculum Development: Twelve Case Studies*, Schools Council Research Studies. Macmillan, London.

Terry, C. (1984) *Using Microcomputers in Schools*, Croom Helm, Beckenham.

Tinson, P.A. and Smith, P.R. (1986) Portability of computer based teaching software: ESPE experience, *Computers and Education*, Vol.10, No.3.

Tyler, R. (1949) *Basic Principles of Curriculum and Instruction*, University of Chicago Press.

Walker, D. (1983) The evaluation of computer assisted learning, in J. Megarry, D.R.F. Walker, S. Nisbet and E. Hoyle (eds.) *Computers and Education*. Kogan Page, London.

Want, D.L. (1982) Keyword driven interaction in computer assisted learning, in R.E.J. Lewis and
    E.D. Tagg (eds.) *Involving Micros in Education*, North Holland, Amsterdam.
Watson, D. (1981) Computer assisted learning in the humanities, in R. Lewis and E.D. Tagg (eds.)
    Computers in Education, North Holland, Amsterdam.
Watson, D. (1982) Some implications of micros on curriculum development, in R. Lewis and E.D.
    Tagg (eds.) *Involving Micros in Education*, North Holland, Amsterdam.
Watson, D. (1983) A model for the production of CAL, *Computers and Education*, Vol. 7, No. 3.
Watson, D. (1984a) *Exploring Geography with Microcomputers*, Council for Educational
    Technology on behalf of the Microelectronics Education Programme, London.
Watson, D. (1984b) Microcomputers in secondary education – a perspective with particular
    reference to the humanities, in A.V. Kelly (ed.) *Microcomputers and the Curriculum*, Harper &
    Row, London.
Watson, D. (1984c) *Enabling School Pupils to Interrogate Census Data*. Historical Social
    Research, Paper No.29.
Watson, D. (1984d) In-service training via CAL development, Case Study 4 in Blakeley, B. H.,
    Teacher training in the UK, in F.B. Lovis and E.D. Tagg (eds.) *Informatics and Teacher
    Training*, North Holland, Amsterdam.
Watson, D. (1984e) The role of CAL in decision-making in the humanities, *Computers and
    Education*, Vol.8, No.1.
Watson, D. (1985) Software to encourage learning, in B. Rasmussen (ed.) *The Information Edge*,
    Queensland Computer Education Group, Australia.
Watson, D. (1986) Developing CAL: the Computers in the Curriculum model, in T Plomp (ed.)
    Proceedings of EURIT 86, Pergamon, Oxford (in press).
Watson D. and McCormick, S. (1981) *Lecture Training Courses*, Project Paper 21, Computers in
    the Curriculum Project, London.
Weigand, P. (1984) Listening at the classroom keyhole, in D. Watson (ed.) *Exploring Geography
    with Microcomputers*, Council for Educational Technology on behalf of the Microelectronics
    Education Programme, London.
Wellington, J.J. (1985) *Children, Computers and the Curriculum*, Harper & Row, London.
Wilkes, J. (1985) *Exploring History with Microcomputers*, Council for Educational Technology
    on behalf of the Microelectronics Education Programme, London.
Willson, A. (1984) A chip off the old block diagram, in D. Watson (ed.) *Exploring Geography
    with Microcomputers*, Council for Educational Technology, London.
Zinn, K.L. (1981) An overview of current developments in computer-assisted learning in the
    United States, in N. Rushby (ed.) *Selected Readings in Computer Based Learning*, Kogan Page,
    London.

AUTHOR INDEX

SUBJECT INDEX